Tony Stankus
Editor

D0148828

Electronic Expectations: Science Journals on the Web

Electronic Expectations: Science Journals on the Web has been co-published simultaneously as *Science & Technology Libraries*, Volume 18, Numbers 2/3 1999

Pre-Publication
REVIEWS,
COMMENTARIES,
EVALUATIONS . . .

"**W**ith characteristic wit and the authority gained from years of careful study of scientific journals, Tony Stankus has given us a very timely work in *Electronic Expectations: Science Journals on the Web.* While there is something for everyone involved in scientific scholarly communication in the various chapters, the work should be especially useful to library science students.

The work should be mandatory reading for all library chief collection development officers, especially those without a science background, the group comprising the vast majority of library CDOs and administrators."

Gary Wiggins, BA, MA
MLS, PhD
Head, Chemistry Library
Coordinator
Science Libraries
Indiana University

"**T**ony Stankus, a well-known writer and critic of issues relating to science librarianship offers a new work advising his readers of situations relating to the proliferation of electronic journals. It supplements and updates a series on this subject published in *Science & Technology Libraries* in 1997. He successfully provides a review of topics discussed in over 300 recent articles in the primary literature.

The articles are written for science librarians, library science students, scientific publishers, aggregators, and internet managers who are involved with print and electronic journals. This reviewer believes that the first article that summarizes important trends in the use of electronic journals is the most significant. Stankus concludes that electronic journals will not replace their print counterparts and that e-journal technology will not lower the cost of technical journals.

I was also impressed by the list of the most important titles in science, medicine and engineering compiled by the author. He provides web addresses for the home page of each journal. Librarians who must evaluate titles for their respective collections will find this quite useful.

I highly recommend this book for science, engineering, and medical libraries.

Bruce Slutsky, MS
Library and Information Science,
Technical Reference Librarians
New Jersey Institute of Technology

"**W**hat are the real issues in the rapidly changing electronic journal scene? This book tells you all about the in's and out's. How editorial functions are evolving, and the personal agendas of the corporate players. Which competition points are driving the market, and why American publisher's tactics will have to parallel those in Europe. Relationships between writers and publishers are examined. You get the scoop on what the major Internet browsers did to get so powerful. Historical trends from the first decade up to now are surveyed. This book answers why print journals will continue to survive in an e-journal environment.

Specifically for librarians are other topics. A short technology instruction explains the mechanics of getting an e-journal to the desktop. Viewing, printing, and scripting software are overviewed. Archiving concerns, librarian's influences over publishers, and power buying with consortia are discussed in depth. This book says why librarians must have an in-depth knowledge of site licenses. A treasury of over 300 references consulted to write this book, along with the world's core scientific journals, including current web addresses, are listed which is most helpful. Scientific authors, publishers, librarians, and internet managers will all find this a must reading, before having their first exposure with e-journals.

Cheryl R. Banick, MLIS
Independent Information Specialist

Electronic Expectations: Science Journals on the Web

Electronic Expectations: Science Journals on the Web, has been co-published simultaneously as *Science & Technology Libraries,* Volume 18, Numbers 2/3 1999.

The *Science & Technology Libraries* Monographic "Separates"

Below is a list of "separates," which in serials librarianship means a special issue simultaneously published as a special journal issue or double-issue *and* as a "separate" hardbound monograph. (This is a format which we also call a "DocuSerial.")

"Separates" are published because specialized libraries or professionals may wish to purchase a specific thematic issue by itself in a format which can be separately cataloged and shelved, as opposed to purchasing the journal on an on-going basis. Faculty members may also more easily consider a "separate" for classroom adoption.

"Separates" are carefully classified separately with the major book jobbers so that the journal tie-in can be noted on new book order slips to avoid duplicate purchasing.

You may wish to visit Haworth's website at . . .

http://www.haworthpressinc.com

. . . to search our online catalog for complete tables of contents of these separates and related publications.

You may also call 1-800-HAWORTH (outside US/Canada: 607-722-5857), or Fax: 1-800-895-0582 (outside US/Canada: 607-771-0012), or e-mail at:

getinfo@haworthpressinc.com

Electronic Expectations: Science Journals on the Web, by Tony Stankus, MLS (Vol. 18, No. 2/3, 1999). *Separates the hype about electronic journals from the realities that they will bring. This book provides a complete tutorial review of the literature that relates to the rise of electronic journals in the sciences and explores the many cost factors that may prevent electronic journals from becoming revolutionary in the research industry.*

Sci/Tech Librarianship: Education and Training, edited by Julie Hallmark, PhD, and Ruth K. Seidman, MSLS (Vol. 17, No. 2, 1998). *"Insightful, informative, and right-on-the-mark. . . . This collection provides a much-needed view of the education of sci/tech librarians." (Michael R. Leach, AB, Director, Physics Research Library, Harvard University)*

Chemical Librarianship: Challenges and Opportunities, edited by Arleen N. Somerville (Vol. 16, No. 3/4, 1997). *"Presents a most satisfying collection of articles that will be of interest, first and foremost, to chemistry librarians, but also to science librarians working in other science disciplines within academic settings." (Barbara List, Director, Science and Engineering Libraries, Columbia University, New York, New York)*

History of Science and Technology: A Sampler of Centers and Collections of Distinction, edited by Cynthia Steinke, MS (Vol. 14, No. 4, 1995). *"A 'grand tour' of history of science and technology collections that is of great interest to scholars, students and librarians." (Jay K. Lucker, AB, MSLS, Director of Libraries, Massachusetts Institute of Technology; Lecturer in Science and Technology, ?Simmons College, Graduate School of Library and Information Science)*

Instruction for Information Access in Sci-Tech Libraries, edited by Cynthia Steinke, MS (Vol. 14, No. 2, 1994). *"A refreshing mix of user education programs and contain[s] many examples of good practice." (Library Review and Reference Reviews)*

Scientific and Clinical Literature for the Decade of the Brain, edited by Tony Stankus, MLS (Vol. 13, No. 3/4, 1993). *"This format combined with selected book and journal title lists is very convenient for life science, social science, or general reference librarians/bibliographers who wish to review the area or get up to speed quickly." (Ruth Lewis, MLS, Biology Librarian, Washington University, St. Louis, Missouri)*

Sci-Tech Libraries of the Future, edited by Cynthia Steinke, MS (Vol. 12, No. 4 and Vol. 13, No. 1, 1993). *"Very timely. . . . Will be of interest to all libraries confronted with changes in technology, information formats, and user expectations." (LA Record)*

Science Librarianship at America's Liberal Arts Colleges, Working Librarians Tell Their Stories, edited by Tony Stankus, MLS (Vol. 12, No. 3, 1992). *"For those teetering on the tightrope between the needs and desires of science faculty and liberal arts librarianship, this book brings a sense of balance." (Teresa R. Faust, MLS, Science Reference Librarian, Wake Forest University)*

Biographies of Scientists for Sci-Tech Libraries, Adding Faces to the Facts, edited by Tony Stankus, MLS (Vol. 11, No 4, 1992). *"A guide to biographies of scientists from a wide variety of scientific fields, identifying titles that reveal the personality of the biographee as well as contributions to his/her field." (Sci Tech Book News)*

Information Seeking and Communicating Behavior of Scientists and Engineers, edited by Cynthia Steinke, MS (Vol. 11, No 3, 1991). *"Unequivocally recommended. . . . The subject is one of importance to most university libraries, which are actively engaged in addressing user needs as a framework for library services." (New Library World)*

Technology Transfer: The Role of the Sci-Tech Librarian, edited by Cynthia Steinke, MS (Vol. 11, No. 2, 1991). *"Educates the reader about the role of information professionals in the multifaceted technology transfer process." (Journal of Chemical Information and Computer Sciences)*

Electronic Information Systems in Sci-Tech Libraries, edited by Cynthia Steinke, MS (Vol. 11, No. 1, 1990). *"Serves to illustrate the possibilities for effective networking from any library/information facility to any other geographical point." (Library Journal)*

The Role of Trade Literature in Sci-Tech Libraries, edited by Ellis Mount, DLS (Vol. 10, No. 4, 1990). *"A highly useful resource to identify and discuss the subject of manufacturers' catalogs and their historical as well as practical value to the profession of librarianship. Dr. Mount has made an outstanding contribution." (Academic Library Book Review)*

Role of Standards in Sci-Tech Libraries, edited by Ellis Mount, DLS (Vol. 10, No. 3, 1990). *Required reading for any librarian who has been asked to identify standards and specifications.*

Relation of Sci-Tech Information to Environmental Studies, edited by Ellis Mount, DLS (Vol. 10, No. 2, 1990). *"A timely and important book that illustrates the nature and use of sci-tech information in relation to the environment." (The Bulletin of Science, Technology & Society)*

End-User Training for Sci-Tech Databases, edited by Ellis Mount, DLS (Vol. 10, No. 1, 1990). *"This is a timely publication for those of use involved in conducting online searches in special libraries where our users have a detailed knowledge of their subject areas." (Australian Library Review)*

Sci-Tech Archives and Manuscript Collections, edited by Ellis Mount, DLS (Vol. 9, No. 4, 1989). *Gain valuable information on the ways in which sci-tech archival material is being handled and preserved in various institutions and organizations.*

Collection Management in Sci-Tech Libraries, edited by Ellis Mount, DLS (Vol. 9, No. 3, 1989). *"An interesting and timely survey of current issues in collection management as they pertain to science and technology libraries." Barbara A. List, AMLS, Coordinator of Collection Development, Science & Technology Research Center, and Editor, New Technical Books, The Research Libraries, New York Public Library)*

The Role of Conference Literature in Sci-Tech Libraries, edited by Ellis Mount, DLS (Vol. 9, No. 2, 1989). *"The volume constitutes a valuable overview of the issues posed for librarians and users by one of the most frustrating and yet important sources of scientific and technical information." (Australian Library Review)*

Adaptation of Turnkey Computer Systems in Sci-Tech Libraries, edited by Ellis Mount, DLS (Vol. 9, No. 1, 1989). *"Interesting and useful. . . . The book addresses the problems and benefits associated with the installation of a turnkey or ready-made computer system in a scientific or technical library." (Information Retrieval & Library Automation)*

Sci-Tech Libraries Serving Zoological Gardens, edited by Ellis Mount, DLS (Vol. 8, No. 4, 1989). *"Reviews the history and development of six major zoological garden libraries in the U.S." (Australian Library Review)*

Libraries Serving Science-Oriented and Vocational High Schools, edited by Ellis Mount, DLS (Vol. 8, No. 3, 1989). *A wealth of information on the special collections of science-oriented and vocational high schools, with a look at their services, students, activities, and problems.*

Sci-Tech Library Networks Within Organizations, edited by Ellis Mount, DLS (Vol. 8, No. 2, 1988). *Offers thorough descriptions of sci-tech library networks in which their members have a common sponsorship or ownership.*

One Hundred Years of Sci-Tech Libraries: A Brief History, edited by Ellis Mount, DLS (Vol. 8, No. 1, 1988). *"Should be read by all those considering, or who are already involved in, information retrieval, whether in Sci-tech libraries or others." (Library Resources & Technical Services)*

Alternative Careers in Sci-Tech Information Service, edited by Ellis Mount, DLS (Vol. 7, No. 4, 1987). *Here is an eye-opening look at alternative careers for professionals with a sci-tech background, including librarians, scientists, and engineers.*

Preservation and Conservation of Sci-Tech Materials, edited by Ellis Mount, DLS (Vol. 7, No. 3, 1987). *"This cleverly coordinated work is essential reading for library school students and practicing librarians. . . . Recommended reading." (Science Books and Films)*

Sci-Tech Libraries Serving Societies and Institutions, edited by Ellis Mount, DLS (Vol. 7, No. 2, 1987). *"Of most interest to special librarians, providing them with some insight into sci-tech libraries and their activities as well as a means of identifying specialized services and collections which may be of use to them." (Sci-Tech Libraries)*

Innovations in Planning Facilities for Sci-Tech Libraries, edited by Ellis Mount, DLS (Vol. 7, No. 1, 1986). *"Will prove invaluable to any librarian establishing a new library or contemplating expansion." (Australasian College Libraries)*

Role of Computers in Sci-Tech Libraries, edited by Ellis Mount, DLS (Vol. 6, No. 4, 1986). *"A very readable text. . . . I am including a number of the articles in the student reading list." (C. Bull, Kingstec Community College, Kentville, Nova Scotia, Canada)*

Weeding of Collections in Sci-Tech Libraries, edited by Ellis Mount, DLS (Vol. 6, No. 3, 1986). *"A useful publication. . . . Should be in every science and technology library." (Rivernia Library Review)*

Sci-Tech Libraries in Museums and Aquariums, edited by Ellis Mount, DLS (Vol. 6, No. 1/2, 1985). *"Useful to libraries in museums and aquariums for its descriptive and practical information." (The Association for Information Management)*

Data Manipulation in Sci-Tech Libraries, edited by Ellis Mount, DLS (Vol. 5, No. 4, 1985). *"Papers in this volume present evidence of the growing sophistication in the manipulation of data by information personnel." (Sci-Tech Book News)*

Role of Maps in Sci-Tech Libraries, edited by Ellis Mount, DLS (Vol. 5, No. 3, 1985). *Learn all about the acquisition of maps and the special problems of their storage and preservation in this insightful book.*

Fee-Based Services in Sci-Tech Libraries, edited by Ellis Mount, DLS (Vol. 5, No. 2, 1985). *"Highly recommended. Any librarian will find something of interest in this volume." (Australasian College Libraries)*

Serving End-Users in Sci-Tech Libraries, edited by Ellis Mount, DLS (Vol. 5, No. 1, 1984). *"Welcome and indeed interesting reading. . . . a useful acquisition for anyone starting out in one or more of the areas covered." (Australasian College Libraries)*

Management of Sci-Tech Libraries, edited by Ellis Mount, DLS (Vol. 4, No. 3/4, 1984). *Become better equipped to tackle difficult staffing, budgeting, and personnel challenges with this essential volume on managing different types of sci-tech libraries.*

Collection Development in Sci-Tech Libraries, edited by Ellis Mount, DLS (Vol. 4, No. 2, 1984). *"Well-written by authors who work in the field they are discussing. Should be of value to librarians whose collections cover a wide range of scientific and technical fields." (Library Acquisitions: Practice and Theory)*

Role of Serials in Sci-Tech Libraries, edited by Ellis Mount, DLS (Vol. 4, No. 1, 1983). *"Some interesting nuggets to offer dedicated serials librarians and users of scientific journal literature. . . . Outlines the direction of some major changes already occurring in scientific journal publishing and serials management." (Serials Review)*

Planning Facilities for Sci-Tech Libraries, edited by Ellis Mount, DLS (Vol. 3, No 4, 1983). *"Will be of interest to special librarians who are contemplating the building of new facilities or the renovating and adaptation of existing facilities in the near future. . . . A useful manual based on actual experiences." (Sci-Tech News)*

Monographs in Sci-Tech Libraries, edited by Ellis Mount, DLS (Vol. 3, No. 3, 1983). *This insightful book addresses the present contributions monographs are making in sci-tech libraries as well as their probable role in the future.*

Role of Translations in Sci-Tech Libraries, edited by Ellis Mount, DLS (Vol. 3, No. 2, 1983). *"Good required reading in a course on special libraries in library school. It would also be useful to any librarian who handles the ordering of translations." (Sci-Tech News)*

Online versus Manual Searching in Sci-Tech Libraries, edited by Ellis Mount, DLS (Vol. 3, No. 1, 1982). *An authoritative volume that examines the role that manual searches play in academic, public, corporate, and hospital libraries.*

Document Delivery for Sci-Tech Libraries, edited by Ellis Mount, DLS (Vol. 2, No. 4, 1982). *Touches on important aspects of document delivery and the place each aspect hold in the overall scheme of things.*

Cataloging and Indexing for Sci-Tech Libraries, edited by Ellis Mount, DLS (Vol. 2, No. 3, 1982). *Diverse and authoritative views on the problems of cataloging and indexing in sci-tech libraries.*

Role of Patents in Sci-Tech Libraries, edited by Ellis Mount, DLS (Vol. 2, No. 2, 1982). *A fascinating look at the nature of patents and the complicated, ever-changing set of indexes and computerized databases devoted to facilitating the identification and retrieval of patents.*

Current Awareness Services in Sci-Tech Libraries, edited by Ellis Mount, DLS (Vol. 2, No. 1, 1982). *An interesting and comprehensive look at the many forms of current awareness services that sci-tech libraries offer.*

Role of Technical Reports in Sci-Tech Libraries, edited by Ellis Mount, DLS (Vol. 1, No. 4, 1982). *Recommended reading not only for science and technology librarians, this unique volume is specifically devoted to the analysis of problems, innovative practices, and advances relating to the control and servicing of technical reports.*

Training of Sci-Tech Librarians and Library Users, edited by Ellis Mount, DLS (Vol. 1, No. 3, 1981). *Here is a crucial overview of the current and future issues in the training of science and engineering librarians as well as instruction for users of these libraries.*

Networking in Sci-Tech Libraries and Information Centers, edited by Ellis Mount, DLS (Vol. 1, No. 2, 1981). *Here is an entire volume devoted to the topic of cooperative projects and library networks among sci-tech libraries.*

Planning for Online Search Service in Sci-Tech Libraries, edited by Ellis Mount, DLS (Vol. 1, No. 1, 1981). *Covers the most important issue to consider when planning for online search services.*

Electronic Expectations: Science Journals on the Web has been co-published simultaneously as *Science & Technology Libraries,* Volume 18, Numbers 2/3 1999.

The development, preparation, and publication of this work has been undertaken with great care. However, the publisher, employees, editors, and agents of The Haworth Press and all imprints of The Haworth Press, Inc., including The Haworth Medical Press® and Pharmaceutical Products Press®, are not responsible for any errors contained herein or for consequences that may ensue from use of materials or information contained in this work. Opinions expressed by the author(s) are not necessarily those of The Haworth Press, Inc.

The Haworth Press, Inc., 10 Alice Street, Binghamton, NY 13904-1580, USA

Cover design by Thomas J. Mayshock Jr.

Library of Congress Cataloging-in-Publication Data

Library of Congress number: 99052014

ISBN 0-7890-0836-X (alk. paper)–ISBN 0-7890-0846-7

Electronic Expectations: Science Journals on the Web

Tony Stankus, MLS

Electronic Expectations: Science Journals on the Web, has been co-published simultaneously as *Science & Technology Libraries*, Volume 18, Numbers 2/3 1999.

The Haworth Press, Inc.
New York • London • Oxford

INDEXING & ABSTRACTING

Contributions to this publication are selectively indexed or abstracted in print, electronic, online, or CD-ROM version(s) of the reference tools and information services listed below. This list is current as of the copyright date of this publication. See the end of this section for additional notes.

- *AGRICOLA Database*

- *Biosciences Information Service of Biological Abstracts (BIOSIS)*

- *BUBL Information Service: An Internet-Based Information Service for the UK Higher Education Community, <URL: http//bubl.ac.uk/>*

- *Cambridge Scientific Abstracts*

- *Chemical Abstracts*

- *CNPIEC Reference Guide: Chinese National Directory of Foreign Periodicals*

- *Current Awareness Abstracts of Library & Information Management Literature, ASLIB (UK)*

- *Current Index to Journals in Education*

- *Educational Administration Abstracts (EAA)*

- *Engineering Information (PAGE ONE)*

- *Environment Abstracts*

- *IBZ International Bibliography of Periodical Literature*

- *Index to Periodical Articles Related to Law*

- *Information Science Abstracts*

- *Informed Librarian, The*

- *INSPEC*

- *Konyvtari Figyelo-Library Review*

(continued)

- *Library & Information Science Abstracts (LISA)*
- *Library & Information Science Annual (LISCA)*
- *Library Literature*
- *Medicinal & Aromatic Plants Abstracts (MAPA)*
- *Newsletter of Library and Information Services*
- *PAIS (Public Affairs Information Service) NYC*
- *PASCAL Institute de L'information Scientifique et Technique*
- *Referativnyi Zhurnal (Abstracts Journal of the All-Russian Institute of Scientific and Technical Information)*

Special Bibliographic Notes related to special journal issues (separates) and indexing/abstracting:

- indexing/abstracting services in this list will also cover material in any "separate" that is co-published simultaneously with Haworth's special thematic journal issue or DocuSerial. Indexing/abstracting usually covers material at the article/chapter level.
- monographic co-editions are intended for either non-subscribers or libraries which intend to purchase a second copy for their circulating collections.
- monographic co-editions are reported to all jobbers/wholesalers/approval plans. The source journal is listed as the "series" to assist the prevention of duplicate purchasing in the same manner utilized for books-in-series.
- to facilitate user/access services all indexing/abstracting services are encouraged to utilize the co-indexing entry note indicated at the bottom of the first page of each article/chapter/contribution.
- this is intended to assist a library user of any reference tool (whether print, electronic, online, or CD-ROM) to locate the monographic version if the library has purchased this version but not a subscription to the source journal.
- individual articles/chapters in any Haworth publication are also available through the Haworth Document Delivery Service (HDDS).

Electronic Expectations: Science Journals on the Web

CONTENTS

ABOUT THE AUTHOR

Tony Stankus, MLS, graduated, *Summa Cum Laude,* from the College of the Holy Cross in Worcester, Mass., and has been that institution's Science Librarian since 1974. He completed his MLS from the University of Rhode Island's Graduate School of Library and Information Studies in 1975, and has been their Adjunct Professor for courses in Special Librarianship and Sci-Tech Information since 1982. In 1992, URI gave him its Distinguished Alumnus Award. He has served as a columnist and contributing editor for *Library Acquisitions: Practice and Theory, Reference and User Services Quarterly, Science and Technology Libraries,* and *Technicalities*. In addition to over 60 papers, mostly on the science journal industry and libraries, he has authored or edited the following Haworth Press books, all of which remain in print.

Special Format Serials and Issues: Annual Review of . . ., Advances in . . ., Symposia on . . ., Methods in . . . 1995. ISBN: 1-56024-799-1.
Scientific and Clinical Literature for the Decade of the Brain. 1993. ISBN: 1-56024-481-X.
Science Librarianship at America's Liberal Arts Colleges: Working Librarians Tell Their Stories. 1992. ISBN: 1-56024-357-0.
Making Sense of Journals in the Life Sciences. 1992. ISBN: 1-56024-181-0.
Making Sense of Journals in the Physical Sciences. 1992. ISBN: 1-56024-180-2.
Biographies of Scientists for Sci-Tech Libraries: Adding Faces to the Facts. 1991. ISBN: 1-5602-214-0.
Scientific Journals: Improving Library Collections Through Analysis of Publishing Trends. 1990. ISBN: 0-86656-905-7.
Scientific Journals: Issues in Library Selection and Management. 1987. ISBN: 0-86656-616-3.

During the past year of scanning and integrating the literature on electronic journals (largely drawn from 1996-1998, but including selected antecedents for context), Tony has buried his father (at age 101), bought a house (age 109), survived his college reunion (the 25th), and celebrated his 20th wedding anniversary with Mary Frances (Doyle) Stankus (an ageless beauty). He also had additional support on completing this project and maintaining his sanity from On High via the intercession of Deacon Jim Quinlivan of St. Paul's Cathedral, where Tony and Mary Frances (a Nursing instructor at nearby Quinsigamond Community College) serve as lectors. Each Sunday after Mass, the upbeat deacon would good-naturedly ask this weary author: "How's that 'book' coming along?" This author shall finally say, be able to say, that it's done. (But only Heaven knows if he's still sane!)

ABOUT THE JOURNAL WEB SITE HUNTERS

The hopefully useful directory of addresses for electronic versions of important journals (with ranking) accompanying these essays could not have been done without the determined assistance of two students in the author's Science and Technology course at the University of Rhode Island's Graduate School of Library and Information Studies. **Jeanne Marie Clavin** took her undergraduate degree at Providence College in Rhode Island, while **Richard Joslin** is a graduate of Charter Oak College in Connecticut.

Introduction

This volume is devoted to a series of tutorial reviews of the literature broadly relating to the rise of electronic journals in the sciences. *Science & Technology Libraries* has already begun some valuable bibliographic updates on electronic journals from Suzanne T. Weiner, Editor for Electronic Resources in Science and Technology, for this journal. This work is, in no way, a replacement for her four-part series focused aimed at keeping our regular target audience, professional science librarians, up to date, a task that will be necessary for years to come. Rather, the reviews in this volume are intended for all the segments involved in e-journals: science librarians, scientific authors, publishers, aggregators, and Internet managers. While some of the material in each review might seem too elementary for one or two segments of this larger audience, it is likely that it will fill in the gaps of knowledge of another. It is hoped that this work will be particularly beneficial to science librarians in training, most of whom continue to be drawn from the ranks of humanities and social studies backgrounds, and are therefore likely to be unaware of even some of the major issues in this newest version of an old battle over allocation of library resources by disciplines. These reviews were based on some traditional literature searching techniques, a good deal of web surfing, and a reformulation of the discovered material in the light of two overriding themes that came to the fore early on in this process.

The first major theme is that while a survey of the literature of librarianship on this topic is needed and very worthwhile–over 100 new papers have appeared in the last two years–it provides insufficient perspective on a development that involves many other players and factors. The influence of libraries and librarians on electronic journals naturally would seem the most important to librarians like this author, but inspection of only our own entrails makes for bad divination in this case. We librarians are a vital but very small organ within the larger virtual body of e-publishing, and all e-publishing put together is, in a larger sense, a small part of e-commerce. E-Commerce,

[Haworth co-indexing entry note]: "Introduction." Stankus, Tony. Co-published simultaneously in *Science & Technology Libraries* (The Haworth Press, Inc.) Vol. 18, No. 2/3, 1999, pp. 1-4; and: *Electronic Expectations: Science Journals on the Web* (Tony Stankus) The Haworth Press, Inc., 1999, pp. 1-4. Single or multiple copies of this article are available for a fee from The Haworth Document Delivery Service [1-800-342-9678, 9:00 a.m. - 5:00 p.m. (EST). E-mail address: getinfo@haworthpressinc.com].

which we can see developing before our very eyes (if we are paying attention) and business and technological warfare in the computer industry (where
the battles can be seen but the outcomes are hard to predict), will probably be
more influential in what happens to the Internet as a whole than what we as a
profession can say or do on our own. Most librarians would acknowledge that
the literatures of academic science and higher education (with which we tend
to have some familiarity) are at least as important as our own in determining
scholarly publishing trends. After all, academic scientists invented the web,
and use it all the time. But they scarcely have control of it anymore. Arguably
as important in mapping developments in e-publishing on the Internet may be
the more practical literature of the printing and publishing industries, including the book, newspaper, popular magazine, and trade publication segments
that many academic science librarians might disdain as irrelevant because
scholarly journal publishing is supposed to be so very unique. Yet all these
segments tend to have some influence in current journal publishing through
either shared ownership, shared production or distribution personnel, and
shared dependence on raw materials markets and ancillary service providers.
This author argues that while the contents of the scholarly electronic publications make them somewhat unique in terms of marketing and therefore somewhat susceptible to control by academic librarians, their principal buyers, the
technological and business contexts in which all Internet publications operate
will still be more alike than some Internet utopian thinkers imagine. The
hard-nosed people in publishing, printing, and even advertising have been
well aware of what the rise of e-publishing could mean for their traditional
businesses, and don't want to lose those sectors over which they have some
control without a fight. They are not merely being statically reactionary,
however, and see that e-publishing may well be something that they can
co-opt while sustaining their traditional business as well. They have long
been working to leverage their considerable trade relations with both the
computing software and hardware industries to develop products and shape
protocols that help them with both their print *and* Internet applications. While
this strategy will not give them absolute control over their own electronic
futures on the Internet (virtually no segment can manage that apart from total
abstinence from even trying) , it has made them much more prepared and
more resilient in the face of radical initiatives against their existing practices
and economic position than is generally suspected. Librarians who argue that
this industry gearing up has either not been happening, or is of no conse-
quence, do not appear to recognize some signs that it is indeed taking place,
and that it is aimed at scientific authors and readers, who are the consumers
of journals, even if they are not often the direct buyers. There have been
improvements in traditional print journals in terms of their promptness of
issuance, design, readability, and even their artwork, even if not in what

librarians might argue is the critical issue, their prices. Consider the covers of life sciences journals which have become veritable eye magnets in recent years, after decades of drabness. Evidence of crossover-to-electronic efforts includes the enormous portion of the digital graphics we see on our web computers that is directly derived from the multi-billion dollar computer-assisted printing industry (which supports the Graphic Arts Technical Foundation, the Research and Engineering Council of the Graphic Arts Industry, the National Association of Printers and Lithographers, and the Seybold Seminars). Evidence about the commercial direction of the Internet also includes the abundance of advertising just about everywhere on it. (Virtually the only source of earned income, as opposed to the investor-gambled money of stock offerings, for most Internet search engine companies and portals is advertising.) Consider also the formation of industry alliances and mergers of publishers with each other and with computer hardware and software companies. (Librarians who breathed a sigh of relief that Reed-Elsevier did not merge with Wolters-Kluwer are apparently unaware that Elsevier is already a technology partner of Microsoft, and that merger overtures have been repeatedly reported in responsible financial publications.) Most of all, print and electronic publishing are united on profiting on content secured by copyright.

The second major theme is that it is also disingenuous to expect that the electronic journal movement ought to be seen as so revolutionary, that it will dramatically change or improve everything about science in libraries. Some for-profit publishers talk about its "value-added" virtue, as if librarians could readily afford everything that improves information access for scientists and yet still have enough monies left over to serve all the non-scientists. Some not-for-profit and largely electronically self-publishing scientists see the rise of electronic journals as part of an "information liberationist movement" that initially will put for-profit publishers out of business, earning the support of librarians, but then in more muted tones, suggest that it may also diminish the physical library and put conventional librarians largely out to pasture as an unneeded intermediary. Librarians are notably altruistic, and in many respects, anti-capitalistic on issues of information, but surely they are not occupationally suicidal or passive partners in information handling who have no information market leverage themselves. Moreover, their electronic experiences thus far in other areas of librarianship have informed at least some of them that there probably is no free electronic lunch for long.

It is certainly true that many librarians are constantly battling a crisis of money caused largely–in the minds of many of them, at least–by conventional print scholarly journals in the sciences. Libraries have been trying and will continue to try cancellations, shared buying, traditional interlibrary loans, and document delivery in an effort to regain control of their print science journal situation. When they see electronic journals they exhibit a three-step cascade of instinctive reactions, honed by their often justified budgetary siege mentality. Their first instinct is to interpret them primarily as cost-fighting weapons, whatever else anyone else thinks they are. Their second instinct is to try integrating these new weapons into their own library's cost-fighting armory as soon as possible, combining their use with the other cost-fighting measures they will keep on using. Finally, their third instinct is to rally interest and coordinate policies on electronic journals as cost-fighting tools through library consortia and associations. Librarians, acting singly or in unison, however, may find that opening that carton containing the web-linked PC that they use to access e-journals will be more like opening Pandora's box, rather than opening some sort of war chest that allows them to gain control over the ongoing scholarly record of science at little or no new cost to them in the near future. Just as importantly, even if librarians were to judge wholly new electronic journals in the sciences as their preferred solution, they have yet to convince significant numbers of their scientist customers that this is the case, quite possibly because many librarians have long regarded the scientists as much as the science publishers to be the problem.

There is at least one area, however, in which the opinions of science librarians, informed by the manuscript submission and reading habits of their own academic scientist customers, are pretty decisive, and in which the other segments involved in e-publishing and e-commerce have less sway, and frankly less influence and competence. That is in the ranking and recommending of specific science journals that have electronic versions. The final section of this work is just one such an effort by this author, supplemented by electronic addresses for those titles, supplied by diligent searches from two of the author's graduate students in the Science and Technology course conducted at the University of Rhode Island Graduate School of Library and Information Studies.

Tony Stankus

REFERENCES

Dewan, Rajiv M. "Marshall L. Freimer, and Abraham Seidman. "Internet Service Providers, Proprietary Content, and the Battle for Users' Dollars." *Communications of the ACM* 41 (8): 43-48, 1998.

Weiner, Suzanne T. "Electronic Journals: Four Part Series: An Introduction." *Science and Technology Libraries* 16 (2): 65-68, 1997.

The Key Trends
Emerging in the First Decade
of Electronic Journals in the Sciences

Tony Stankus

It should be admitted that there is no unanimity of historical recounting or consensus of forecasting in the literature surveyed by this author. Contrary assessments are readily to be found in the several reference lists following each paper within this work. These include many that will disagree with the author's opinions. Nonetheless, a scan of over 300 recent papers (including over 150 pertinent to this work, but outside the scope of the more narrowly defined literature of librarianship) that are cited throughout this volume prompts the following summary assessments that are intended to set the table for the longer reviews that follow. These assessments represent some of this author's central theses, and are presented straightway in the time-management interests of busy readers who need to get to the main points first, and then can hash out any underlying issues and reasons later by reading items in the bibliographies that follow this and other papers in this work for themselves.

The three bibliographies that follow this opening paper are the most general in nature. The first list of readings focuses on other "news, trends and opinion" pieces relating to electronic journals and electronic publishing, mostly in the sciences. The second focuses on some of the major concerted strategies, past and present, of libraries acting together (or of many libraries acting separately, but having a cumulative effect) when facing a general crisis in scholarly journals, most often those in the sciences. It is in the context of these collective cost-control and resource sharing strategies that most librarians are going to determine their electronic journal strategies. The third bibli-

[Haworth co-indexing entry note]: "The Key Trends Emerging in the First Decade of Electronic Journals in the Sciences." Stankus, Tony. Co-published simultaneously in *Science & Technology Libraries* (The Haworth Press, Inc.) Vol. 18, No. 2/3, 1999, pp. 5-20; and: *Electronic Expectations: Science Journals on the Web* (Tony Stankus) The Haworth Press, Inc., 1999, pp. 5-20. Single or multiple copies of this article are available for a fee from The Haworth Document Delivery Service [1-800-342-9678, 9:00 a.m. - 5:00 p.m. (EST). E-mail address: getinfo@haworthpressinc.com].

5

ography discusses the still unresolved dilemma of how archives for electronic journals will be set up and maintained. Given a lack of consensus, archiving will not be discussed in detail further in this work, although papers noting some pioneering or self published electronic journals or preprint archives will be listed at the end of the next paper.

TREND ONE

Electronic journals will not replace print journals any time soon: subscription prices are the biggest threats to print subscriptions, not e-journal technology per se.

Print and electronic journals will have a very long period of co-existence: at least 10 years and perhaps longer. There is little or no evidence that the technological feasibility of producing electronic versions of most print journals of science has, of itself, encouraged the wholesale discontinuance of their print versions by their publishers. Subscription prices have caused, and will continue to cause, most reductions in print holdings in libraries of the main categories of science journals. Nonetheless, most academic institutions that customarily take more than a 100 journals or so (the largest market) still appear to spend much more on their print journals than on their electronic versions, and still take more print journals (with or without a concurrent electronic versions) than electronic only journals. Only in holdings of cumbersome and complicated indexing/abstracting services are we seeing substantial abandonment of print products with direct replacement by access to electronic versions. Much of this drop off is due to unique advantages in electronic searching and the possibility that pay-as-you-go searching can be cheaper than the complete cost of a traditional print subscription for some libraries. (A great many libraries are hoping that electronically based Interlibrary Loan or Document Delivery will do the same, but this approach is still based on cost avoidance more than on a fundamental belief, that all things being equal, buying individual documents as needed is more satisfying for their customers, than having complete runs if they can be afforded.) Aware of these trends, and fearing them to some extent, most publishers will require both print *and* electronic subscriptions, or will at least adjust pricing that favors dual subscriptions and push all-their-publications package plans, especially to consortia. Discounts for electronic-only subscriptions, when available, will continue to be minimal. The presence of over 7,000 electronic versions of print journals, however, has given companion e-journals a critical mass that suggests an end to any notion that somehow they are merely experimental. They are here to stay, although likely to remain coupled to print. Purely electronic journals are, and will continue to be, wildly popular as personal, institutional, or professional society experiments, but are still warily regarded by most scientific authors as a reliable depository for their best work on a continuing basis. Even with over a thousand electronic journals that have no formal print version, and even though some have endured for several years by now, there is insufficient evidence to suggest that they are the inevitable wave of the future. Few of them are emerging as serious contenders for leadership in a major scientific discipline, largely because the combination of print-plus-electronic journal provides more of the advantages of both old and new publishing with less risk of anything but higher costs that scientific authors and readers generally do not have to bear personally.

TREND TWO

Electronic journals will not be substantially cheaper than print in the long run, if cheaper at all. Mergers and partnerships among publishers will increase to spread technology costs, to maintain cash flow, and to reduce risks of the electronic publishing systems already adopted by partners being by-passed by developments in the larger commercial publishing marketplace or internet community.

While some costs for some familiar components of the print journal production, distribution, accessing and archival process will be reduced during the very slow transition from solely print to largely print-with-electronic journals, the overall financial burden will remain high for both print and electronic formats and among all parties involved in journals. While the initial cost for add-on electronic versions involving a small number of journals is somewhat smaller than expected owing to the dual use of the same computer infrastructure for print based operations in electronic publishing roles, large scale scale-up costs and demands for global around-the-clock server operations will increase a publisher's "after-production" costs over time, as geo-dispersed mirror sites multiply and the possibility of a fracture of the Internet owing to competing *Java* versions or high-speed versus low-speed capacities looms. Decisions made in the computer software and hardware industries, an area over which scientific authors, libraries and publishers have only moderate bargaining power, will add a substantial degree of uncertainty to cost planning. For-profit publishers in particular will continue to merge to reduce technology costs, gain a greater voice in Internet standards decision-making, and as a hedge against decreases in library market share from rising coalitions of not-for-profit publishers and libraries in electronic publishing.

TREND THREE

Libraries and librarians will remain important because of buying power, unanticipated technical services complications, and a lack of resolution to electronic archiving that favors sustaining print archives. Consortia of libraries will become even more important as a power in buying, licensing and archiving.

Libraries and their staffs–with some job description changes, perhaps–will remain very essential to publishers and to scientific authors. Despite phenomenally strained relations with librarians, publishers know that libraries buy most of the journals for scientists, and scientists are not gladly going to begin paying directly. Therefore, most journals will continue to be sold to libraries whose librarians will administer the local Internet domains through which licensed electronic versions of journals will be made available to be read by the scientists. Moreover, publishers, scientists, and even most library administrators have largely overlooked the resilience of catalogers (now becoming "metadata" analysts, by the way) and other library professionals in making electronic journal work for themselves, some of the need for which is clearly obvious to library users already, and some of which is obvious only to other catalogers (who may, however, simply be more prescient than the rest of us). Clearly, there is going to be a dramatically greater need for librarians to develop expertise in negotiating site licensing agreements for individual electronic journals and electronic journal packages, for their own institutions, and as is increasingly the case, for consortia of libraries as well. Furthermore, even less computer-capable librarians should take some comfort in that the archival medium will remain primarily print and a responsibility for individual libraries or library consortia for the next several years. This will be largely the case until major bibliographic utilities sign with significant numbers of scientific publishers for a significant number of science journals (as opposed to signing mostly with general or humanities publishers and having comparatively few science publishers or publications). Terms are likely to focus on long-term storage or access rights, rather than on attempting to secure any rights to resell content at a profit. Right now, preserving readability of text regardless of computer platform used seems to be triumphing over applying modern hypertext navigation capabilities to old text, so that most electronic archives resemble electronic microfilm much than most hot-linked e-journals.

TREND FOUR

Libraries are not likely to become successful electronic publishers if they keep trying to change heavily publishing scientists into publishing execu-

tives willing to commit a great deal of time and attention. Libraries will gain somewhat greater leverage over prices if they become financially committed, but otherwise silent, partners with the society presses that scientists value most.

Despite pleadings by some librarians, most scientists will not participate in any sustained joint drive to overthrow existing publishing empires to set up and continuously administer some kind of low cost people's publishing cyberocracy, involving only libraries and ad-hoc groups of individual scientists, similar to today's pre-print servers. (Two efforts, HighWire from Stanford and Project Muse from Johns Hopkins, have been successful in facilitating scientific e-journal publication. But HighWire mainly assists existing not-for-profit print science publishers, and is not itself a publisher. Johns Hopkins is a publisher but most of its titles are older and nonscientific.) Coalitions formed between library consortia and well-established not-for-profit scientific journal publishers and the few university presses that are scientifically sympathetic and journal-oriented are more sustainable, but only with the established publishers controlling much more of the production aspects than will the libraries, and the libraries committing most of the money. Part of this reluctance of scientists to deal directly with libraries as de-facto publishers has to do with the lack of a refereeing system in individual library-based publishing that would inspire the trust of colleagues at other institutions. Part of this may also have to do with the look and feel of a kind of disjointed vanity publishing program that such an individual library-based publication is likely to present. Additionally, relations between science faculty and the library community have grown almost as resentful as those between libraries and publishers because there remains a substantial lack of common ground on the need and value of scientific journals as a genre, owing a good deal to a dearth of scientists in librarianship. There are still many librarians who still expect to transform scientific mores in much the same way some partners engage to marry: "The marriage will be great once I get him to change." Moreover, there is also a critical and underappreciated problem of time commitment based on the continuing reliance of most print-plus-electronic journals today on an issue-by-issue production schedule inherited from the era of print-only journals. Issue-by-issue editing and packaging demands adherence to deadlines in the interests of not only timeliness (at which print-only has been failing through backlogs, and at which e-journals should excel) but it can also mean problems of issue-indigestion on the part of readers unless issue frequency actually keeps increasing, and with it, issue deadline pressures on either the librarians or scientists involved. (Without this adherence to more frequent issues, e-journals would serve up even more titanically indigestible screen-after-screen-after-screen-just-for-the-table-of-contents "issues.") Managing and integrating the flow of even just the already-scientist-approved manuscripts into timely produced issues has always been a time-consuming part of the journal cycle and neither libraries nor individual scientists have a proven track record of doing this without hiring, or themselves becoming, full-time, committed publishing professionals. An all-amateur publishing framework would also mean not only the assumption of the financial uncertainties that even some well-organized not-for-profit publishers are currently facing–but would take the scientist's time away from doing science: a cost most scientists would not bear, even if some librarians seem willing to abandon their traditional duties. The "conservation of their own time and energy feature" of having someone else handle publishing details is still valued by scientists more than any manuscript backlog reduction promised by institutionally self-published web-based journals. However, even this proposed benefit of backlog reduction in electronic-only journals appears moot. While many purely electronic journals have announced that they will publish article by article immediately after acceptance, most are frankly starving for articles, owing to a largely justified lack of author confidence in them. The advance electronic publishing of articles accepted in established print journals, but not yet in print, will actually serve to reinforce the current dual-version print-and-electronic journal system.

TREND FIVE

"Middlepeople" can still make money: some aggregators will continue to do well in the e-journal world, largely by doing more than their traditional job descriptions might suggest.

Most publishers will continue to work with aggregators–a mixed group for whom they have long had mixed feelings–if it can be shown that those aggregators will provide electronic distribution networks that reduce their own in-house electronic workload, will adopt electronic publishing technical standards and practices that will reinforce the ones the publishers have chosen for themselves, or will provide royalty revenues from aggregator electronic products that offset losses from subscriber cancellations. Not all aggregators will do equally well or follow the same path to success. The major subscription services, bolstered by long-standing library buying habits, and better public relations with the library community will probably do the best, particularly in dealing with small libraries and small publishers who could use their rapidly accumulating electronic expertise. Traditional indexing-abstracting services will remain reasonably secure in their relations with larger libraries and with larger publishers on issues of Internet technology, although favorable financial arrangements with the publishers may become somewhat stressed over the issue of any indexing-abstracting alliances with third-party document delivery firms that the publishers regard as inimical. Partly to counter any loss of business with those traditional indexing and abstracting services, more of the document delivery systems will continue their own evolution into low-cost, electronic defacto indexing-abstracting services that are especially appealing to small libraries who have been opting out of both large journal collections and to subscriptions, print or electronic to the major and generally expensive indexing-abstracting services.

BIBLIOGRAPHIES

Bibliography on Electronic Publishing and Electronic Journals in General, Including Pro and Con Assessments

Anonymous. "Electronic Publishing Explodes on the Web." *ARL Newsletter* 187. *http:www.arl.org/newsltr/187/explode.html*

Anonymous. "Publishing, Perishing, and Peer Review." *The Economist* 346 (January 24, 1998): 77-78.

Association of Research Libraries. *E-Journal Forum. [A listserv] http://www.cni.org/Hforums/arl-ejournal/*

Bailey, Charles, compiler. *Scholarly Electronic Publishing Bulletin.* A growing electronic bibliography from a major figure in e-journal cataloging issues at the University of Houston Libraries. *http://info.lib.uh.edu/sepb/sepb.html*

Beattie, David, and David McCallum. "Electronic Scholarly Publishing Initiatives at Industry Canada." *The Serials Librarian* 33(3-4): 223-232, 1998.

Bennett, Jo. "If You Build it, They Won't Necessarily Come." *Folio: The Magazine for Magazine Management* 27(2): 49, Feb 1, 1998.

Budd, John. "The Future is Us." *Library Acquisitions: Practice and Theory* 22 (2): 228-229, 1998.

Budd, John, and Lynn Silipigni Conaway. " University Faculty and Networked Information: Results of a Survey." *Journal of the American Society for Information Science* 48: 843-852, 1997.

Cox, John. "The Role of the Paper-Based Journal in an Era of Electronic Information." *The Serials Librarian* 30 (3-4): 41-54, 1997.

Crawford, Susan Y., Julie Hurd, and Ann C. Walker. *From Print to Electronic: The Transformation of Scientific Communication.* Information Today, 1996.

Cummings, Anthony M. and others. "University Libraries and Scholarly Communication: A Study Prepared for the Andrew Mellon Foundation." *Journal of Library Administration* 23 (3-4): 1-247, 1996.

Davis, Susan A. "Surviving the Serials Crisis: Are E-Journals an Answer?" *Serials Review* 21: 95-96. Winter, 1995.

Duranceau, Ellen Finnie. "Old Wine in New Bottles?: Defining Electronic Serials." *Serials Review.* 22: 69-79, Spring 1996.

Ekman, R. and R. Quandt. *Technology and Scholarly Communication.* University of California Press, 1998.

Elliott, Roger. "The Impact of Electronic Publishing on the Scientific Information Chain." *IFLA Journal* 23(5-6): 351-5, 1997.

Garigliano, Jeff. "Web Titles are Falling Fast." *Folio: The Magazine for Magazine Management* 27(2): 13, 1998.

Ginsparg, Paul. "Winners and Losers in the Global Research Village." *The Serials Librarian* 30 (3-4): 83-95, 1997.

Gomes, Suely, A.J. Meadows. "Perceptions of Electronic Journals in British Universities." *Journal of Scholarly Publishing* 29(3): 174-81, 1998.

Hafner, Katie. "Scientists Are Publishing More On Line." *New York Times* (January 21, 1999): E4.

Hamaker, Charles A. "Chaos–Journals Electronic Style." *Against the Grain* 9(6): 90-1, Dec. 1997/Jan. 1998.

Harnad, Stevan, and M. Hemus. "All-or-None: No Stable Hybrid or Half-Way Solutions for Launching the Learned Periodical Literature into the Post-Gutenberg Galaxy." *In The Impact of Scholarly Publishing on the Academic Community.* London: Portland Press, 18-27, 1997.

Harnad, Stevan R.. "How to Fast-Forward Learned Serials to the Inevitable and the Optimal for Scholars and Scientists." *The Serials Librarian* 30 (3-4): 73-81, 1997.

Harnad, Stevan R. "The Paper House of Cards, and Why It's Taking So Long to Collapse." *Ariadne* 8, March, 1997. *http://ariadne.ac.uk/issue8/harnad/*

Harter, Stephan P. "Scholarly Communication and Electronic Journals: an Impact Study." *Journal of the American Society for Information Science* 49(6): 507-16, 1998.

Hilts, Paul. "Confronting Publishing's New Paradigm." *Publishers Weekly* 245 (23): 29, June 8, 1998.

Hsu, Richard C., and William E. Mitchell. "After 400 Years, Print is Still Superior." *Communications of the ACM* 40 (10): 27-28, October, 1997.

Jenkins, Clare. "User Studies: Electronic Journals and User Response to New Modes of Information Delivery." *Library Acquisitions: Practice and Theory* 21 (Fall, 1997): 355-363.

Kennan, Mary Anne. "The Impact of Electronic Scholarly Publishing." *LASIE* 28(3): 24-33, 1997

Ketcham, Lee and Kathleen Born. "Projecting the Electronic Revolution While Budgeting for the Status Quo." *Library Journal* 121 (7): 45-51, 1996.

Kidd, Tony. "Electronic Journals: Their Introduction and Exploitation in Academic Libraries in the United Kingdom." *Serials Review* 24 (1): 7-14, 1998.

Lienhard, John. "Reinventing Journals, Reinventing Knowledge." *The Serials Librarian* 30 (3-4): 29-40, 1997.

Milliot, Jim. "WK Sees Gradual Electronic Growth." *Publishers Weekly* 245 (16): 17, 1998.

Mogge, Dru, and others. *Directory of Electronic Journals, Newsletters and Academic Discussion Lists.* 7th ed. Association of Research Libraries, 1998.

Muth, Anne Marie. *By the Numbers: Electronic and Online Publishing: A Statistical Guide to the Electronic and Online Publishing Industry.* Gale Research, 1998.

Neal, James G.."The Electronic Revolution: Vision, Innovation, Tradition." *The Serials Librarian* 30 (3-4): 97-105, 1997.

NewJour [a listserv, based at the University of Pennsylvania, reporting new electronic journals or electronic versions of print journals. Performing quite a vital service] *http://gort.ucsd.edu/newjour/*

Odlyzko, Andrew. "Silicon Dreams and Silicon Bricks: The Continuing Evolution of Libraries." *Library Trends* 46(1): 152-67, 1997.

Odlyzko, Andrew M. "Tragic Loss or Good Riddance: The Impending Demise of Traditional Scholarly Journals." (A number of versions are available of this seminal critique.) One is at *http://www.iicm.edu/jucs-0-0/tragic-loss-or-good/html/paper.html*

Orr, Alicia. "'You Can't Take a Laptop into the Bathtub'. . . and Other Reasons why Print Media isn't Dead (or Dying) in the Electronic Age." *Target Marketing.* 21(8): 31, 1998.

Peek, Robin P. and Gregory G. Newby. *Scholarly Publishing: The Electronic Frontier.* MIT Press, 1996.

Peek, Robin, Jeffrey Pomerantz, and Stephen Paling. "The Traditional Scholarly Journals Legitimize the Web." *Journal of the American Society for Information Science* 49 (11): 983-989, September, 1998.

Pikowsky, Robert A. "Electronic Journals as a Potential Solution to Escalating Serials Costs." *The Serials Librarian.* 32(3-4): 31-56, 1997.

Porteous, James. "Plugging Into Electronic Journals." *Nature* 389: 137-138, 1997.

Quandt, Richard E. "Electronic Publishing and Virtual Libraries: Issues and an Agenda for the Andrew W. Mellon Foundation." *Serials Review* 22 (1): 9-24, Summer, 1996.

Rogers, Sharon J. and Charlene S. Hurt. " New Electronic Scholarship and Libraries: Or the Medium Became the Message." *Journal of Library Administration* 25 (4): 239-249, September-October, 1998.

Rowland, Fytton. "Print Journals: Fit for the Future." *Ariadne* 7, January, 1997. *Http://www.ariadne.ac.ul/issue7/fytton/*

Schaffner, Ann C. "The Future of Scientific Journals: Lessons from the Past." *Information Technology and Libraries.* 13: 239-47, 1994.

Schatz, Bruce, and Hsinchun Chen. "Building large-scale libraries." *Computer* 29(5): 22-26, May, 1996.

Stamps, David. "Why Paper Won't Go Away." *Training* 35 (4): 37-38, April, 1998.

Stankus, Tony. "Electronic Journals: Questions For Today With Answers For Now." *Technicalities* 18(5): 1+, May 1998.

Stankus, Tony. "*Spam* and *Spam-Lite*: A Parable About Retaining Science Department Loyalties During the Transition from Print to Electronic Journals." *Science and Technology Libraries* 17 (1) 87-89, 1997.

Stein, M.L. "Don't Sweat the Internet." *Editor & Publisher* 131 (34): 40-41, August 22, 1998.

Stewart, Linda Guyotte. "User Acceptance of Electronic Journals: Interviews with Chemists at Cornell University." *College and Research Libraries* 57: 339-349, 1996.

Tenopir, Carol and Donald King. "Managing Scientific Journals in the Digital Age." *Information Outlook* (February, 1997): 40-41.

Tenopir, Carol, and Donald Ward King. "Trends in Scientific Scholarly Journal Publishing in the United States." *Journal of Scholarly Publishing* 28(3): 135-70, Apr. 1997.

Tomlins, Christopher L. "The Wave of the Present: The Printed Scholarly Journal on the Edge of the Internet." *Journal of Scholarly Publishing* 29 (3): 133-150, 1998.

Valauskas, Edward J. "Electronic Journals and Their Roles on the Internet." *The Serials Librarian* 33 (1-2): 45-54, 1998.

Wilkinson, Sophie R. "Electronic Publishing Takes Journals Into a New Realm." *Chemical and Engineering News* 76 (20): 10-18, May 18, 1998.

Woodward, Hazel M., J.F.B. Rowland, and Cliff McKnight. "Electronic Journals: Myths and Realities." *OCLC Systems and Services* 13 (4): 144-151, 1997.

Bibliography of Organized Library Responses, or Aggregate Effects of Individual Library Actions, in The Sci-Tech-Med Journal Crisis Including

- *Traditional Interlibrary Loan and Newer Document Delivery*
- *Consortial Collection Development, Cancellations, Electronic Networks*
- *Coalitions with Preferred Publishing Partners*

Alexander, Julie S. "Cooperative Collection Development and Consortia." *Library Acquisitions: Practice and Theory* 21 (4): 533-535, Winter, 1997.

Allen, Barabara McFadden. "CIC and OCLC Transform Interlibrary Loan Services with New Agreement." *OCLC Newsletter* (November/December, 1998): 8-9.

Allen, Barbara McFadden. "The CIC-EJO as a Model for Management of Internet-Accessible E-Journals." *Library Hi-Tech* 15 (3-4): 45-49, 1997.

Allen, Barbara McFadden. "Hanging Together to Avoid Hanging Separately: Opportunities for Academic Libraries and Consortia." *Information Technology and Libraries* 17 (1): 36-44, 1998.

Anonymous. "ARL's SPARC Invites Expanded Membership." *Information Today* 15 (9): 19, October, 1998.

Anonymous. "CIC Quick Delivery." *Library Journal* 121 (1): 22, 1996.

Anonymous. "Library Groups Endorse SPARC Initiative." *Computers in Libraries* 18 (9): 16, October, 1998.

Anonymous. "Low Cost E-Journal Scheme Begun." *The Library Association Record* 100 (12): 625, 1998.

Anonymous. "SPARC Announces Partnership with the Royal Society of Chemistry." *Information Today* 15 (11): 19, December, 1998.

Berry, John, and Eric Bryant. "ARL Venture to Redefine Scholarly Publishing Model." *Library Journal* 123 (11): 14, June 15, 1998.

Billings, Harold. "TexShare and GALILEO: Comments on Managed Information Sharing." *Texas Library Journal* 73 (4): 155, 1997.

Bradley, Doreen R., Julia Ann Kelly, and Wilhelm Cara. "HealthWeb: an Internet Collaboration." *College and Research Libraries News* 59 (5): 338-340, 1998.

Case, Mary M. "Library Associations Endorse Principles for Licensing Electronic Resources." *ARL Newsletter* 194.
http://www.arl.org/newsltr/194 /licensing.html

Case, Mary M. "Serial Cancellation Rates Increase After 1995 Drop." *ARL Newsletter* 188.
Http://www.arl.org/newsltr/188/serial.html

Chrzastowski, Toma E. and Karen A. Schmidt. "The Serials Cancellation Crisis: National Trends in Academic Library Serials Collections." *Library Acquisitions: Practice and Theory* 21 (4): 431-443, 1997.

Chrzastowski, Tina E. "National Trends in Academic Serial Collections, 1992-1994. *Science & Technology Libraries* 16 (3-4): 191-207, 1997.

Chrzastowski, Tina E., and Mary A. Anthes. "Seeking the 99% Chemistry Library: Extending the Serial Collection Through the Use of Decentralized Document Delivery." *Library Acquisitions: Practice and Theory* 19: 141-152, 1995.

Dannelly, Gay N. "Remote Access Through Consortial Agreement and Other Collection Initiatives." *Against the Grain* 8 (November, 1996): 24.

Dijkstra, Joost. "Journals in Transition: From Paper to Electronic Access: The DECOMATE Project." *The Serials Librarian* 33(3-4): 243-70, 1998.

Dowling, Thomas P. "OhioLINK–The Ohio Library and Information Network." *Library Hi Tech* 15 (3-4): 136-139, 1997.

Etschmaier, Gale and Marifran Bustion. "Document Delivery and Collection Development: An Evolving Relationship." *The Serials Librarian* 31 (3): 13-27, 1997.

Fedunok, Suzanne "A Perspective on U.S. Cooperative Development." *INSPEL* 31 (2): 47-53, 1997.

Fedunok, Suzanne. "Proposals for Interinstitutional Cooperation at the SUNY Centers." *The Serials Librarian* 29 (3-4): 67-77, 1996.

Frazier, Ken. "Liberating Scholarship." *Library Journal* 123 (17): 40, October 15, 1998.

Garwin, Laura. "Journal Prices Lead Libraries to Back Less Costly Initiatives." *Nature* 393: 719, 1998.

Geffner, Mira, and Bonnie J. MacEwen. "A Learning Experience: The CIC Electronic Journals Collection Project." *The Serials Librarian* 33 (3-4): 271-277, 1998.

Goodyear, Dennis L. "Serials Management Issues: Current Problems and Future Opportunities." *Colorado Libraries* 23 (4): 37-40, 1997.

Halgren, Joanne V. "Resource Sharing, Interlibrary Loan, and Orbis: How Did We Get Here and Where Are We Going?" *Journal of Interlibrary Loan, Document Delivery and Information Supply* 8 (4): 5-18, 1998.

Hane, Paula. "Academic Mega-Consortium Negotiates LEXIS-NEXIS Access." *Information Today* 15 (8): 1, 1998.

Helmer, John F. "Special Issue: Library Consortia." *Information Technology and Libraries* 17 (1): 5-50, 1998.

Hewett, Stephen. "Journals in Transition: From Paper to Electronic Access: the European Union project DECOMATE: a Case Study." *Serials Review* 23 (2): 79-83, 1997.

Hilts, Paul. "Plan for Low-Cost Journals Online." *Publishers Weekly* 245 (29): 114, June 20, 1998.

Hirshon, Arnold. "Library Strategic Alliances and the Digital Library in the 1990s: The OhioLINK Experience." *The Journal of Academic Librarianship* 21: 383-386, 1995.

Hodge, S. P. "CIC Electronic Journals Collection." *Choice* 35 (August, 1998) p. 62.

International Coalition of Library Consortia. "Statement of Current Perspective and Preferred Practices for the Selection and Purchase of Electronic Information." *Information Technology and Libraries* 17 (1): 45-50, 1998.

Jackson, Mary. "A Spotlight on High-Performing ILL/DD Operations in Research Libraries." *ARL Newsletter* 198 *http://www.arl.org/newsltr/illdd.html*

Jaffe, John Gabriel. "The VIVA Private College Funding Initiative." *Virginia Libraries* 43 (4): 6-7, 1997.

Johnson, Bruce. *Economics of Access versus Ownership: The Costs &*

Benefits of Access to Scholarly Articles via ILL and Journal Subscription. Binghamton, NY: The Haworth Press, Inc. 1996.

Johnson, Richard K. "Introducing a Response to Soaring Journal Prices: SPARC, the Scholarly Publishing and Academic Resources Coalition." *Http://www.arl/sparc/factsheet.html*

Johnson, Steven D. "Chaos: Electronic Style." *Library Acquisitions: Practice and Theory* 22 (2): 198-201, Summer, 1998.

Kara, William J. "The USDA/Mann Library Partnership: A Collaboration Between Public Agencies and an Academic Library." *The Serials Librarian* 30 (3-4): 235-242, 1997.

Kendall, Mark F. "Collection Development, Full Text, and Document Delivery, A Panel Discussion." *Library Acquisitions: Practice and Theory* 21: 255-260, 1997.

Kendall, Mark F. "How We Did It: Resource Sharing and License Agreements, A Report." *Library Acquisitions: Practice and Theory* 21: 253-255, 1997.

Kiernan, Vincent. "Paying By the Article: Libraries Test a New Model for Scholarly Journals." *Chronicle of Higher Education* 44 (49): A21-A22, August 14, 1998.

Kiernan, Vincent. "University Libraries Join with Chemical Society to Create a New, Low-Cost Journal." *Chronicle of Higher Education* 44 (44): A20, July 10, 1998.

Kochan, Carol Ann, and Daniel R. Lee. "Utah Article Delivery: A New Model for Consortial Resource Sharing." *Computers in Libraries* 18 (4): 24-28, 1998.

Kohl, David F. "How the Virtual Library Transforms Interlibrary Loans: The OhioLINK Experience." *Interlending and Document Supply* 26 (2): 65-69, 1998.

Kohl, David F. "OhioLINK: A Vision for the 21st Century." *Library Hi Tech* 12 (4): 29-34, 1994.

Kohl, David F. "Resource Sharing in a Changing Ohio Environment." *Library Trends* 45: 435-447, 1997.

Kopp, James J. "Don't Overlook the Human Factor." *Alki* 13 (July, 1997): 25-26.

Kopp, James J. "Library Consortia and Information Technology: The Past, the Present, the Promise." *Information Technology and Libraries* 17 (1): 7-12, 1998.

Lynden, Frederick C. "Will Electronic Information Finally Result in Real Resource Sharing?" *Journal of Library Administration* 24 (1-2): 47-72, 1996.

MacEwen, Bonnie J. and Mira Geffner. "The CIC Electronic Journals Collection Project." *The Serials Librarian 31 (1-2): 191-203, 1997.*

McKnight, Cliff. "Many Projects That Depend on Collaboration." *Communications of the ACM* 41 (4): 86-87, 1998.

Malakoff, David. "Academic Publishing: New Journals Launched to Fight Rising Prices." *Science* 282: 853-854, 1998.

Martin, Robert S. "TexShare in Transition." *Texas Library Journal* 73 (4): 152-154, 1997.

Millson-Martula, Christopher A. "VIVA: In the Vanguard for Cooperative Collection Development in Virginia." *Virginia Libraries* 43: 16-18, 1997.

Milton, Suzanne. "Has the Availability of Electronic Journals in Full Text Affected Interlibrary Loan Usage? An EWU Case Study." *Alki* 14(1): 18-19, March 1998.

Morgan, Eric L. "Resource Sharing and Consortia, or, Becoming a 600 Pound Gorilla." *Computers in Libraries* 18 (4): 40-41, 1998.

Mosher, Paul H. "Real Access as the Paradigm of the Nineties." *Journal of Library Administration* 21 (1-2): 39-48, 1995.

Myers, Myrtle. "Union Listing on OCLC: Past Present and Future." *Serials Review* 22: 45-56, Summer, 1996.

Nevins, Kate. "An Ongoing Revolution: Resource Sharing and OCLC." *Journal of Library Administration* 25 (2-3): 65-71, 1998.

O'Connor, Phyllis, Susan Wehmeyer, and Susan Weldon. "The Future of Using an Integrated Approach: the OhioLINK Experience." *Journal of Library Administration* 21 (102): 109-120, 1995.

Patel, Kim. "Libraries Join to Cut Prices of Journals." *The Times [of London] Higher Education Supplement* (October 16, 1998) p.6.

Payne, Lizanne. "The Washington Research Library Consortium: A Real Organization for a Virtual Library." *Information Technology and Libraries* 17 (1): 13-17, 1998.

Payne, Valerie J., and Mary A. Burke. "A Cost Effectiveness Study of Ownership versus Access." *The Serials Librarian* 32 (3-4): 139-152, 1997.

Penson, Meryll. "The University System of Georgia's GALILEO." *Journal of Library Administration* 25 (2-3): 97-109, 1998.

Potter, William Gray. "GALILEO: Georgia's Electronic Library." *Library Hi Tech* 14 (2-3): 9-18, 1996.

Potter, William Gray. "Recent Trends in Statewide Academic Library Consortia." *Library Trends* 45: 416-434, 1997.

Prabha, Chandra G. and Elizabeth C. Marsh. "Commercial Document Suppliers: How Many of the ILL/DD Periodical Article Requests Can They Fulfill?" *Library Trends* 45: 551-568, 1997.

Rambler, Mark. "Do It Yourself? A New Solution to the Journals Crisis." *Lingua Franca* (December, 1998/January, 1999), p. 61.

Rea, Jay Weston. "The Washington State Cooperative Library Project: Quo Vadis?" *Alki* 14 (1): 13-14, 1998.

Reed-Scott, Jutta. "Future of Resource Sharing in Research Libraries." *Journal of Library Administration* 21 (1-2): 67-75, 1995.

Saint-Lifer, Evan. "ARL's SPARC, Chemists in Deal." *Library Journal* 123 (13): 14, 1998.

Saint-Lifer, Evan and Michael Rogers. "University Libraries Testing Model for E-Journal Prices." *Library Journal* 123 (15): 14, September 15, 1998.

Saunders, LaVerna. "ARL's SPARC Alliance Bears Fruit: ARL/ACS Electronic Publishing Venture." *Information Today* 15 (8): 25, 1998.

Saunders, LaVerna. "Research Libraries Initiate Scholarly Publishing Collaboration." *Computers in Libraries* 18 (8): 20-21, 1998.

Simpson, Donald B. "Solving the Challenges Presented by Electronic Resources: Creating Opportunities Through Inter-Institutional Collaboration." *Journal of Library Administration* 24 (4): 49-60, 1997.

Stankus, Tony, and Carolyn Virginia Mills. "Which Life Science Journals will Constitute the Locally Sustainable Core Collection of the 1990s and which will Become 'Fax-Access' Only? Predictions Based on Citation and Price Patterns 1979-1989." *Science & Technology Libraries* 13: 73-114, Fall 1992.

Taylor-Roe, Jill. "'United We Stand, Divided We Spend.'": Current Purchasing Trends in Serials Acquisitions in the UK Academic Sector." *Serials Review* 24 (1): 3-6, 1998.

Treloar, Andrew E. "Libraries' New Role in Electronic Scholarly Publishing." *Communications of the ACM* 41 (4): 88-89, 1998.

Van Dam, Scott, Jennifer Block, and Richard N. Pettitt. "The Impact of the OhioLINK Network on Traditional Interlibrary Loan. " *Journal of Interlibrary Loan, Document Delivery, and Information Supply* 8 (1): 1-19, 1997.

Vikor, Desider L., George Gaumond, and Fred M. Heath. "Building Electronic Cooperation in the 1990s–The Maryland, Georgia, and texas Experiences." *The Journal of Academic Librarianship* 23 (November, 1997): 511-514.

Weiser, Allison. "Two More Groups Endorse SPARC." *Library Journal* 123 (15): 20, September 15, 1998.

Wilder, Stanley. "Reflections." *Library Resources and Technical Services* 42 (3): 243, 1998.

Wilkinson, Sophie. "En Route: Less Costly Journals." *Chemical and Engineering News* (July 6, 1998),: 4.

Wilkinson, Sophie. "Movement to Cheaper Journals Gains Ground." *Chemical and Engineering News* (November 2, 1998): 9.

Yoon, Carol Kaesuk. "Soaring Prices Spur a Revolt in Scientific Publishing." *New York Times* (December 8, 1998), p. D2.

Zappen, Susan H. "From Cancellations to Collaboration: Some Thoughts." *Against the Grain* 9 (June, 1997): 1.

Zappen, Susan H. "Two Libraries, One Direction." *The Bottom Line* 9 (2): 21-24, 1996.

Bibliography on the Still Unresolved Archival Dilemma: Some Progress Reports

Day, Michael William. "Online Serials: Preservation Issues." *The Serials Librarian.* 33(3-4): 199-221, 1998.

Guthrie, Kevin M. "JSTOR: From Project to Independent Organization." *D-Lib Magazine* *http://www.dloib.org/dlib/july97/07guthrie.html*

Kelly, Robert A. "Digital Archiving in the Physics Literature: Author to Archive and Beyond ; the American Physical Society." *The Serials Librarian* 30 (3-4): 163-170, 1997.

Kirsner, Scott. "The Archival Black Hole." *Editor and Publisher* (September 19, 1998) p. 24 +.

Sully, Sarah E. "JSTOR: an IP Practitioner's Perspective." *D-Lib Magazine* *http://www.dloib.org/dliob/january97/-1sully.html*

Tagler, John. "The Electronic Archive: The Publisher's View." *The Serials Librarian* 34 (1-2): 225-232, 1998.

Thomas, Spencer W., Ken Alexander and Kevin Guthrie. "Technology Choices for the JSTOR Archive." *Communications of the ACM* 32 (2): 65, 1999.

A Review of the Print Journal System in the Sciences, with Prospects for Improvement in Deficiencies and Costs Through Electronic Publishing: Practices and Attitudes of Publishers and Printers, Librarians, and Scientific Authors

Tony Stankus

The drive for electronic journals on the Internet in the sciences has at least as much to do with the perceived deficiencies of the current system of print journals as with any certain advantages of the new technology. (It also has a lot to do with an industry-wide instinct that somehow, if one player in the journal game seems to be taking a leap into electronic publishing, then all the rest feel compelled to take theirs too.) While many of the disadvantages of print journals occur to some degree in any subject field, they seem increasingly acute in the sciences. Journals are the archetypal medium for information exchange in the sciences and journal articles are the predominant denomination of science faculty-career-building currency. The complaints of publishers, library subscribers, authors, and readers concerning the current system are sometimes similar and mutually reinforcing, and, at other times, a matter of sharp disagreement. Some causes for complaint in the cycle of print serials in the sciences have remained well-grounded or worsened over the last decade,

[Haworth co-indexing entry note]: "A Review of the Print Journal System in the Sciences, with Prospects for Improvement in Deficiencies and Costs Through Electronic Publishing: Practices and Attitudes of Publishers and Printers, Librarians, and Scientific Authors." Stankus, Tony. Co-published simultaneously in *Science & Technology Libraries* (The Haworth Press, Inc.) Vol. 18, No. 2/3, 1999, pp. 21-41; and: *Electronic Expectations: Science Journals on the Web* (Tony Stankus) The Haworth Press, Inc., 1999, pp. 21-41. Single or multiple copies of this article are available for a fee from The Haworth Document Delivery Service [1-800-342-9678, 9:00 a.m. - 5:00 p.m. (EST). E-mail address: getinfo@haworth pressinc.com].

while others have been substantially diminished, and have minimal continuing validity. A review of the players in the scientific information process, their take on the current cost factors in the print journal economy, and the possibilities for benefit by moving to electronic delivery of journal content via the web portion of the Internet seems warranted. This is particularly true given that print is going to be around for a long time yet.

MOST PRINT PUBLISHERS
ARE LIKE GENERAL CONTRACTORS:
DEALING WITH SUBCONTRACTORS
CAN BE AS IMPORTANT TO THEIR SUCCESS
AS DEALING WITH SUBSCRIBERS

It is often incorrectly supposed that publishers are the sole, internally unified and coordinated intermediary between authors and library-based journal readers. This is only rarely true. (The Haworth Press, Inc. the publisher of many of the journals within which I publish is one of the exceptions.) The role of publishers today is more akin to general contractors on a large construction project that never seems to end, with many suppliers, subcontractors, silent partners, agents, and brokers, all having some say in the process. While it is the publisher/general contractor who gets to negotiate initial arrangements with many of his collaborators in a project, and can presumably come to terms that are favorable to the firm's own interests, the publisher also has to front his collaborators some money, assume oversight, and provide for a number of contingencies that are not always apparent at the start of a new venture. Publishers, like general contractors, have to keep their clients (subscribers) as tolerant as possible with what is seen by the client as chronically high prices without incurring additional client wrath for failures caused by the delayed or defective performance of subcontractors who find they cannot function well in the long run, or are otherwise no longer content, with the initial arrangement as negotiated. Today, publishers also have to avoid having some of their traditional subcontractors take over the project or displace them by an a separately negotiated deal with the clients. Up until the 1970s, that occurrence was rare because it was difficult for subcontractors to accumulate sufficient physical and financial capital, and to have as ready an access as had the general contractors to clients. With each passing decade, these limitations have been weakened. New publishers generally spring from entrepreneurially-minded former employees and subcontractors of existing publishers.

Paper journals have historically had substantial costs with respect to production space, conventional printing equipment, editorial processing, expendable materials and shipping, and marketing and revenue collection. It is at least partly because these costs have been escalating at a time of a tremendous expansion in the numbers of acceptable manuscripts–without any relaxation in the need to make a profit in many cases–that virtually all print publishers have been raising subscription prices in the sciences faster than in any other major subject or form of library material. While there is steadily mounting disbelief on the part of academic librarians that increases in costs are the prime factor in the rise of serial prices, it is at least fair to qualitatively review some of the cost factors in conventional print publishing in the United States for domestic publishers and for foreign publishers who have a substantial American market. Likewise it might be appropriate to review the costs libraries incur in processing, servicing, and maintaining the current print journal, with a view as to whether or not costs apart from subscription prices are likely to decline in an increasingly electronic journal world.

EXISTING COSTS TO PUBLISHERS OF PHYSICAL OVERHEAD: OFFICES, PRODUCTION EQUIPMENT, SHIPPING AND SOME WAREHOUSING

Virtually all science publishers today must maintain at least one "white collar" office usually in or near a major American metropolitan or academic center, and the larger firms often have two to five geographically scattered centers across the country. (Wolters-Kluwer US, with its newly acquired biomedical subsidiaries, for example, currently has at least three offices with about 400 employees, although admittedly not all of them are white collar.) Those publishers with an international market usually have several foreign offices in addition. A small percentage own "blue collar" production facilities as well. Somewhat to the surprise of many in the library profession, the actual printing and distribution of scientific journals has been done apart from their editorial handling for well over 20 years in most major firms.

This divorce began with the migration of physical production out of urban centers and into industrial parks, or even to foreign settings. This shift was largely due to high building overhead, unfavorable tax climates, and deteriorating infrastructure in traditional American urban publishing centers, as well as the greater presence of higher cost, unionized labor in the printing and shipping trades. With time, an ever increasing portion of the physical production and distribution of print journals has been outsourced to relatively anonymous competitive bidders, as a form of overhead cost control on the part of publishers. (Indeed, one of the surprise developments caused by the decline in the number of subscriptions of many formerly larger run journals is that more of the printing can now be done by entrepreneurial "on-demand" printers, who used to depend on the local advertising or small brochure market.) Nonetheless, overhead costs for virtually all conventional publishing operations require outlays for space for the largely computerized office equipment in white collar operations, and publishers must cover, directly or indirectly through fees to contractors, the capital costs of the purchasing, maintaining, and housing fairly sophisticated (and now also largely computer-driven) print machinery in their blue collar operations. Postal costs can be manipulated only through various trans-shipment schemes, where production in a high cost postal area is bundled off to a low cost postal area for individual unit mailings . . . something that can be accomplished in Europe but is not feasible in the U.S. Warehousing of back issues has already seen about all the savings that can be expected since many publishers abandoned long-term back issue retention owing to unfavorable decisions on deductibility as a business expense, and since contemporary computerized printing (particularly Computer-to-Plate or CTP technology) already allows for eccentrically small runs that can exactly match already paid-for demand. (STM publishers no longer round up to the nearest 1,000, or 500, or even 100 subscribers, a common practice that allowed for easy replacement of issues missing from libraries, by the way.) What little warehousing remains, moreover, has long been outsourced in prior cost reduction campaigns.

Prospects for Changes in Costs in These Areas–In a world of internet science journals, it might be argued that the spatial and capital portion of overhead costs devoted to contracting for blue-collar physical production will likely decrease for publishers, as servers substitute for printing presses and production lines, and costs for warehousing and traditional postage largely disappear. The substitution of Internet access fees and 24-hour white collar web server rooms with administrators for blue collar printers and postage may, however, be more expensive, although there is some movement to outsourcing the "warehouse server" function from initial editorial processing by computer. This will increasingly be the case when the electronic infrastructure worldwide increases and more and more scientists in different countries will be able to access web journals. The most immediate practical solution will be time-zone based mirror sites–most online searching empires maintain at least three already–probably serving more than one publisher. Interestingly, the reduced spatial costs of electronic infrastructure and the relative scarcity of competent high-end computer help has reversed, somewhat, the migration of electronic production and warehousing out of traditional publishing cities and academic centers in the US. The best web administrators do not necessarily wish to migrate to industrial parks or offshore, although a certain amount of telecommuting might offset their necessity of doing so in person.

EXISTING EDITORIAL PROCESSING COSTS:
COPY ONE GETS NO CHEAPER

While many scientific manuscripts, having been written by PhDs and survived a refereeing process of their peers, are alleged to arrive ready for publishing, there are many significant details, not immediately obvious to authors or to readers, that require the hidden hand of full-time paid editorial staff at the publisher's headquarters. The following of "Instructions for Authors" by scientific authors is the start of an involved process of journal composition by publishing professionals, not a self-sufficient end point.

There is a long-standing division of labor in science journal editing, and it involves a number of ironic misnomers. The publisher's headquarters folk, who handle a great many details of a journal's fit-and-finish, and whose education is most often in English or Journalism, are termed "technical" editors, despite their utter lack of "technical" engineering training in most cases. By contrast, most of the scholarly, scientific "editors" on science journal mastheads have advanced degrees in science, engineering, or medicine, but have no particular training in compositional "editing" or publication management. The latter work part-time as "editors" and are often unpaid, or only modestly reimbursed for expenses. (The most common expenses are ironically for secretarial help, postage/fax/telecommunications, and travel to editorial board meetings.) Scientific editors are necessarily more qualified and more focused on gauging the factual validity and relative importance of the manuscripts submitted than anyone else in the journal process, and undertake their editor's jobs as part of their professional responsibilities as scientists. Often chosen because of their own productivity as scientific authors or as professors at major scientific institutions, scientific editors have little time or inclination to put together smoothly the sequential packages that readers customarily regard as finished, professional appearing print journal issues. While scientific editors or editorial boards meet with technical editors and publishing staff on an annual or semiannual basis, and set certain broad policies for the coming year, most scientific editors are relatively uninvolved with the actual details of modulating manuscript flow, page budgeting and layout. It is generally not their job to integrate freely submitted, refereed material with recurring features and columns. That is the work of the technical editors.

The work of technical editors includes changes in covers, tables of contents, sequentially numbered manuscript pages, inserting indexes, book and media reviews, job listings, notices of upcoming meetings, and the like, as well as product advertising. Technical editors often are responsible for tracking of the various stages of manuscript revisions and tallying the accumulation of finally accepted papers, a job that is often shared with the editor's secretary. While the presence of spell-checkers and author-supplied diskette-

based graphics packages have tremendously diminished much of the traditional copy editing and virtually eliminated the redrafting of figures that
technical editors used to do, the total look-and-feel of a journal is still largely
theirs. Otherwise, one finds journals that look like a collection of term papers,
and does not tend to attract the attention or readers or advertisers. While that
minimalist format is common among some rather distinguished letters journals (particularly in physics and chemistry), that genre accounts for less than
10% of existing print journals, particularly in the life sciences and medicine.
Even in the many cases where a professional society is the official publisher
and would appear to have a captive audience of member readers, an editorial
production team at association headquarters (or at a for-profit firm that is
handling the account), is necessary once the print journal evolves past the
stage of an informal technical bulletin or straightforward "letters" journal in
order for the journal to compete with other finished look publications in the
same field.

Prospects for Changing Costs in This Area–It is not yet clear whether
some of the behind-the-scenes work of print technical editors will be diminished or transformed by electronic publishing, in a way that leads to cost
savings. It is safe to say that the editorial staff shrinkage current desktop
technology has allowed for seems to be modest, involved low-end clerical
skills, and has resulted in few published cost savings thus far that have not
been reduced somewhat by loss of economies of scale. Part of this may
result from the perceived need to maintain both print and electronic versions
of journals. A continued dependency on, or preference for, the print journal
model for familiar journal formats with recurring features, apart from pure
research content, is likely to continue a demand for publishing professionals
who will electronically choreograph their issuance and appearance. Indeed,
journals whose purely research content is increased in every electronic issue
as a means of reducing backlogs may find themselves less read owing to a
kind of information overload problem in which the proportion of papers of
interest to a specialist will ironically fall, even if the number of papers
published overall increases. This can be solved either by more frequent
smaller electronic issues with a concomitant increase in frequent general
research or professional interest material integrated, or by further subdivid-
ing electronically giant electronic journals into more digestible subspecialty
journals, where the purely topical research level material is focused enough
to encourage frequent reading. Both approaches are likely to require more
publishing professionals, not fewer. Estimates that suggest that 60%-70% of
the costs of a journal are incurred before its physical production remain
unchanged.

COSTS OF EXPENDABLE PRODUCTION MATERIALS

All print journals require paper and ink, as well as covers or some exterior packaging that holds the articles together, and is capable of being addressed for shipment to subscribers. While the unit costs of newsprint for newspapers and paper for some slim humanities journals are generally quite modest, few scholarly journals now use cheap paper. Librarians, who are the buyers of most scholarly journals, have lobbied most scholarly publishers successfully for the use of more expensive "acid-free" papers and non-corrosive inks than mass market publishers have been accustomed to using. Many research societies or governmentally funded agencies have either been naturally sympathetic, or are under regulatory agency mandate, to using papers containing a certain measure of recycled content, and non-toxic soy inks, often putting those demands in some collision with requirements for archival quality, and raising materials costs even higher. Furthermore, scientific journals often have requirements for specially coated papers and inks for purposes of optimal illustration and slick, technical advertising.

Prospects for Changes in Cost in This Area–Despite (and perhaps because of premature predictions of an eventually "paperless Information society"), there have been substantial shortfalls in the supply of journal quality papers in the late 1990s, as paper producers besieged by both environmental regulators and doubts about the future of print have deferred or canceled new paper production facilities, ironically driving up high quality paper prices. While it is clear that the increasing dissemination of science journals via the Internet will diminish the acute need for the publishers to consume vast quantities of high grade paper and ink, the publishers will lose certain economies of scale in their purchasing, and will still have to maintain a fairly delicate balance of power in price setting with their suppliers. Their use of high-grade paper (although not necessarily ink–there is a wider print industry market for the ink) cannot fall so low that more and more competitors from among their suppliers will again be tempted to go out of business, for this will empower the remaining suppliers to raise their prices. A drop in demand for journal quality paper and any changes in the ink market will not lower prices appreciably for the printer paper and toner that libraries use in their printers, because they are largely different segments of the paper and "ink" industry and producers have limited ability to shift production from one type to another. Most critics of the production costs of print journals suggest that under the current system, library subscribers pay for the printing of all the papers and ink within a journal, including many that readers will never need. It is not clear, however, that having most readers print everything they need whenever they need it for more than a few minutes of screen viewing will lower world demand for paper and toner in the long run, resulting in lower paper and toner prices. The opposite, an increase in world printer paper and toner usage with concomitant upward push in prices, is at least as likely. (Indeed a recent downward trend in prices is likely to be arrested owing to a merger of some major producers, who are very likely to both cut labor costs and be once again in a position to raise prices.) This is particularly the case, since the competition for these resources is the much larger business world, and libraries have no competitive advantage that will force down those prices.

THE LIBRARY'S VIEWPOINT OF THE DISADVANTAGES OF PRINT JOURNALS

Librarians are, as a group, the most critical of the print journal publishing process, particularly as it applies to the sciences, and arguably the most concerned with initial subscription costs and the costs of print journal aftercare. While it could often be said that the wishes of librarians and their social sciences and humanities customers are one and the same, this is increasingly not the case with scientists and their libraries. Librarians are overwhelmingly drawn from the humanities and social sciences before taking their graduate training in library and information science. Nothing in their undergraduate literature, nor even in their professional reading today, comes close to the volume and the critical emphasis that scientific journal literature holds for scientists. There is consequently a substantial dissonance of cognitive and value systems in force between scientists, and the librarians who attempt to serve those scientists at the same time they are trying to accommodate library users in other disciplines. Both scientists and librarians want some restraint, some fairness and some excellence in science journal literature, but their views of the right proportions when deciding on a winning journal collection strategy are quite different.

Scientists view the journal literature as a very large arena for identifying the most significant factual ideas and interpretations in science in as fair a manner as possible. They welcome as many qualified entrants (many refereed papers in many reputable journals) as possible for each field, with the restraint in participation coming only through eliminating papers and/or journals that referees dismiss as factually inaccurate, or as reporting only trivially new facts or insights. For them, the only fair judges are other scientists who have run the race–scientists who award in the course of the race countable indicators of journal or article excellence, such as citations, for publishing the works of other scientists in the field that help set the pace and direction for the science encompassing a field. Essentially, scientists in a given field like the format of the Boston Marathon: 20,000 runners who all have a shot to compete and win. The scientists think that it is worthwhile to support 20,000 scientists in a field to get an unambiguous winner of best-in-race each year, but insist that the race must be run year after year to keep that winning journal and other contending journals on their toes. In science, the marathon never seems to end, and having fewer journal-entrants in the race is often taken as a sign of a weakening field.

Librarians, by contrast, value highly restrained competition, with a great deal of *a priori* screening and exclusion being "fairest to library budgets" in their opinion. They like the Olympic event model of academic contests. The librarians view the selection of perhaps a few dozen multiply screened athletes, the athletes being journals with a few contestant authors and their few contestant papers, but every contestant would be a finalist from many preliminary events that the library did not have to sponsor. The library would only have to sponsor an event for the finalists in each department. Finding out exactly which runner is the very best worldwide by a highly inclusive marathon with many possible contenders is not as important as being able to fund an event race for every department. The librarians see the scientific marathon as only one contest among many at the Olympics, and are glad that it comes around only every four years.

COSTS OF LIBRARY PROCESSING OF INCOMING ISSUES

Journals typically come in many separate issues annually, and when many print journals are taken by a library, the costs of recording the arrival or non-arrival of issues, mounts greatly. The bar-coding of journal issues has not progressed to anything near the degree that is seen in grocery stores, despite some industry supported pilot projects. Consequently journal check-in includes a great deal of clerical-level mail-opening and yet requires some sophistication in title and journal section or part discernment, given many look-alike titles, many title changes, and cancer-cell-like multiplications of new subsections. The subscriber may also stamp dates of receipt, marks of ownership, and attach anti-theft strips and routing slips as well. The subscriber also may have a burden in dealing with more than one copy, with each going to a separate location on campus. All-in-all, almost every change in a print journal, whether of its packaging, frequency of issue, title, organization of content, or subsectioning, generates both increased direct costs in subscription fees, and a good deal of hidden handling costs.

Prospects for Change in Processing Costs–It is heartening to report that this is one area where migration to electronic journals will largely eliminate a great deal of clerical and semi-skilled work. However, there is already an astounding amount of library literature that suggests that catalogers, in particular, have detected problems in alerting library customers to the presence of electronic journals within their integrated library systems catalogs, and are attacking these problems with zeal, if with no clear prospect of a resolution that will decrease the employment of catalogers.

COSTS OF HOUSING, SHORT-TERM INVENTORY RETENTION AND THEFT REPLACEMENT, AND LONG-TERM ARCHIVING

Most libraries that subscribe to print journals must maintain both current display capacity and back year storage in dry, well lit, climate-controlled areas. This housing generally involves two different forms of shelving, often in two widely separated locations within a library or library system. Annual runs of many science journals consume as much as three feet a year of shelf space, so that a library of 1,000 science journals must have something like a quarter to half a mile of available shelf space each year. Based on long-standing experience in many libraries that loose journal issues tend to get lost, misplaced or prematurely worn out, most libraries also opt to send loose issues to bindery. The gathering together of these issues, their collation, labeling and packing for shipment to the bindery, and the processing of their return from the bindery all represent additional costs attributable to housing and security. The billings from the binder probably add something on the order of 5-10% of the costs of a typical university journal budget. These costs are growing, not so much because binders are increasing their per-volume charges as because journals are increasing the number and thickness of their issues, requiring more physical volumes per subscription. One hidden cost in preparing for bindery is the replacement of missing issues, often at a cost that is at least 15% over original cost, assuming that replacement issues are available from the publisher. Back-issue resellers charge even more. Rebinding is also not uncommon and even more costs may be required when photocopying engenders sufficient wear and tear to break the spine, or when mutilation results in missing or defaced pages. Nonetheless, binding has the advantage that the printed word is well preserved and not subject to much serious degradation or lack of readability through technological obsolescence. The substitution of microforms for bound volumes saves dramatically on space, but remains wildly unpopular when done by most end-users, and incurs additional expense for reader-printers and in time and opportunity costs for users, as noted below.

Prospects for Change in Costs in This Area–With electronic journals, there are no back issues to physically bind. There is virtually no chance of theft or mutilation, because all but the most dedicated hackers are unable to get at the publisher's server and alter or delete journal content. Issues go missing only if the library fails to pay its bill, or the servers at either the publisher or at the library crash, and that is regarded as a less common occurrence than lost or misplaced bound volumes in even a well-maintained print library. Even the simultaneous user problem–a journal is missing to a user even if the library in fact owns it for as long as another user has it–is greatly reduced by electronic journals. No longer is a journal "missing" if someone else in the library wants to use it, and your customer also needs to photocopy it. The problem of long-term archiving remains a library responsibility. Publishers have long abandoned maintaining comprehensive back runs of even their own journals, and have shown limited willingness to convert what computer files they may have retained to mount electronically readable back files, because of limited demand. Most projects to build electronic archives from the pre-computer-driven print era have been small-scale, have not involved scientific journals, and have few automated steps. Scanning has been shown to be a viable but expensive process, and most pilot projects have been grant-funded. CD-ROMs are serving a stop-gap electronic archive for now, and while CD-ROM players are becoming common on PCs, networking them on campus is already a greater headache than maintaining current web-based distribution of current electronic journals. Furthermore, changes in the hardware portion of CD-ROM platforms may require re-encoding of their content whenever a new standard or technological platform becomes popular, because the data-storage segment of the CD-ROM industry is trivial in influence relative to the dominant entertainment use of CDs (consider DVD-ROM and DVX-ROM), adding an additional uncertainty and discouragement of investment in existing CD-ROMs. Most libraries are sticking with print, for despite its storage disadvantages, its platform, the Class A bound volume, is clearly stable.

THE DISADVANTAGES OF PRINT JOURNALS FOR SCIENTIFIC READER-AUTHORS

Probably the biggest complaint of most active scientists with print journals is that their libraries no longer take as many as the scientists would like, usually for reasons of costs but in some cases also for reasons of space. While scientists on the whole feel that their institutions and their libraries under-spend on science journals relative to what scientists bring in to those institutions by way of grant money, they are ironically somewhat sympathetic to the space and retrievability issues mentioned above. Even when scientists pay as little as 10% of what their library must pay for the same journal, personal subscriptions to science journals taken by faculty members have fallen off dramatically, largely because faculty offices are easily overrun in a very short time by today's bulky and many-issued print journals. It is often easier to retrieve an article from the library than it is to find it in one's own office.

LAG-TIMES AND OPPORTUNITY COSTS FOR AUTHORS

Authors must generally wait some time after the acceptance of a manuscript in a print journal for its appearance. Lag times run from something like two months for some letters journals in the experimental life and physical sciences, to two years in overcrowded fields like mathematics. While some fields compensate by having an informal pre-print distribution service–and the one within physics is truly remarkable–with costs born by the author or the author's institution, and many journals publish brief notices of forthcoming papers, it can be reasonably argued that relatively few authors can gain in professional visibility and reader-feedback via citations in other literature and through the applications of their work by other authors through preprints the way they do through the prompt publication of their finished works.

Prospects for Change in Costs in This Area–It is likely that as long there are sufficient publishing industry personnel to keep electronically posting the number of manuscripts deemed acceptable by editors and referees–and this is a big "if" unless real publishing professionals are in charge–lag times will be less of a problem. The problem will then be finding only the papers you want from among the many that are constantly being added to the electronic issues or cumulative archive. Speed and abundance have their own problems, and will probably require more intelligent indexing/abstracting than the self-assigned indexing provided by authors, on which most preprint servers currently depend for their own search engines. (This represents a great opportunity for librarians with competencies in both the concerned subject and indexing/abstracting fundamentals.) Moreover, scientists will still have to watch out for library reticence to commit a large proportion of general library revenues to their special electronic needs. Money, not technology, will remain the real wedge issue dividing librarians from scientists. Librarians, justifiably unsure of future archiving modalities, will find themselves paying for both print and electronic versions for a long time to come.

BIBLIOGRAPHIES

Bibliography of Financial Analyses of the Publishing Industry Including Critiques of Pricing and the Economic Consequences for Libraries of the Propensity of Academic Scientists to Publish Heavily, or Why Librarians Have the Attitudes They Have About the Publishing Industry and Faculty Demands for Expensive and Voluminous Science Journals

Amiran, Eyal. "The Rhetoric of Serials at the Present Time." *The Serials Librarian* 28 (3-4): 209-221, 1996.

Anonymous. "Industry Stocks: July Performance." *Publishers Weekly* 245 (32): 237, August 10, 1998.

Birdsall, William F. "I Am Read, Therefore I Am: Faculty and the Psychology of Journal Cancellations." *Journal of Academic Librarianship* 24 (3): 240-241, 1998.

Branin, J.J., and Mary Case. "Reforming Scholarly Publishing in the Sciences: A Librarian Perspective." *Notices of the American Mathematical Society* 45: 475-486, 1998.

Butler, H. Julene. "Where Does Scholarly Electronic Publishing Get You?" *Journal of Scholarly Publishing* 26: 234-246, July, 1995.

Carrigan, Dennis P. "Commercial Journal Publishers and University Libraries: Retrospect and Prospect." *Journal of Scholarly Publishing* 27: 208-221, 1996.

Case, Mary. "Views of the Current Marketplace for Scholarly Journals." *ARL Newsletter* 200
http://www.arl.org/newsltr/200/intro.html

Cox, John. "The Changing Economic Model of Scholarly Publishing: Uncertainty, Complexity, and Multimedia Serials." *Against the Grain* 10 (2): 24+, April, 1998.

David, Sue. "The Future Structure of Scholarly Communication Holds No Place for Commercial Publishers: A Debate Organised by the University College & Research Group (London Section) of the Library Association." *Http://www/mdx.ac.uk/www/UCRL/debrep2.thm*

Drew, Barbara, ed. *The Financial Management of Scientific Journals.* Council of Biology Editors, 1989.

Duranceau, Ellen Finnie. "The Economics of Electronic Publishing." *Serials Review* 21(1): 77-90, 1995.

Duranceau, Ellen Finnie. "Exchange Rates and the Serials Marketplace." *Serials Review* 21(3): 83-96, 1995.

Fialkoff, Francine. "We Need to Talk: Despite Shared Concerns, Pricing/ Format Issues Separate Librarians and Publishers." *Library Journal* 121 (3) 136, February 15, 1996.

Giambi, Dina. "ACRL Journal Costs in Academic Libraries Discussion." *Library Acquisitions: Practice and Theory* 21: 68-70, Spring, 1997.

Guernsey, Lisa. "Librarians' Newsletter Takes Aim at Commercial Publishers of Scholarly Journals." *Chronicle of Higher Education* (November 13, 1998) p. A25.

Henderson, Albert. "Forecasting Prices of Foreign Science Journals." *The Serials Librarian* 23(1-2): 129-34, 1992.

Henderson, Albert. "The $160 Million Question: What Happens to the

Federal Money Paid for University Research Libraries?" *Against the Grain* 9: 28-9, Nov., 1997.

Henderson, Albert. "Research Journals: A Question of Economic Value." *Logos* 16(1): 43-46, 1995.

Henderson, Albert. "A Solution to the Futility of Cost-Effective Librarianship." *Science & Technology Libraries* 12: 99-107, Fall 1991.

Ivins, October. "Joint Discussion Group Meeting: ALCTS SS Journal Costs in Libraries Discussion Group and SS Research Libraries Discussion Group." *Library Acquisitions: Practice and Theory* 21 (4): 535-537, 1997.

Keating, Michael. "Open the Book on Library Subs." *Folio: The Magazine for Magazine Management* 27 (8): 53, June, 1998.

Kerwin, Ann Marie. "Recent Media Mergers Valued at 2.55 Bil." *Advertising Age* 69 (19): 56, May 11, 1998.

Ketcham-Van Orsdel, Lee and Kathleen Born. "E-Journals Come of Age." *Library Journal* 123: (7): 40-45, April 15, 1998.

King, Donald Ward, and Jose-Marie Griffiths. "Economic Issues Concerning Electronic Publishing and Distribution of Scholarly Articles." *Library Trends* 43: 713-40, Spring 1995.

King, Donald W. "Some Economic Aspects of the Internet." *Journal of the American Society for Information Science* 49(11): 990-1002, 1998.

Kingma, Bruce. *The Economics of Information: A Guide to Economic and Cost-Benefit Analysis for Information Professionals.* Englewood, CO: Libraries Unlimited, 1996.

Kronenfeld, Michael R. "Update on Inflation of Journal Prices in the Brandon-Hill List of Journals." *Bulletin of the Medical Library Association* 84: 260-263, 1996.

Lichtenberg, James. "Academic Librarians Warn Publishers on Journal Prices." *Publisher's Weekly* 245 (29): 114, June 20, 1998.

McCabe, Mark J. "The Impact of Publisher Mergers on Journal Prices: A Preliminary Report." *ARL Newsletter* 200 *http://www.arl.org/newsltr/200/html*

Massa, Michelle. "Great Balls of Fire." *Graphic Arts Monthly* 70 (6): 66-68, June, 1998.

Meyer, Richard W. "Monopoly Power and Electronic Journals." *Library Quarterly* 67 (4): 325-349, 1997.

Milliot, Jim. "Salary Survey: Bigger the Company, Bigger the Paycheck." *Publishers Weekly* 245 (27): 33-36, July 6, 1998.

Newsletter on Serials Pricing Issues. [Moderated by Marcia Tuttle, the recently retired doyenne of serials librarianship in America. The most influential single listserv on the subject.]
http://www.lib.unc.edu/prices/

Quandt, Richard E. "Simulation Model for Journal Subscription by Libraries." *Journal of the American Society for Information Science* 47: 610-617, 1996.

Robnett, William E. "Online Journal Pricing." *The Serials Librarian* 33 (1-2): 55-69, 1998.

Roth, Alison C. "ACRL Electronic Pricing Discussion." *Serials Review* 21 (3): 1-9-110, 1995.

Ruschin, Siegfried. "Why are Foreign Subscription Rates Higher for American Libraries than they Are for Subscribers Elsewhere?" *The Serials Librarian* 9: 7-17, Spring 1985.

Schad, Jasper G. "Scientific Societies and Their Journals: Issues of Cost and Relevance." *Journal of Academic Librarianship* 23 (5): 406-407, 1997.

Schmidt, Kathy Wodrich. "Throwing Out the Bathwater But Keeping the Baby: Managing Serials in an Age of Precarious Pricing and Burdened Budgets." *Library Acquisitions: Practice and Theory* 21 (4): 486-489, 1997.

Snyder, Herbert W. "Allocating Costs: Is it a Program Worth Keeping?" *Library Administration & Management.* 12(3): 166-8, Summer 1998.

Sosteric, Mike. "At the Speed of Thought: Pursuing Non-Commerical Alternatives to Scholarly Communication." *ARL Newsletter* 200
http://www.arl.org/newltr/200/sosteric.html

Stankus, Tony. "Cash Cows, Sacred Cows, and Mad Cow Disease." *Technicalities.*16: 2-3, June 1996.

Stankus, Tony. "Could Long Term Shifts of Publishing Sector Dominance among the Top 100 Physical Science Journals Slow Rates of Invoice Inflation?" *Science and Technology Libraries* 15(3): 77-89, 1995.

Stankus, Tony. "Making the Scientist a Library Ally in the Real Research Journal Funding Wars: Those with Our Treasures and with Our Own Mistaken Notions." *Library Acquisitions* 14(1): 113-119, 1990.

Stoller, Michael A., Robert Christopherson, and Michael A. Miranda. "The Economics of Professional Journal Pricing." *College and Research Libraries 57: 9-21, 1996.*

Surowiecki, James. "The Publisher's Curse." *New York Times Magazine* (May 31, 1998) p. 6+.

Varian, Hal R. "Pricing Electronic Journals." *D-Lib Magazine*
http:// www.dlib.org.dlib/june96/06varian.html

Walker, Thomas J. "Free Internet Access to Traditional Journals." *American Scientist* 86 (5): 463-471, September-October, 1998.

Wilder, Stanley J.."Comparing Value and Estimated Revenue of SciTech Journals." *ARL Newsletter* 200
http://www.arl.org/newsltr/200/wilder.html
Wyly, Brendan J. "Competition in Scholarly Publishing? What Publisher Profits Reveal." *ARL Newsletter* 200
http://www.arl.org/newsltr/200/wyly.html

Bibliography of the Nuts, Bolts, Work and Worries of the Preprint Portion of Publishing Operations, Print Operations Today, Including Crossover Efforts*

(*Excluding REFERENCES to Specific Computer Hardware (e.g., Apple Computers) and Software (e.g., SGML), Which Can Be Found in the Bibliography Following the Next Paper, and the Larger Strategic Concerns of Publishers Which Follow in the Paper After That)

Adams, Richard M. *Computer-to-Plate: Automating the Printing Industry.* Pittsburgh: Graphic Arts Technical Foundation, 1996.

Andrews, Lynne. *Handbook for Managing a Productive Digital Environment.* National Association of Printers and Lithographers Research and Educational Foundation, 1995.

Anonymous. "Evolution of the Press." *Graphic Arts Monthly* (July-August, 1998 Supplement): 60-61.

Anonymous. "Mapping a Digital Path." *Graphic Arts Monthly* 70 (4) 29, April, 1998.

Anonymous. "Mid-Year Report on Publishing Technology." *Graphic Arts Monthly* (July-August, 1998 Supplement): 41-96.

Anonymous. "Seven Tips for Selecting a Printer." *Folio: The Magazine for Magazine Management* 27 (7): 54, May, 1998.

Charlesworth, Eric. "New Plants May Affect Coated Paper Market." *Folio: The Magazine for Magazine Management* 27 (7): 17, May, 1998.

Crim, Elias. "Digital Diagnosis for 1998." *American Printer* 220 (January, 1998), p. 24-26.

Cross, Lisa. "Remote Proofing Closes the Gap." *Graphic Arts Monthly* 70 (1): 44-46+, 1998.

Dzilna, Dzintars. "Anticipate Apple's Rhapsody." *Folio: The Magazine for Magazine Management.* 27(3): 27, Mar. 1, 1998.

Dzilna, Dzintars. "Printing Presses Forward." *Folio: The Magazine for Magazine Management* 27 (7): 52-54, May, 1998.

Fishel, Catherine. "Cross-Media Publishing." *Graphic Arts Monthly* (July-August, 1998 Supplement): 37-39.

Fitzgerald, Mark. "Unions Gain Ground at Paper Web Sites." *Editor and Publisher* 131 (37): 46, September 12, 1998.

Forbes, Thom. "How to Compete in Online Publishing." *Folio: the Magazine for Magazine Management* 26 (Special Sourcebook Issue, 1998): 240.

Garigliano, Jeff. "A Guide to Foreign Mail Distribution." *Folio: The Magazine for Magazine Management* (1998 Supplement): 247-249.

Graham, Anne. "Rethinking the Workplace." *Folio: The Magazine for Magazine Management* 27 (7): 65-66, May, 1998.

Hilts, Paul. "Approaching the Point of No Returns." *Publishers Weekly* 245 (25): 64-65, 1998.

Hilts, Paul "On Beyond On Demand." *Publishers Weekly* 245 (43): 36-37, 1998.

Hilts, Paul. "Seybold SF: Toward a New Vision of Publishing Technology." *Publishers Weekly* 245 (40): 16, 1998.

Krepchin, Ira P. " Smart Materials Handling Costs Little, Saves a Lot." *Modern Materials Handling* 47 (12): 54, 1992.

Lamparter, William C. "The Second Time Around." *American Printer* 221 (4): 46+, July, 1998.

Lawson, Cree. "Between a Rock and a Hard Place." *Village Voice* 43 (32): 78, August 11, 1998.

Levins, Hoag. "Connections Adapts with Changing Industry." *Editor and Publisher* 131 (26): 20-22, June 27, 1998.

Lichtenberg, James. "Lurching Towards the Millennium." *Publishers Weekly* 245 (35): 26-28, April 31, 1998.

Love, Barabara. "How Our Jobs Have Changed." *Folio: The Magazine for Magazine Management* 27 (5): 46-55, April, 1998.

Maurer, Rolf. "Cover to Cover." *Folio: The Magazine for Magazine Management.* 27(2): 94, Feb 1, 1998.

McAllister, Robin B. *The Business Side: For Preparers of Desktop Published Documents for Printing.* Delmar, 1997.

Nickerson, Nate. "The ABCs of CTP." *Folio: The Magazine for Magazine Manaegment* 27 (7): 51, May, 1998.

O'Quinn, Donnie et al. *Digital Prepress Complete.* Hayden, 1996.

Peterson, Ivars. "Rethinking Ink." *Science News* 153 (25): 396-397, June 20, 1998.

Poyssick, Gary and Steve Hannaford. *Workflow Reengineering.* Hayden: 1996.

Robidoux, Michelle. "Select a New System Systematically." *Folio: The Magazine for Magazine Management* 27 (8): 49, June 1998.

Romano, Frank J. *Digital Media: Publishing Technologies for the 21st Century.* MicroPub Press, 1996.

Romano, Frank. "The Information Factory." *American Printer* 214 (2): 58, 1994.

Romano, Richard M. and Frank J. Romano, eds. *Graphic Arts Technical Foundation Encyclopedia of Graphic Communications.* Prentice Hall, 1998.

Rosenberg, Jim. "Outlook for Technology." *Editor and Publisher* 131 (January 3, 1998): 39.

Rosenberg, Jim. "Spending Spree for Printing Plant Upgrades." *Editor and Publisher* 131 (33): 12+, August 15, 1998.

Ruggles, Philip Kent. *Printing Estimating: Costing Methods for Digital and Traditional Graphic Imaging.* Delmar, 1996.

Schavey, Aaron. "Publishing's Future in Electronic Commerce." *Business America* 119 (January, 1998): 39.

Sharples, Hadley. "Distance Proofing, Closer Customers." *Graphic Arts Monthly* 69 (11): 41-44, November, 1997.

Sharples, Hadley. "Digital Printers Bet on Innovation." *Graphic Arts Monthly* 70 (4): 66+, April, 1998.

Sharples, Hadley. "Managing Content to Link Print & Web." *Graphic Arts Monthly* 70 (4): 94, April, 1998.

Small, Jay. "The Perfect Size for an Opening Home Page." *Editor and Publisher* 131 (13): 20-22, March 28, 1998.

Spinner, Jenni. "Be Prepared." *American Printer* 220 (December, 1997): 50+

Stankus, Tony. "Desktop Publishing and Camera-Ready-Copy Science Journals." *The Serials Librarian* 15(1-2): 17-27, 1988.

Stephenson, G.A. "Electronic Publishing Resources on the Web." *Computer Networks and ISDN Systems* 30(13): 1263-72, Aug. 3, 1998.

Sucov, Jenifer. "Custom E-Publishing: 10 Questions." *Folio: The Magazine for Magazine Management* (1998 Supplement): 237-239.

Van Roden, Wendy. "What Drives Paper Prices?" *Folio: The Magazine for Magazine Management* 27(3): 76-80, Mar. 1, 1998.

Whitcher, Joann Strashun. "Networked Printers Gain Strength." *Graphic Arts Monthly* 70 (4): 72-74, April 1998.

Zollman, Peter M. "The Numbers Racket." *Editor & Publisher* 131(30): 4, July 25, 1998.

A Bibliography of Some Traditional Tasks in Serials Management in Libraries Along with Expanding Duties for Librarians in the Management of Electronic Journals

Allen, Barbara McFadden. "Negotiating Digital Information System Licenses Without Losing Your Shirt or Your Soul." *Journal of Library Administration* 24 (4): 15-26, 1997.

Anderson, Bill. "CONSER on the Internet: Facilitating Access to Serials Information." *The Serials Librarian* 32 (1-2): 77-94, 1997.

Basch, N. Bernard, and Judy McQueen. *Buying Serials.* Neal-Schuman, 1990.

Bates, Mary Ellen. "How to Implement Electronic Subscriptions: Replacing the Routing List Hassle." *Online* 22 (3): 80-84+, May-June, 1998.

Buchanan, Nancy L. "Navigating the Electronic River: Electronic Product Licensing and Contracts." *The Serials Librarian* 30 (3-4): 171-182, 1997.

Chen, Chiou-sen Dora. *Serials Managment.* Chicago: American Library Association, 1995.

Cline, Lynn S. "Highlights of the ALCTS Serials Section Research Libraries Discussion Group." *Library Acquisitions: Practice and Theory* 21 (4): 481-483, 1997.

Cook, Eleanor I. "Taking the Good with the Bad: How Migration to an Integrated Library System Can Affect Serials Work Flow." *The Serials Librarian* 32 (1-2): 1-7-122, 1997.

Daigle, Leslie, Ron Daniel, and Cecilia M. Preston. "Uniform Resource Identifiers and Online Serials." *The Serials Librarian* 33(3-4): 325-41, 1998.

Demas, Samuel G., Peter McDonald, and Gregory W. Lawrence. "The Internet and Collection Development: Mainstreaming Selection of Internet Resources." *Library Resources and Technical Services* 39 (3): 275-290, 1996.

Duranceau, Ellen Finnie. "Beyond Print: Revisioning Serials Acquisitions for the Digital Age." *The Serials Librarian* 33(1-2): 83-106, 1998.

Duranceau, Ellen Finnie. "Cataloging Remote-Access Electronic Serials: Rethinking the Role of the OPAC." *Serials Review* 21: 67-77, Winter 1995.

Duranceau, Ellen Finnie. "Naming and Describing Networked Electronic Resources: The Role of Uniform Resource Identifiers." *Serials Review* 20(4): 31-44, 1994.

Duranceau, Ellen Finnie. "Why You Can't Learn License Negotiation in Three Easy Lessons: A Conversation with Georgia Harper, Office of General Counsel, University of Texas." *Serials Review* 23(3): 69-71, Fall 1997.

Duranceau, Ellen Finnie, Margret G. Lippert, and Marlene Manoff. "Electronic Journals in the MIT Libraries: Report of the 1995 E-Journal Subgroup." *Serials Review* 22: 47-56+, Spring 1996.

Ford, Charlotte E. and Stephen P. Harter. "The Downside of Scholarly Electronic Publishing: Problems in Accessing Electronic Journals Through Online Directories and Catalogs." *College and Research Libraries* 59(5): 448-456, 1998.

Gabriel, Joseph A. "Managing and Coping with Electronic Serials: A Report from the ACRL New England Chapter Serials Interest Group, Fall, 1996 Program." *The Bottom Line* 11 (1): 14-17, 1998.

Gerhard, Kristin H. "Cataloging Internet Resources: Practical Issues and Concerns." *The Serials Librarian* 32 (1-2): 123-137, 1997.

Hawkins, Les. "Serials Published on the World Wide Web: Cataloging Problems and Decisions. " *The Serials Librarian* 33 (1-2): 123-145, 1998.

Kaag, Cynthia Stewart. "Collection Development for Online Serials: Who Needs to Do What, and Why, and When." *The Serials Librarian* 33(1-2): 107-22, 1998.

Landesman, Betty. "Keeping the Jello Nailed to the Wall: Maintaining and Managing the Library's Virtual Collection." *The Serials Librarian* 30 (3-4): 137-147, 1997.

Leach, Bruce A. "A Simple Program Simplifies Moving and Integrating Serial Collections." *The Serials Librarian* 32 (3-4): 93-106, 1997.

Leonhardt, Thomas W. "The Alarmists Versus the Equilibrists: Reexamining the Role of the Serials Professional in the Information Age." *The Serials Librarian* 28 (3-4): 187-195, 1996.

LIBLICENSE-L discussion list. [Yale's web site for discussion and advisory on e-journal licenses and related matters].
http://www.library.yale.edu/~llicense/index.shtml

Luther, Judy. "Selection of Full-Text Online Resources: What You Need to Know." *Library Acquisitions: Practice & Theory* 21 (4): 522-525, 1997.

Mouw, James R. "Changing Roles in the Electronic Age-the Library Perspective." *Library Acquisitions: Practice & Theory* 22(1): 15-21, 1998.

Okerson, Ann. "Buy or Lease? Two Models for Scholarly Information at the End (or the Beginning) of an Era." *Daedalus* 125 (4): 55-76, 1996.

Olivieri, Rene. "Site Licenses: A New Economic Paradigm." *The Serials Librarian* 30 (3-4): 183-190, 1997.

Osborn, Andrew. *Serial Publications: Their Place and Treatment in Libraries.* Chicago: American Library Association, 1980.

Pelzer, Nancy. "Monographic Analysis of Serial Issues in the Online Environment." *The Serials Librarian* 32 (3-4): 67-82, 1997.

Rentschler, Cathy. "Indexing Electronic Journals." *The Serials Librarian.* 33(3-4): 319-24, 1998.

Rioux, Margaret. "Hunting and Gathering in Cyberspace: Finding and Selecting Web Resources for the Library''s Virtual Collection." *The Serials Librarian* 30 (3-4): 129-136, 1997.

Roth, Alison. "From Overdrive to Cyberdrive: The Impact of Technology on Technical Services." *Serials Review* 23 (3): 87-88, 1987.

Schwartz, Charles A. "Restructuring Serials Management to Generate New Resources and Services." *College and Research Libraries* 59 (2): 115-124, 1998.

Shadle, Steven and Others. "Electronic Serials Cataloging: Now That We're Here, What Do We Do?" *The Serials Librarian* 30 (3-4): 109-127, 1997.

Simpson, Pamela and Robert S. Seeds. "Electronic Journals in the Online Catalog: Selection and Bibliographic Control." *Library Resources & Technical Services* 42(2): 126-32, Apr. 1998.

Stankus, Tony. "Binding is Still Good Discipline." *Technicalities* 15: 1+, Dec. 1995.

Stankus, Tony. "Which Format and Frequency Changes Should Librarians Favor?" *Technicalities* 15 (5): 13.

Tuttle, Marcia, Luke Swindler and Frieda B. Rosenberg. *Managing Serials.* JAI Press, 1996.

Van Goethem, Geraldine. "Acquiring and Managing Electronic Journals: Integrated Workload or Special Handling." *Library Acquisitions: Practice and Theory* 21 (4): 507, 1997.

Weintraub, Jennifer. "The Development and Use of a Genre Statement for Electronic Journals in the Sciences." *Issues in Science and Technology Librarianship* no. 17

Williams, James W. "Serials Cataloging, 1991-1996: A Review." *The Serials Librarian* 32 (1-2): 3-26, 1977.

Wood, Elizabeth J. "At Issue: Dimensions of Seriality in an Electronic World." *Library Acquisitions: Practice and Theory* 21 (4): 517-519. 1997.

Bibliography on PrePrint Archives and Self-Publishing as Forerunners to Electronic Journals or as Models for Electronic Journal Development, Case Studies of Pioneering Electronic Journals, Self-Published or from Already Established Publishers

Bachrach, Steven M., Darin C. Burleigh, and Anatoli Krassivine. " Designing the Next-Generation Chemistry Journal: the *Internet Journal of Chemistry.*" *Issues in Science and Technology Librarianship* no.17, 1998.

Boyce, Peter, Evan Owens, and Chris Biemesderfer. "Electronic Publishing: Experience is Telling Us Something." *Serials Review* 23(3): 1-9, Fall 1997.

Brown, Ladd. "It's not your Father's Journal: It takes Links, Permanence and a Whole New Process." *Library Acquisitions: Practice & Theory* 22(2): 227-8, Summer 1998.

Butler, Declan. "US Biologists Propose Launch of Electronic Preprint Archive." *Nature* 397 (6715): 91, 1999.

Goodman, Laurie. "Free Tips for Experimenters." *Nature* 395 (6698): 135, 1998.

Heller, Dennis. "Evaluation of Electronic Journals Related to the Internet." *The Reference Librarian* 58: 121-33, 1997.

Homes, Todd C. "Brains on Call." *Nature* 395 (6698): 129 September 10, 1998.

Taubes, Gary. "Electronic Preprints Point the Way to Author Empowerment," *Science* 271: 767-768, 1996.

Walker, Thomas J. "Electronic Reprints–Segueing Into Electronic Publication of Biological Journals." *BioScience* 45: 171, 1996.

Widzinski, Lori J. "The Evolution of *MC Journal.*" *Serials Review* 23 (2): 59-72, 1997.

Youngen, Gregory K. "Citation Patterns to Traditional and Electronic Preprints in the Published Literature." *College and Research Libraries* 59 (5): 448-456, 1998.

The Business and Technological Warfare Affecting the Internet and Electronic Journals: Terminology of Major Hardware and Software Components and Competing Strategies of Major Players

Tony Stankus

Fortunately for libraries and librarians, e-journal terminology and software are heading for at least a momentary plateau in which certain winning terms and technologies are being accepted as standard. Today's library administrators, already preoccupied by issues of how much they have to pay for their subscriptions and what kind of deals can be gotten through site licenses for their e-journals or those of their consortium must now focus on the key technological issue of the perceived necessity–or lack of it–of having to buy new hardware and software every 18 months or so. This is because what these librarians spend on technology tends to be subtracted from what they have available for content. What follows is the recent history of current e-journal terminology and technology, with discussion on the remaining unresolved issues.

THE NATURAL LANGUAGES OF JOURNAL TEXT AND THE HELP SCREENS

Despite the personal multilingualism of scientists as individuals coming from many countries, one thing is absolutely clear: while a tiny minority of

[Haworth co-indexing entry note]: "The Business and Technological Warfare Affecting the Internet and Electronic Journals: Terminology of Major Hardware and Software Components and Competing Strategies of Major Players." Stankus, Tony. Co-published simultaneously in *Science & Technology Libraries* (The Haworth Press, Inc.) Vol. 18, No. 2/3, 1999, pp. 43-74; and: *Electronic Expectations: Science Journals on the Web* (Tony Stankus) The Haworth Press, Inc., 1999, pp. 43-74. Single or multiple copies of this article are available for a fee from The Haworth Document Delivery Service [1-800-342-9678, 9:00 a.m. - 5:00 p.m. (EST). E-mail address: getinfo@haworthpressinc.com].

43

science journals on the web will be non-English or offer a full-text alternative non-English version in addition to English, the overwhelming majority of science e-journals will be in English. This is despite the fact that the relatively ancient, traditional computer-to-computer character language for text file transmissions, *ASCII (American Standard Code for Information Interchange)*, is capable in its expanded form of handling most non-English Roman alphabet languages, with a wide number of accent or diacritical marks available–and despite the fact that Japanese word-processing is now routine despite its being non-ASCII. The linguistic imperialism of English has been so long firmly entrenched in the world of print journals of science long before desktop or laptop computers became widespread that a reversal is simply unlikely.

By contrast, any help screens and search directions in the front-ends (what you see on the screen when you first click on a e-journal, a *Graphical User Interface (GUI)*) of e-journals, however, will likely have multilingual options, and most major publishers that offer e-journals also offer German, Japanese, French and Spanish already at their home pages.

BASIC COMPUTER PLATFORM AND NETWORK CONCEPTS

Individual publishers have had to gamble time and again when selecting from one or more forks in the technology road with the hope that they choose the right fork so they wouldn't have to back-track. Their first goal was finding computer help with their ongoing print journal operations. Their second hope was that somehow the particular hardware and software they invested in for computer-assisted printing operations could evolve into a *platform* that would be eventually adopted as the publishing industry's standard for electronic publications, whenever it came to pass, with as small a disruption and equipment and software reinvestment as possible. Publishers have spent a good deal of the 1990s with an uneasy feeling that if they didn't get into electronic publishing somehow, their publications line would suffer a loss of prestige and sales to more technologically aggressive competitors. This was balanced by the fear they would spend all that money and still end up with the wrong system, and still get beaten by their competitors. They have felt that they would be damned if they did, and damned if they didn't.

Ironically, much the same could be said of libraries seeking help with automating a number of their old-hard copy files: card catalogs, circulation records, reserves, and journal check-ins. They too sought to identify and adopt a stable platform that would be standardized across libraries. It is almost serendipitous that the development of electronic journals would eventually cause both the journal publishing and library sectors to focus on some of the same technologies and issues of platform compatibility and stability.

A *platform* is a combination of a fundamental category of computer hardware along with the primary computer software operating system that maximizes its operation. Today's primary computer platforms are:

- Personal computers using Windows operating software
- Personal computers using MacOS operating software
- Workstations (very powerful PCs) that generally use UNIX operating software or Windows NT
- A small but enthusiastic and growing number of personal computers and workstations, mostly at sci-tech institutions in Europe, that use LINUX, a derivative of UNIX.
- Big Iron mainframes (historically refrigerator-sized computers, most commonly made in the past by Digital and IBM, although most are now much smaller) with dumb terminals, some of which operate under old Big Iron systems like Digital's VMS, but most of which now also operate with UNIX or Windows NT.

All of these platforms systems, except the dumb terminal portion of the Big Iron system, can work as *stand-alone* computers. Historically most of their benchmark design specifications for individual PCs, workstations, and Big Iron machines were set in terms of how large and sophisticated a computer task they could quickly and reasonably do on their own, as *stand-alones*. The principal difference between a dumb terminal and stand-alones like PCs or workstations was that PCs and workstations contained enough computer memory and had sufficient internal hard-drives and processors so they could perform a substantial variety of tasks independently, and dumb terminals did not have these tools and could not do these tasks. Dumb terminals were stations where queries could be initiated and results received, with all the processing really done by the Big Iron computer. Big Iron systems went out of style largely because any fault with the Big Iron machine tended to cripple all the dumb terminals connected to it.

Nonetheless, computers based on all of these platforms can also be strung together in a *local network*, and *all the local networks that adopt certain networking standards and invest in some additional telecommunications hardware are what constitutes the Internet.* A classic example of a *local network* can be found in most academic and larger special libraries today in the form of their integrated library systems (on-line catalog, circulation system, reserves, etc.) Campus-based networks, when linked to the great external network of the Internet, are rapidly becoming the preferred approach to the distribution of electronic journal content. It is quite important to understand competing views on optimal network platforms when considering important collateral costs of administering an e-journal network. As a practical matter, the relative discrediting of the expensive Big Iron-cheap dumb terminal network concept has led to a race among rival concepts of networks based largely on PCs and workstations.

Today the performance of these member platforms as distributors of computerized content (their *server* role) in a network is an increasingly important benchmarking characteristic, as well as their performance as a receiver and processor of computerized content (their *client* role). Historically, based on the example of Big Iron computers and their dumb terminals–the progenitor of today's modern network, and the way the first generation of most library integrated systems were mounted–it used to be both a logical and correct assumption that, generally, *servers* in a network must be at least as powerful as *clients*, and are generally much more so. It was also historically true, but no longer currently the case, that any network strung together had to have all of its components matching or at least highly compatible in hardware and operating systems (*a homogenous* or *uniform platform*).

Today a wide variety of software and telecommunications advances and adherence to formal policies (standards) adopted by the makers of most of these differing platforms no longer makes this the case, and heterogeneous platforms are common in both local networks and on the Internet. Moreover, if all the PCs included in the network are sufficiently powerful and fast, the *servers* need not be more powerful or faster than the *clients*. As discussions of the computer industry conducted later in this chapter will show, some major players in the computer industry favor this "every one is an All-Star approach" for at least local networks. This approach gained favor in business and academia because it allowed individual businessmen and scholars in local networks the ability to keep on working at their individual tasks with minimal disruption and maximum freedom without having to worry too much about breakdowns or logjams with the Big Iron machine. Rivals, particularly the seemingly odd couple of makers of lower-cost, more modestly capable PCs and makers of very powerful workstations, suggest that for some operations, including electronic journal distribution over the Internet, that preserving a sharp distinction of *client-server* division of labor in their kind of network makes more sense, and is cheaper for libraries.

SGML FOR HEAVY DUTY PRIMARY FORMATTING OF ARTICLES AND HTML FOR SOME PRIMARY ARTICLE FORMATTING AND FOR MOST LINKING AND NAVIGATION WITHIN AND AMONG ARTICLES

Whatever the network or platform chosen, a text and formatting language that worked across all these platforms seemed absolutely essential. The first choice facing the publishing industry was the selection of one or advanced encoding languages that would give electronically typeset journals the look and feel of high quality traditionally typeset print, with a helpful and attractive assortment of print fonts, point ranges, and layout options. As it turns out, the majority of today's print and electronic journals are initially encoded in some version of *SGML, Standardized Graphical Mark-up Language,* the most powerful software that has passed the critical *across-all-platforms* standards test.

SGML is a formatting language standard with a 1960s ancestry that was initially designed at IBM (as *GML, Graphical Mark-up Language*) for researchers who were filing reports or making official proposals or bids to the US federal government or military. The goal then is much like the goal of science journal publishers today: so that the journal or report composition and layout on screen and in print would be compatible between the submitting and receiving parties, and that this held true over a wide variety of different computer platforms. Not too surprisingly, software packages adherent to *SGML* have long been customized by a variety of software engineers and sold to commercial printers in proprietary versions to drive computerized typesetting and layout for print publications. While it was not originally very necessary for publishers' staffs to know much about SGML to mark up print manuscripts in the electronic typesetting and editing phase of operations, a certain amount of familiarity with SGML has crept into the consciousness of the technical and style staffs of print publishes as more and more of their work was done on PCs. Most publishing software vended over the last two decades for this higher-end publishing-printing audience has had an SGML-compatible backbone, even if it looked like it was just like any desktop other word processing package. Most publishers today who require that journal article manuscripts sent in by authors be accompanied by diskettes in a major popular word processing language do not print directly from the author's diskette, but rather machine translate that author's diskette into something SGML-compatible first.

Perhaps the biggest initial milestone that hinted that fidelity to SGML standards was going to pay off came when on-line indexing and abstracting databases were being developed in the late 1970s. The mark up tags long assigned by indexers that designated given portions of an abstract with differing typography (authors, abstract numbers, subject terms, etc.) turned out to be computer-sortable to form the basis of differing computer-searchable fields. In other words, the instructions for the printer could be transformed into labeled-electronic handles for retrieving electronic documents and parts of documents based on some common mark up characteristic, generally a combination of words or numbers and some assignment to a designated index or field (like author or journal source). The habit of using SGML-compatible software packages in the publishing industry then has had substantial advantages in the reduced amount of added cost and training time required of publishers and of their technical and style editorial staffs to make their historic print journals electronically transmittable today. SGML maintains its appeals for many publishers because it supports more *attachments* and *extensions (special functions or features in addition to core scripting capabilities, like files for illustrations, side-bars, and arrays of complex mathematical equations)* without altering the main flow of the text or page layout. It should be noted that some formatting languages, like the TeX family, are essentially devoted to these exceptions, particularly to the special problems of mathematics, and will be discussed shortly.

HTML is a nimble, light-weight evolutionary offspring of SGML that is actually much better known than its parent outside the print publishing industry, largely because it is the visually or graphically-oriented software language of the modern web page. If you bought a web-page/home-page composing software package, it is most likely written in, and dependent on HTML. (This is not to say that software like C++ or Perl is also not heavily used by professional web site designers.) While an increasing array of format, font and type point options are also present in HTML, and whole documents and entire journals can be composed and displayed on the web in HTML, its real strength lies in enabling the viewer on any modestly powerful PC to bounce back and forth between specially HTML tagged and linked portions of an individual document, and even among different articles in other journals and databases. (This can be done with SGML, but not quite so readily in documents that are not designed by mark up professionals.) Consider HTML to be the "linking" language, more so than a primary "layout" language. That's really *SGML's raison d'être*. It should be noted that while HTML is less robust in its carrying capacity for attachments and extensions, it continues to evolve and gain new fans in scholarly e-journal publishing. With time we will see even more adherents of *XML* (Extensible Mark-Up Language) an advanced formatting language with even more multimedia capacity. While multimedia has some future in scientific journal publishing, its use in scholarly scientific e-journals is much less common than a lay person might guess given the many commercial and entertainment uses of sound and moving images encountered all the time by the average web-surfer.

ELECTRONIC TRANSFER AND DESTINATION CODES: TCP-IP AND DOMAINS, HTTP AND URLs

Computer scientists have developed and superimposed a few linguistic flourishes that enable encoded electronic journal content to travel along the electronic mail route between networks that we call the Internet. The most important basic language development here revolves around *TCP-IP (Trans-*

mission Control Protocol-Internet Protocol). A TCP-IP processed and labeled ASCII document is ready to be distributed throughout the Internet. TCP-IP has two components. The TCP part tells the electronic mailman how the bits of information ought to be bundled for best shipping (many convenient packages rather than one giant package, as it turns out actually). The IP part gets all these convenient packages to the right destination. One of the first things a librarian has to do when gearing up to receive electronic journals is to tell the publisher or subscription service just what the proper IP mail address is.

As a practical matter, few of us readily remember, use or provide the all-numerical IP code. It can be something like a multi-digit zip code or phone exchange, with its length dependent on the size and extent of branching of its servers and their clients. Punctuation in these addresses is important, as the intervening periods or decimal points among these numbers are hierarchical, with the initial clusters of numbers having greater scope like a Dewey or a Cutter number. To add somewhat to the confusion, each numerical cluster is given an alphabetical terminology with the "A" cluster covering a larger computer network territory, than the subsequent "B" cluster, which in turn covers more territory than a "C" cluster. A typical IP code address might be 123.123.12.1. The first 123 (the "A" class number) would indicate a major regional bank of the highest powered servers and switching stations within a country. The second 123 (the "B" class number) might indicate a district node of high power servers and switching hardware encompassing a number of academic or research institutions, or a particularly large given institution or firm. The third 12 (the "C" class number) generally designates a "subnet" server "12" on a particular campus, often one that serves the desktop machines of an academic department or library system. As a practical matter, most e-journal licenses are sold with "Class C" licenses. This means that clients with hierarchical addresses to the right of Class C server 12, like 12.1 12.2, 12.3, etc., are licensed to receive the electronic journal. In some institutions, Class C licenses will cover a range of servers that are assigned to a task on a "server-available" basis. (This approach is also used by commercial internet service providers like America On-Line operate.) In these cases a *Dynamical IP Address* is provided and the license is more likely tied to a *Domain Address.*

It has long been recognized that routinely remembering and using such a lengthy code is impractical, based on the experiences of the conventional mail and phone businesses. Most people do not use even recall or use the last four digits of their now nine-digit zip code but recall and use a mixed numerical and verbal address when addressing conventional mail. And depending largely on mnemonic advertising campaigns, many people use either a mixed letter-plus-number code for dialing long distance or collect, or use all numerical digits, but generally stop at attempting to memorize and use more than 15 digits. Most librarians are likely to recall and use something more conveniently memorable like a mixed verbal and numerical code in our electronic journal dealings, and we routinely electronically supply and use a domain address in our internet mail traffic. Consider it a kind of triumph for LC class think over DDC class think.

Portions of the domain address tend to acronymically or allegorically identify the institution (the College of the Holy Cross, my place, uses the compressed HolyCross, no spaces in its domain address). Sometimes the particular server within the institution is also identified in the domain (Mine is called Clinton, named after a nearby town, not the President). There are also a few characteristic internet linguistic conventions at the end of each domain address, within the US in particular. These are called *"root domains."* Educational institutions, for example, append an "edu" at the end. Government agencies a "gov". Not-for-profit publishers use "org", while for-profit publishers use "com". In Europe, addresses end with national root domains: "uk" for the British, "nl" for the Dutch, etc.

Along the Internet, usually at each institution, a special server called a *Directory Name Server*, essentially a Name and Address router, translates these domain addresses back and forth into all-numerical IP addresses, not unlike the touch-tone keypad on your phone translates the mnemonically-favored mixed letter and number phone numbers into all-number phone numbers. Having made this conversion, it then routes incoming electronic mail to given desktops.

Most e-journals in science contain much more than simple ASCII text, however, and accessing and interacting with them require additional mailing and receiving language. Suffice to say that the special formatting and interactivity features of today's e-journals–what technical people really mean when they describe something as having hypertext quality–requires and receives special handling along the *World-Wide Web (WWW)* portion of the Internet. (Indeed the first version of the WWW was developed by an American, Tim Berners-Lee, for scientists to share scientific information in a graphical format–one with images as well as text–at CERN, a giant particle accelerator facility, centered in Switzerland, but serving all Europe). That means that an additional or special encoded language is involved along with the TCP-IP transmission of text. That special code is *HTTP,* the *Hypertext Transfer Protocol.* Most hypertext documents (with their TCP-IP and HTTP encoding) that you seek find their way to an appropriate and unique address on the web, usually one that contains a substantial addition to the basic IP address: the *URL (Universal Resource Locator)* address. Once again, this address involves either an all-numeric version or a mixed verbal and punctuation-important format, with the latter overwhelmingly preferred. Indeed, punctuation, including assorted slash marks, is characteristic of virtually all the URLs that matter to e-journals.

UNSCRAMBLING THE CONTENT
AND LETTING YOU VIEW IT AND PRINT IT
OFF IN A FAMILIAR FORMAT:
DOCUMENT FORMATTERS FOR CLIENT COMPUTERS

PDF

Your PC generally needs an in-house simultaneous translator to turn the TCP-IP and HTTP routed (and usually *SGML* and *HTML* encoded) stream of transmitted electronic packages into what looks like a journal page as it develops on your screen and is eventually routed to your printer. Many publishers have assumed the cost of making available to electronic journal subscribers a "downloadable" program, or "helper application," a *Portable Document Formatter* or *PDF*, most often Adobe Acrobat, to do just that. Loading this helper application to your own PC is often done surreptitiously and transparently while you, your technical services people or your computer support staff fill out interactively on-line what amounts to a step-by-step electronic registration form while visiting the publisher's or subscription service's web site. A few of the steps required during these interactive enroll-ment sessions actually involve the routing of some of the name-address and local server network and type of workstation or PC information through a server at Adobe, the owner of the proprietary formatting language (or at a licensed and metered mirror site authorized by Adobe but maintained by the individual publisher). That server then opens your PC's hard-drive into which the enabling PDF software is read (through a process called *FTP: File Trans-fer Protocol*), constructing a pathway through which e-journal contents will automatically be routed for translation, entirely without your being aware of it. This program also contain instructions that tell your printer how to format the text as well, whenever you want to print off your document. (Experience has already told most e-journal publishers that most of the time, subscribers are more likely to print off the document after scanning just the abstract or the first few e-pages, rather than sitting there and reading it through entirely.) Just think of your PDF as a benevolent incubus of sorts: somehow (via very fast and silent FTP) the little devil got inside you, and gets you what you want without your thinking about how the devil got into you, or how the devil works.

It should be noted that you can have a document that includes PDF coding, but is not hypertext-navigable because it was not also encoded in HTML.

Likewise, it is possible to print off an article that is encoded only in HTML, but has no PDF software attached. It will be hypertext-navigable on screen, but most likely not have quite the finished look of a document that has been PDF-processed (although it can be quite jazzy given today's web designers). HTML-only documents tend to look like computer frame printouts or direct "screen dumps," and have that limited amount of large screen-size text, whereas PDF documents look virtually identical to a photocopy from a print journal. Students who have not seen many print journals find HTML print-outs quite acceptable, because they look like the web pages they are used to seeing when surfing the net for other reasons. Students don't mind the often greater number of pages that the HTML print-out requires (particularly if there is no per-page payment meter attached to the printer). Their visual literacy and layout expectations seem very much to have co-evolved with the onset of the web. Faculty who have long been used to print journal page layouts, find the PDF versions reassuringly familiar, and much more space efficient. (Journal layout and typography have evolved over centuries for factors of readability, attractiveness, and space utilization, long before computers of any kind!) Faculty have been known to find the HTML-only frame print-outs vaguely disconcerting, the way large-print *Reader's Digest* for the visually-impaired appears to the normally-sighted.

PostScript

Adobe also makes available *PostScript* programs in much the same vein as a PDF, although only about 5% of the science journals this author has seen so far seem offer this as a reader's document translating/formatting option. (PostScript files are hugely important, however, as a printer's formatting tool.) Although most users are scarcely aware of it, PDFs actually omit much of the encoded information in an electronic article file in the interests of ease and speed of electronic journal article transmission and reception, although most of it is intended not to be seen by the readers in any case. This reduction also uses up less working space (*"cache"*) on the PC that accepts it, and makes it less likely that receiving a transmitted article will freeze up a PC by overflowing its cache. (A cache is the holding area where your PC stores material that you will work on some time in the near future. More on cache later.)

As a practical matter, the small amount of viewer fidelity or resolution as lost in PDFs matters little to most text and graphs within an electronic journal article, but could be more important in the hyperfine details of some illustrations, and PostScript is particularly good at handling some cumbersome mathematical equations. A PostScript file is actually the closest that one gets to the actual electronic file that the computer-driven typesetter has used for the print version. It is not only technically possible to generate a PDF file from a PostScript file (most electronic journals that have print analogues are based on just such a conversion), but not generally vice-versa. PostScript has some advantages as an alternative document formatter in that it loses slightly less of the total encoded mapping information for text and figures, even if it takes somewhat longer to load. At the higher end of PCs–those with 400 megahertz clock speed, for example–the added time is insignificant, given equally fast transmission lines, but at workaday 200 megahertz machines, it takes about twice as long and more than twice the cache. PostScript has a special advantage for the mathematics, physics, and computer science community in that virtually all versions are robust enough to handle the special attachments and extensions in those fields, including TeX prepared articles (see below).

RealPage

A third type of view-and-print software is *RealPage*, from Catchword, a largely British-based provider of electronic publishing services to print publishers. It is seen in less than 5% of the electronic journals this author has encountered. Like PDF from Adobe, ReaPage is derived from PostScript files with some editing and somewhat more effective data compressing than PDF to speed the transmission of e-journal content and reduce cache requirements in client computers. Some of its fonts, however, only approximate the original fonts of the original PostScript file, although the font differences are really minor. Nonetheless, fewer fonts saves some translation processing time before the mounting of the papers on the web and also marginally reduces transmission time when clients finally seek the paper. Like PDF, RealPage is available free for e-journal readers from its company's web-site, or those web-sites of electronic publishers who use Catchword as their electronic publishing contractor. It takes just a little more knowledge of executive commands to install RealPage than PDF. Even that comparative disadvantage is fading as Catchword is developing a Java-version that obviates almost any software skill or special cache requirements. (More on Java shortly.)

A Special Case Family:
TeX, LaTeX, and AMSTeX

A fourth scripting software encountered in electronic publishing is *TeX* (pronounced "Tech"), its companions *LaTeX* (Pronounced Lah-Tech, not Lay-Teks like the condom), and *AMSTeX*. This software must always be present in the article preparer's workstation or PC, as well as on the publisher's servers, and sometimes must also be especially enabled in the client's PC, workstation, or printer as well, unless the article has been further processed in some version of PostScript, or the most recent PDF. This trio was developed for the Math, Computer Science, and Physics community with the protean Donald Knuth (now of Stanford) being the initial author of TeX, Leslie Lamport (from Digital) the author of the somewhat more user-friendly LaTeX, and staff at the American Mathematical Society, the corporate author of AMSTeX. These tools and their many variants have something of a cult status, for they represented 1980s solutions to the centuries-old problems of the multiple characters, type fonts (Knuth developed the companion Meta-font software as well), and the layered arrays of long equations that have historically slowed the typesetting and production of math journals in partic-ular. (An old adage among mathematicians was that the only thing harder than getting the equations right was finding and correcting all the errors in the proof sheets from the publisher.)

This is not to say that learning TeX or even its more user-friendly versions is all that easy. It's a skill that tends to get mastered only during the Ph.D. dissertation stage, and not only for reasons of preparing that document but also the articles that are to be submitted based on that work. Many mathemat-ical society press journals will now only accept TeX type manuscripts. None-theless, despite this implied endorsement, and the fact that many versions are freeware (a tradition started by Knuth), a number of problems are cropping up within the TeX family. Most versions are actually preferentially UNIX friendly–not surprisingly given that most high level math research really requires a real workstation, as opposed to an average PC, so that most mathe-maticians have UNIX workstations–even though TeX has long been philo-sophically committed to being compatible across all platforms, a concept they tend to characterize as *DVI, device-independent*. Many versions of TeX were developed before the web, and making these documents hypertext navi-gable presents special challenges. Even printer compatibility can be some-thing of a problem. Nonetheless, mathematicians pride themselves on both their inventiveness and their eccentricity, and are unlikely to quickly abandon using some variant of TeX as the scripting core with an overlay of SGML, HTML, and PDF or PostScript for web publishing, with HTML being used most often for searchable fields in the author, title, affiliation, journal source, and abstracts portion of the paper and PostScript or the most advanced PDF being used for the main body, with all those equations.

NAVIGATING THROUGH DOCUMENTS AND FILES

More on HTML and Java Applets

Some critics argue that merely delivering a reasonable electronic facsimile of a print page is a waste of the presentation opportunities that electronic publishing allows for. While moving picture sequences, sound and other enhancements are possible and occasionally encountered, the hypertextability of text and illustrations–the mobility forte of HTML–is the daily show that matters for now.

Hypertext allows the PC user hooked up to the web the ability to bounce back and forth between texts, images, literature references and the like. It is one of the core software technologies of the web portion of the Internet. In order for the rare ASCII document or the much more common SGML text to become hypertextable, it must be further translated into some version of HTML–Hypertext Mark-Up Language. As mentioned earlier, HTML has some of the features of SGML, indicating when a caption might be rendered in bold face, or increased in point size for example, but the most important HTML tags mark the location of objects within a file, such as literature references or captions in such a way that clicking on that citation will bounce the reader to the actual article mentioned in the cited reference, or clicking on the caption, will pull up the illustration.

Initially, both individuals creating home-pages for themselves using HTML, and publishers converting their journal articles in some other programming language or format needed to do this additional HTML marking up and tagging "by hand." That is, they had to examine their existing documents and laboriously key-in the marks using a kind of start (<>) and stop (</>) code where given letters, numbers, or acronyms within these angled brackets indicated the format adjustments desired and provided information on what other links it would activate and what links would be activated by it, in return. All this "tagging" and "linking" notation is typically quite visible in what is called the source file version of an electronic article, but these lines of code are generally and mercifully suppressed by the time they get through to your PC's C drive and on to your screen. While many "over-the-counter," "buy and install yourself" software packages for individual HTML users initially require a fair amount of "hand labor," the amount of work and number of steps has been progressively reduced through a greater automatic (and invisible when not viewing the source file) embedding of intermediate steps through the incorporation of *Java* technology, and *JavaScript,* its document composing companion.

While any software engineer can study a variety of textbooks describing Java, and pass certain exams or courses to become Java-certified, large vended packages using Java are often proprietary software products of Sun Microsystems, or licensed by them. Java takes Internet document preparation, encoding, publishing and searchability by subsequent readers into new levels of ease and offers across-the-platform compatibility. Like any installed software, Java packages use up a fair amount of disk space on the PCs or workstations of article publishers. But Java is also one of the few SGML,

HTML-compatible software packages that can be installed and run on the publisher's servers and not be required to be fully installed and resident on the receiving client's PC in order for the client to view on his or her PC screen some visually attractive and relatively animated display of prose and images.

PCs owned by readers can be minimally Java-enabled to receive portions of programs sent from the publisher's servers–segments called Java Applets–without having all the programs necessary to Java publish also being sent. (You don't need an electronic printing press level of software in order to read an electronic publication, in other words.) This shipping to you of only what you need arrangement has the potential of saving space in your computer's cache.

CACHE WORRIES CAN BE CASH WORRIES FOR LIBRARIES

Without the electronic economy of Java Applets, more incoming messages, and more electronic journal articles, would overflow your cache routinely. You would have to have more and more permanently installed in-baskets covering your desk (you have to add more and more cache capacity) in order to handle the mail, giving you less space to do your work, because each mail package would be so bulky or you'd keep needing to buy bigger and bigger desks. Smaller electronic packages also mean increased computer processing speed through an absence of required instructions on key PC chips and drives, effectively allowing a more modest PC to function like a high-end workstation, at least in the electronic journal contents receiving mode. This economy of cache storage and speed requirements would seem to be a rather moot point since most heavily publishing scientists have high-end workstations running UNIX, but most multi-user library computers do not (they run on Windows or MacOS software). It is no longer unusual for even liberal arts college libraries to have a hundred or so PCs, and for even small campus networks to have over a thousand. Continuously updating and upgrading these can become a real technical and financial problem in a world without Java-type technology.

Java's real thrust then, is making the Internet a place that is easy to use for less technically savvy and lower-end-equipped PC users that most library systems can afford to buy, and afford to continuously update and maintain. This Java-driven advancement in electronic economy and simplicity was originally motivated, however, not by scientific communication concerns for libraries, but by ordinary salesmanship factors. The best business minds in the country suggest that sales of just about anything through the Internet are eventually going to dwarf sales from snail-mailed print catalogs or via telemarketing or cable television. (*PC Magazine* reports that retail and business-to-business sales over the web were already over $20 billion in 1998.) Commercial interests, in fact, would rather you spend your money on something other than the software and hardware that allows you to match the speed, slickness, and animation of their web catalogs as viewed on your own PC. Web marketers want you to spend it on the merchandise they're offering you via their web catalogs! Likewise with receiving electronic journal content: you don't necessarily need a PC as big, fast, and as expensive as that of the servers used by the publishers. Smart journal publishers will foster an appropriate level of software and hardware that will enable multi-user subscribers to spend their money on the journals, not on platforms with their high-end electronic packaging, shipping and delivery system. This is because publishers realize that, in the long run, the greatest buyers of e-journals are going to be the same greatest buyers of print journals: libraries, not individual scientists.

HOW COMPETITION AND PERSONALITIES IN THE SOFTWARE AND HARDWARE WORLD ARE EFFECTING E-JOURNALS: OR WHY READING WEB PUBLICATIONS MAY BE BEST WHEN ACCOMPANIED BY BLACK JAVA WITH NO MICROSOFT CREAM TO CLOUD IT UP

Why would Sun Microsystems develop, widely promote and freely license a software language like Java? Sun currently dominates the telecommunications server portion of the Internet business. The firm's sales slogan "The Computer is the Network" meant that today you didn't have to have the world's most powerful computer on your desktop to get a job done well. Rather, Sun, particularly through its ubiquitous and highly persuasive CEO Scott McNealy, argues that your desktop machine can effectively "borrow the network" to get a web job done. Under this philosophy "Your" computer is not only the desktop machine in front of you, it is your desktop machine plus all the other servers that your machine is using at the time when you are on the net. Sun makes its money by selling their high-end servers to vendors who are effectively loaning out their server's use to you as a customer in the course of some transaction, with the idea that along with the use of the server the customer will, directly or indirectly, make a sale of some sort. Sun machine owners want to keep their money-making websites continuously and reliably open for business from anyone who has any level of PC that is minimally Internet-capable. Sun wisely prides itself on the platform independence features of Java. Java can operate on just about any computer platform or network, high-end, low-end, and offers no discriminatorily preferential treatment to some customers from among those who write code in Java over other similarly certified Java code writers. Nor does Sun favor some companies who offer plug in Java-licensed software packages over others who adopt the same packages. *Java* software can work on Macs, Windows machines, UNIX machines, and even on some "dumb" terminals. It is particularly pertinent to note that *Java* is particularly appealing to the growing numbers of *"network" computer* users.

Just as importantly, Sun is allied with Oracle, a high-end business software company that has also promoted low-end "network" computer software. Oracle has a notoriously competitive president, Lawrence Ellison, who is an open rival of Microsoft's Bill Gates (more on Gates later). Ellison disagrees with Bill Gates' vision of the hardware and software future. Ellison's argument is that low-cost, low-end machines can be networked within a local intranet or externally linked to the Internet, and need only sufficient power and speed to store within their cache the pieces of programs that high-end servers "loan" to the network computer cache for the duration of the task at hand. It is Ellison's view that end-users who are surfing the net, at a library for example, can visit sites where Sun's workstations are working as high-end servers (and not unlikely to be using Oracle's high-end software). These end-users will be able to function in hypertext-navigable environments because the embedded Java Applets sent from the high server to the networked computer do most of the work in an economical fashion, and then "leave" the networked machine when the task is done. In other words, in Ellison's world, more and more former high-end-treadmill buyers of PCs could become network computer users without losing access to web content or features. Libraries using NCs can get out of the rat race of feeling forced to buy higher and higher tech computers for fear of being technologically or budgetarily forced off the Internet. A library might, for example, buy a dozen Oracle-based network computers for the cost of a single high-end server or a half dozen high-end PCs that would require multiple ugradings and high maintenance, and then continue to use those NCs for years. The onus for keeping up with the technology rat-race then falls to the businesses (like journal publishers) who are maintaining their sites and upgrading their servers, who can presumably afford his high-end Oracle software better. As long as the server hardware remains Java-friendly and any revised software is written in pure or "black" Java, which is famous for its intergenerational and interplatform compatibility, the NC computers could remain highly functional and their libraries can avoid repetitive upgrading and maintenance.

LOSING THE FIRST NC BATTLE BUT HELPING TO MAKE SURE THE TEMPORARY DEFEAT WAS PYRRHIC TO AT LEAST SOME OF THE VICTORS

Partly to head off any chance that Oracle-type NCs would make any headway, and coming to realize that high-end PC sales were stalling out for reasons of price resistance, high-end PC makers quickly began to produce stripped down machines with stripped down chip versions that nonetheless retain fairly good web searching capability. This adjustment worked to diminish the NC threat, but cut into their own company's profitability. It did little to deter Oracle, which retained its outstanding high-end business software business, and continues to mount various Windows bypass ventures via pure Java. More importantly, it demonstrated that the race for ever more sophisticated chips in ever more powerful machines requiring ever more frequent Windows upgrades was not the only race in town. In particular, it demonstrated that some of Windows' partners, the chipmakers, Intel in particular, could be forced to react from time to time in a way that might upset their long term strategy, and particularly, might upset the seemingly cozy relationship of Intel with Microsoft.

Ellison and Oracle are not the only allies of McNealy and Sun in battles with Gates and Microsoft. IBM, and its president Louis Gerstner, compete with Sun at the high-end server market, but also writes a lot of web software in Java for their AS servers, and is clearly on Sun's side. But most pertinently for libraries gearing up to receive electronic journals on the web, the makers and marketers of browsers are also drawn into the fray.

THE TWO INTERNATIONAL STANDARDS-SETTING BROWSERS: NETSCAPE AND INTERNET EXPLORER

As a practical matter accessing virtually all electronic journals today require the installation of a recent version of either a Netscape browser or a Microsoft browser on the receiving PC (AOL's browser has, until recently, actually been a licensed variant of Microsoft's) and sooner or later you find yourself working their proprietary GUIs and CGIs. The search engines attached to each of these browsers (they do have their own ones, by the way) are not as important as the fact they way these browsers are designed fundamentally sets the operational parameters of almost all other browsers, search engines, and yes, ultimately even electronic journals.

BROWSERS, SEARCH ENGINES, GUIs AND CGIs

Browsers are essentially the access ramps to the World Wide Web. It is through them that just about everyone gets linked to destinations on the web, originally whenever they didn't have a specific URL to enter, and nowadays, even when they do. First, they generally link you to hundreds of high-powered search engine servers and routers, essentially way station stops. These *search engine servers stand ready to point you to host or content servers,* your ultimate destination. How do browsers do this? Well, first, after you or your computer company has installed your browser, and you click it on, the browser shows you a local signpost called a *Graphical User Interface (GUI)*, with a space on that signpost that lets you enter a description of what you want to see, whenever you do get to your ultimate destination. On the other side of the signpost, the side that faces and is readable at the search engine server, is a *Common Graphical Interface (CGI)*. The CGI does some quick translating of what comes in from your GUI and links you to a menu of possible destinations (host or content servers). Once you make your choice of destination, generally with a double-click), the CGI of the destination host-content server looks over the CGI of the search engine server, including the information you entered voluntarily on your GUI (and some additional password, account or security information that you may or may not be aware of, but which is often gets attached to the CGI). If everything is compatible (and any obligations or restrictions are met) the host or content server's CGI then pushes the search engine servers CGI off to the side (at least visually from the viewpoint of your PC screen, and changes your GUI. (That's why your screen changes once you click onto a web site.) When you get done with the host server's CGI, the search engine's CGI generally takes its place (unless time has expired) and you get the search engine's GUI back. Unless time has expired, you also often get back the menu of possible destinations as well.

MORE ON SEARCH ENGINES

Most large, powerful *search engines–Lycos,* originally from Carnegie-Mellon, *AltaVista* from Compaq-Digital, *Yahoo, Excite, InfoSeek, and HotBot* are perhaps the most popular of these search engines–are themselves composed of two parts. The first part of the search engine, and one with which your PC generally does not make any direct connections, is a constantly roving *"bot"* (a take off on the term "robot") or *"crawler"* that moves through files on the web, picking up tagged terms or phrases, and storing them, along with their URLs. The second part is a high-speed comparison sorter. This is the one you do tend to make most of your connections with. It takes the queries you specifically ask via your GUI–CGI signpost and matches them with what the search engine's "bot" or "crawler" has found over time. It should be understood, however, that since competing search engines have different bots and crawlers, with divergent different software strategies, and variations in the length of time they have been compiling and sorting tags, there can be substantial differences in the quantity and quality of items retrieved.

WHY SEARCH ENGINES, OFTEN INVENTED BY SCHOLARS AS SCHOLARLY HELPERS, ARE BECOMING "PORTALS," AND WHY SEARCH ENGINE BUILDER GEEKS ARE BECOMING MILLIONAIRES EVEN IF THEY'RE NOT AS GOOD AS LIBRARIANS AT THEIR ORIGINAL MISSION

Interestingly, advertising campaigns for competing browsers now engage in warfare over whether "older and more" is better than "fewer but newer and therefore improved." But it is readily apparent that neither new nor old firms seem to pay as much attention as they should to basic indexing and abstracting principles, or to error correction and revisions. This is largely because whatever else search engines started out to be, they have ended up being venues for advertising and for e-commerce as well. (Indeed, since most of them don't charge you for using them, they make their money by charging the advertisers, setting their rates based on the number of visitors or users of their engines. Consequently, many search engines are evolving into *portals*, places on the Internet where you go to find something to buy as much as find facts or information on documents on the web.)

HOW DID THE TWO MAJOR BROWSERS GET THAT POWERFUL? A HISTORY LESSON ENCOMPASSING THE CURIOUS REASON THAT THE BROWSER WARS MATTER TO LIBRARIES

To Paraphrase an Old Political Campaign Slogan: "It's the Java, Stupid!"

While browsers, like highway on-ramps, are hard to construct, they are simple to use. Their simplicity of use has incredibly expanded traffic and commerce on the Internet, and commerce now drives changes to the Internet as much as technology. While it is certainly conceivable that a better on-ramp could be built, any substantial deviance from the core structural plans used by the two leaders is more likely to lead to a road to nowhere than to a great diversion of Internet traffic onto the new style road. It might first appear given that since the search engine owners have become millionaires, that the owners of the two major browsers would just naturally be billionaires (since the browser parameters control the search engine parameters to a great degree) and that this was just going to be a fact of life librarians would have to accept with indifference as to which browser. But it's important to understand that it's not just about specific personalities, or about preferring one company over another, although these people and corporate battle subplots will figure prominently in the following history. For librarians, it's ultimately about Java.

Mosaic, developed by a very young Brian Anderson at the University of illinois, was the first widely used browser (not-for-profit) in the US. Today, it has been largely supplemented by the two commercial versions that we know as bitter rivals. These are on one hand, Netscape's *Navigator* and *Communicator* (developed by the still youthful Andreessen and his new corporate partners at Netscape) and Microsoft's Internet Explorer. Importantly, James Barksdale, CEO of Netscape (he tends to handle the business side of Netscape), is also openly aligned with the anti-Gates group. His Netscape Navigator and Netscape Communicator are relatively low-end in hardware requirements and are also Java enabled and compatible with many different hardware platforms. Indeed, his firms' readily compliant use of Java without much alteration further strengthens Java as the software technology of choice for the web, and therefore for the e-journal business.

THE ALTERNATE VISION
OF BILL GATES/MICROSOFT AND ANDREW GROVE/INTEL

To Hell with Your Budget Waist Line!
Their Specially Attached and Extensioned Java
Goes Best with Cache-Rich Chips
Baked According to the Microsoft Cookbook

Bill Gates is one of the founders and remains the leader of Microsoft. His success and that of his firm has been remarkable for both its extent, and for the extensive criticism it has engendered. While critics may argue that the software products of his firm may not necessarily be the best, they certainly sell the best, almost to the exclusion of some of his competitors' software. Critics suggest that Microsoft's success in sales have made it de-facto the platform software partner whose offer hardware platform partners can't refuse.

The principal business, and most profitable member of the Microsoft product line by far, is the sale of Windows software that runs best on ever more powerful PCs that the computer hardware industry keeps producing. The best guarantee of an endless supply of new Windows customers is the perceived necessity among computer buyers and users, both personal and in business, for continuously more powerful PCs, which generally have to have new Windows software programs written for them in order to optimize their function. Given that a new generation of chips comes out about every 12 to

18 months, and new PCs are built around those chips, it is not surprising that tens of millions of new Windows software packages also get sold, with a majority now pre-installed when the new PC is delivered. In short, there are hot new platforms on the market every calendar year, and over 90% of them automatically have Windows software. It has now gotten to the point that most consumers expect to be sold new Windows software with new chips and new machines and would find it strange if this were not the case.

Leading edge chip design and related PC hardware development costs hundreds of millions of dollars annually for each firm involved. These investments are not a sure thing in terms of guaranteed sales, at least partly because there is always the possibility that another competitor will come up with a better chip at the same time, or drastically cut prices on their older chips, discouraging new purchases. Any alienation of the number one (and in many minds the one and only) software vendor only adds to the risk of business failure, even if technological success is achieved in chip performance. Leading chip makers, such as Intel, therefore, are in close contact (some would say collusional contact) with Microsoft about where forthcoming chip design is headed and this gives Microsoft has a head start, if not an actual veto power concerning changes in platform development.

For years, it looked as if this consultative partnership was mutually beneficial and even genuinely happy. Nonetheless, this had been hard to confirm or deny based on pronouncements in the profession literature or popular press. This is largely because there are more chip leaders to keep track of than software leaders, and few have become quite the celebrities that Mr. Gates has become. Even the leader of the most famous chip company, Intel's Andrew Grove, despite his being named *Time Magazine*'s Man of the Year in 1998, is far more circumspect in his opinions of Mr. Gates and Microsoft than is the professional press at large. More is inferred about his long standing alliance–termed the "Wintel" platform alliance–than has historically been reported in direct quotes. Likewise it is safe to assume that other leading chipmakers such as those with Cyrix, Advanced Micro Devices, Integrated Device Technology, Toshiba, Fujitsu and Motorola have at least a consultative relationship with Microsoft, but are also less flamboyant and more discreet than Mr. Gates or the computer industry press, in freely stating their opinions about what appears to some critics to be a mandatory "voluntary" alliance. This also seems true for computer component assemblers and overall PC builders, in whose finished products the chips are housed, and through which the software operates. These "Wintel" allies appear to include such giants as Compaq, Dell, Packard-Bell and Gateway. Part of their discretion may just be a matter of the personalities involved, but part of this may also be for fear of alienating Mr. Gates, and being punished through market share losses caused by not having Windows' blessing or Windows installations.

(Their machines can run without Windows, but could they ever sell as well as they do?)

It has been shown to be possible to do business without Microsoft's approval or Intel's chips; it's just seemed perilous to do so, and remain independent. Threats to one member of the Wintel coalition tend to be treated as threats to another, and team members seem to try buying out or co-opting any threats for the good of the entire coalition. Apple, a firm that remains number one in publishing software and computer graphics design, for example, has long had a history of making and using only its own chips, as well as having its own excellent Mac software. It thrived until the mid-1980s as an openly anti-Wintel platform. Yet by that time, it saw declining sales, and newer Apples were built to allow for the installation of Windows, in addition to the supplied Mac software. For a variety of reasons, Apple saw its share of the market continue to tumble, despite having good products and the prospects of even better ones down the road. When Apple desperately needed a cash infusion in 1998 to get its next generation of PCs ready, it got its money and presumably some marching orders to tone down its anti-Wintel talk from Microsoft (which had reportedly threatened to cease marketing and supporting the Mac-compatible version of Windows). Less noted was the fact that Apple also started to use other chips, including Intel chips, in addition to its own. For a time, Apple abandoned at least some of its anti-"Wintel" advertising, and seemed to go along Wintel lines in the browser wars. (Given the success of their very recent iMac line, however, and the new, wickedly fast G3 chips, they are resuming their Wintel bashing, and may become more openly a Netscape ally).

The case of Digital seems another instance of Wintel coalition maneuvering. Despite being in financial trouble because of its long overreliance on the declining Big Iron mainframe platform market, Digital remained an extremely attractive takeover target, because of its Intel-beating proprietary Alpha chips. Most observers noted that the purchase of Digital by Compaq, very much a Microsoft and Intel ally, ended a chip threat to Intel. (Indeed, Intel had already lost a chip patent infringement suit to Digital with a settlement in favor of Digital in the hundreds of millions of dollars.) Less appreciated was the fact that Digital also had an army of technicians willing and able to convert literally thousands of still working VAX Big Iron machines, still under service contract from Digital, away from competing software to Microsoft's *Windows NT* ensuring that large numbers of banks, hospitals and academic institutions (the traditional Digital mid-sized institutional markets) would migrate to Wintel and stay there. When those machines finally do die, all the files and loaded software will have to migrate onto Wintel machines, unless their owners wish to lay out prohibitive amounts of money for software rewriting and file restructuring.

Under the Wintel current system, hardware and software will go on happily leapfrogging one another, with a huge number of hardware and software buyers financially mesmerized into joining this purchasing race. Microsoft and Intel, moreover, argue that no one is ever forced to join the race, and that many businesses have voluntarily been doing so and have profited by keeping up. This begs the questions as to whether libraries can do so as well by this continual pressure to upgrade. While Bill Gates has become admittedly a donor to some of America's library systems, it is not clear that his largesse will offset the cost of libraries being required to keep up in a platform improvement race that his own company seems to foster.

DESPITE THE SPEED OF THEIR CHIPS AND SOFTWARE, MICROSOFT AND INTEL SEEMED SLOW TO GRASP E-MAIL, BUSINESS NETWORKING AND THE WEB: THEY THEN USED BUSINESS STRATEGIES TO OFFSET TECHNOLOGICAL TARDINESS

Gates and hardware allies such as Intel have cooperated to encourage desktop computers that might potentially and secondarily be part of a local network or company intranet, but were primarily designed as stand-alone computers. In a way, Gates and his industry allies have long argued that the weakest computer link determines the strength of the entire computer chain and that network reliability and speed may actually be weakened or retarded if too many old, underpowered, low speed PCs are used in a network. To repeat an earlier analogy, they suggested that the best teams or networks are composed of all-stars: machines that function very well alone make for networks that function very well together. They appeared to think that their Wintel coalition would maintain agenda-setting power over any developments in networking through gaining market share dominance of the desktop client components that would probably make up any client-server network. While it was quite clear that Intel chips were certainly going to be used in servers in the evolving client-server framework, Microsoft in particular felt that there would always be fewer "server-coaches" than all-star client-players. Most importantly in terms of unit sales, each player would still have to have its own Microsoftware installed and in need of repeated upgrading. Microsoft felt that it could make up in volume sales of client software anything it lost in the then still developing server software market.

Microsoft only belatedly realized that the growth in inter-computer communications, such as e-mail, and more involved corporate or institutional messaging was going to be so immense that this was a major business opportunity they were going to miss out on. More importantly, it was becoming such a big enough phenomenon that new players might eventually become rich enough able to deflect Microfsoft's hitherto controlling hand in driving overall computer hardware and software technology. (Recall that the Internet was (and is) more than just the graphically oriented World Wide Web, and that e-mail was growing exponentially, even before the web. Millions of people where e-mailing with BITNET long before pictures came on the scene, and it did not require a Microsoft product or even a specifically Intel chip to do so.) Microsoft found that in order to catch up, it had to buy out most of the early pioneers, who were still relatively cash-poor compared to Microsoft and Intel. This included swallowing up, happily or otherwise, some former technology partners that showed signs of wanting to go their own way. Microsoft was not entirely triumphant, however. Novell, for example, gained a great share of that market and successfully fought off Microsoft's subsequent attempts to rein them in.

Microsoft grew determined not to let this sort of thing happen again with other file-sharing and transactional business networking. After a particularly arduous research and product testing cycle, Microsoft finally came up with Windows NT, a network-oriented operating system that makes the most of the team play of the ever-more-powerful PCs with which Microsoft was far more familiar and over whose technological innovation they had a great say. Given the wide installed base of existing Wintel machines (and the conversion of many old Digital Big Iron machines to a server role, as mentioned earlier) Windows NT finally caught up in the business networking market, even if some critics argued, once again, that it was not, or is not, the best product so much as the market dominating product. Importantly, to get the full benefit of the NT software, you eventually have to upgrade the hardware portion of the platform as well to match the software, and this strengthens the hand of the hardware members of the coalition. (Indeed, some libraries today are facing difficulties funding yet another upgrade to higher-end Intel PCs necessary to match campus-wide adoptions of Windows NT.)

Despite the failures of their early warning systems that prompted the forced march development of Windows NT, Microsoft still seemed caught short by the rise of the web. It seemed as if it was either exhausted by the retooling-to-NT effort, or more likely felt satisfied that this was enough product line re-engineering for the time being to maintain control of any future market developments. But once again, to its surprise, it was not. Microsoft belatedly realized that just as Novell had earlier run off with a good deal of the e-mail and messaging business, Netscape, along with its technology partner Sun, was now running off with the World Wide Web business. Microsoft once again found itself facing a crash program over the last two years to stake a claim in the rising web software market. It worried that without a bold move, it could lose both in the obvious short run (no web-access product at a time when the web was getting hot, the mid-1990s) and more subtly in the long run in a way that would threaten its hold on its most profitable individual PC platform technology. Microsoft realized that the web could conceivably undercut the sustained demand for new Windows software, their core product. They effectively asked themselves: Where would the demand for ever more sophisticated Windows software running on ever more sophisticated PCs come from if the public transportation "computer-ridership" of the World Wide Web gave individual PC users –Microsoft's prime market–what they wanted at relatively low-end technology and low cost? Who would be buying instrument packages on Ferraris, as it were, when a low cost bus trip had the potential to satisfy so many basic computer wants?

Large and technically capable as Microsoft was, and despite its ultimately successful development of NT, it still felt it could not develop a consumer-level market web browser with custom software on its own, quickly enough, that was as readily useful and widely accepted as was Netscape with Sun's Java. Since it couldn't buy Netscape, it licensed another little-known pioneering browser from a small firm called Spyglass, and repackaged it. But it still needed the Java, and warily, Sun licensed it as well.

This permission was given, however, subject to conditions that any modestly-altered Microsoft-generated versions not compromise the across-all-platforms readability of one version of Java with another. In other words, Sun expected Microsoft to behave nicely like Netscape and Oracle. It wanted Microsoft Java to strengthen Java's hold as the lingua franca of the web because the vast number of Microsoft speakers would de-facto become Java speakers as well.

Further, there was some expectation that Microsoft's new product, Internet Explorer, would compete on its own technological merits against Netscape. PC buyers could choose to buy and up load either Netscape or the Internet Explorer as they liked, based on their own response to advertising campaigns, columns in the PC press, or via word-of-mouth recommendations on comparative performance from their friends who had used one or both packages and could offer an informed opinion. Instead, Microsoft used its considerable clout with PC makers to pre-install not only the latest version of Windows before delivery of those PCs to the sales floor, an old Microsoft practice, but also bundled in the Internet Explorer in those installations. Consequently, it quickly became difficult to buy a PC that did not have Internet Explorer already in place, reducing the desire and likelihood of new computer buyers from buying Netscape software or even giving Netscape a trial. In a particular hard-nosed competitive tactic, the preloaded software was made so that it would be deliberately hard to replace the Explorer with Netscape, should the new computer purchaser nonetheless wish to do so.

Microsoft followed this practice of mandatory bundling together of Windows software with Internet Explorer for PC owners who already had an older Windows 3.1 package and were seeking to upgrade it with a Windows 90s series. Such PC owners could not upgrade their old Windows software without automatically loading the Explorer as well. Consequently, Microsoft not only seemed poised to block buyers of new computers away from also buying Netscape software, but also any computer users who were merely trying to upgrade their old equipment. To add insult to injury, Microsoft essentially gave away this browser for no added charge to the consumer, undercutting Netscape, which charged for its browser, and appeared to need that revenue to stay in business. Microsoft argued that adding browser software to Windows software was a long-decided strategy, something that was not a short-term predatory price-cutting tactic at all. In fact, they claimed, it was a downright public service. They argued, somewhat disingenuously, that this was a long-planned synergistic intermeshing of Windows and the new browser, like Siamese twins sharing electronic organs. Being forced to remove their give-away browser component from the bundled Windows software would wound the computer and cripple consumers, they maintained.

This development drew a fairly quick response from the Justice Department, who had already cautioned Microsoft about what was seen to be other anti-competitive or monopolistic practices. To be fair, it should be mentioned that the exuberant Scott McNealy of Sun and Java, and the people at Netscape who saw their market share crash and ended up having to give away their product to individual (but not corporate) PC users seemed to be important catalysts in goading the government to action.

Moreover, according to legal news, Microsoft has developed a substantially new dialect of Java, with attachments and extensions that may not be as readily understood by other Java speaking machines on the Internet. This would threaten not only Netscape, but Sun and IBM as well, given that Microsoft has many more customers than either Sun or Netscape. Sun's Java (increasingly termed *Pure Java*) would become something like the Queen's British English, a curious minority dialect in a world of American Microsoft English, with parts of it increasingly difficult to comprehend across continents and in computer terms, across platforms.

Most importantly for libraries, loss of control over Java might threaten the viability of low-cache, low-cost PCs as receiving docks for electronic journal content. The internal cache, drives, and processors of computer networks in libraries connected to the Internet might have to be upgraded more often. Libraries straining to pay for content and licensing agreements for themselves or their consortia, would have to spend more and more money, more and more often, on platforms, soon after a transition to NT network platforms had already cost them money.

MR. BILL GOES TO WASHINGTON,
AND NOT ALL OF HIS ALLIES GO ALONG
(OR GO ALONG HAPPILY AT LEAST) WITH HIM

The year 1998 witnessed the unfolding of two stories where the principals may have had fewer principles than most people would like, but each remained the principal of his respective domain despite this. Both President Clinton and Chairman Gates were depositioned and both experienced painfully obvious difficulties with their memory cache and had unusual difficulty in parsing commands and queries, repeatedly answering in the form of what for most people would be regarded as "Fatal Error Messages." Nonetheless, the response of the PC consumer market to this apparent lying was much more like that of Ms. Clinton than that of Mr. Starr. Both the PC world and she have grown used to any flaws in the characters involved since their respective dealings with these men still fundamentally enable them to get their own personal agenda accomplished. Stories of underlying tensions have nonetheless emerged that suggests that while few major players in either computing or politics can afford to stop working altogether with either Bill for the time being, those players can more openly do business with other partners at the same time as they do business with the Bills, and perhaps one day make decisions to do business without their old partner's approval or involvement if necessary.

This is particularly the case now with AOL whose front end and browser was Internet Explorer based, but will soon switch to Netscape though a merger of AOL and Netscape, a deal that includes making Sun a preferred provider of new technology to the new merged entity. This is a triumph for Pure Java and therefore, in the opinion of this author, for libraries as well.

This has also encouraged speculation that Intel, the longest standing partner of Microsoft, might reconsider its position. The document discovery process during the recent trial disclosed that at times in the recent past, it appeared that Microsoft had actually threatened its most loyal partner's independent initiatives and overtures rather forcefully, suggesting that the Microsoft-Intel alliance was more one of wallets and elbows, not hearts or minds all along. Furthermore, it now appears that Intel suffered disproportionately more market share casualties than did Microsoft in the successful quelling of the NC uprising, a bruising battle in whose outcome both firms had an equally vested interest, and that Microsoft did not offer any offsetting compensation to its more wounded ally. In any case, Intel now has to pioneer not only its high-end Pentium chips, but their stripped down Celeron line as well, essentially fighting a two front war. (And it is important for libraries to note that some early Celeron chip machines had a dearth of L2 cache that would make handling long downloads problematic.)

None of this suggests that either Microsoft or Intel was or is intentionally unfriendly to issues involving scholarly electronic journals and libraries that depend on *Java*. It is entirely likely that they were largely unaware and unconcerned about any collateral effect of their technology and business tussles on our particular business. (To give you some perspective, Microsoft earns every three weeks about what Elsevier, another Microsoft strategic partner and the world's largest STM publisher, makes in an entire year.) It even remains very likely that many, if not most, libraries will continue to use "Wintel" type PCs as client machines for accessing electronic journals. But this writer is inclined to believe that it was a good thing that having some of these issues aired in the courts in a way that will favor keeping the Java as black as possible in both "Wintel" and other platforms adopted by libraries, so that libraries can avoid as much red ink in their budget accounts as possible.

BIBLIOGRAPHY

***Bibliography on Hardware, Software, and Technological Warfare
Affecting the Internet and Electronic Journals:
Terminology of Major Components and Competing Strategies
of Major Players***

Scope Note: These references deal with three interrelated themes:

- *The Internet has co-evolved along with the business of making and selling computers and computer software. Business needs and technological advances both drive changes in the Net, although those needs and breakthroughs are not always forseeable when purchases of hardware and software need to be made.*
- *Software and hardware investments by both libraries and publishers tend to be reaffirmed or threatened by the outcomes of fierce competitions in the computer hardware and software industries, over which libraries and publishers have only a limited amount of control, despite their expensive investments. Fear of premature obsolescence owing to failure of technological allies or partners in standards setting or market-controlling wars, requiring unplanned reinvestment remains very high.*
- *Ironically, libraries and publishers of all types may be able to gain some stability if competitors and standards favoring Pure Java which is co-incidentally also favorable to e-commerce prevail. E-commerce needs will have a far greater sway over the entire Net, and perhaps even over electronic publishing, despite all manner of resolutions by librarians, or publishers, or joint groups, because of its greater economic impact.*

Abram, Stephen and Jane Dysart. "A Conversation with Bill Gates." *Information Outlook* 1 (5): 23-25, May, 1997.

Alper, Joseph. "From Army of Hackers: An Upstart Operating System [Linux]" *Science* 282:1976-1978, 1998.

Alschuler, Liora. *ABCD–SGML: A User's Guide to Structured Information.* International Thomson, 1995.

Anonymous. "Electronic Commerce" [a special issue] *Business America* 119 (January, 1998): 1-44.

Barron, Kelly. "Bill Gates Wants Our Business." *Forbes* 161 (April 6, 1998): 46-47.

Boeri, Robert J., and Martin Hensel. "XML: the New Document Standard." *EMedia Professional* 11 (6): 33, June, 1998.

Boyle, James. "A Blueprint for Managing Documents." *Byte* 22 (5): 75-80, 1997.

Brinkley, Joel. "Gates Testifies He Knew Little of Microsoft-Sun Battle Over Java." *New York Times* (December 3, 1998) p.C5.

Bradley, Neil. *The Concise SGML Companion.* Addison-Wesley, 1997.

Burden, Dorian. "A Beginner's Guide to Page Make-Up." *Folio, the Magazine for Magazine Management* 26 (Special Sourcebook Supplement): 174-175, 1998.

Busse, Torsten, Kristi Essick, and Mary Jo Wagner. "Linux Continues to Pick Up Steam." *InfoWorld* 20 (48): 34, 1998.

Caruso, Denise. "Digital Commerce." *New York Times* (Monday, November 16, 1998): C5.

Chang, Dan and Harkey, Da. *Client/Server Access With Java and XML.* Wiley, 1998.

Clip, Paul. "Servlets: CGI the Java Way." *Byte* 23 (5): 55-56, 1998.

Clyman, John. "Face-Off: Internet Explorer 4.0 vs. Communicator." *PC Magazine* 16 (20): 100-122, November 18, 1997.

Cohen, Adam. "A Tale of Two Bills." *Time* 153: 52, January 25, 1999.

Colby, Martin et al. *Using SGML.* Que Corp., 1996.

Cook, William J. "Guess Who's Number One in E-Commerce?" *U.S. News and World Report* 125 (22): 53, December 7, 1998.

Crosby, Walter. "Generation XML." *Computerworld* 32 (10): 19, March 9, 1998.

Donovan, Truly. *Industrial Strength SGML.* Prentice Hall, 1997.

Dzilna, Dzintars. "Brand-Building in a Wired World." *Folio: The Magazine for Magazine Management* 27 (6):31-33, 1998.

Dzilna, Dzintars. "New Life for an Old Friend: Chip Upgrades." *Folio: the Magazine for Magazine Management* 27 (11): 29, August, 1998.

Dzilna, Dzintars. "Mac versus PC." *Folio: The Magazine for Magazine Management* 27 (5): 60-62, April, 1998.

Dzilna, Dzintars. "PDF Steals the Show." *Folio: The Magazine for Magazine Management* 27 (8): 47. June, 1998.

Gable, Gene. "More on Platform Wars." *Publish* 13 (February, 1998): 20.

Gable, Gene. "Placing Wagers at the Publishing Playoffs." *Publish* 12 (December, 1997): 24.

Garber, Lee. "PC Makers Try to Catch Buyers With the Net." *Computer* 32(2): 16-18, 1999.

Gelertner, David. "Software Strongman." *Time* (December 7, 1998): 200.

Grove, Andrew. "Andy Grove Sees the Future: the iMac Points the Way." *Time* (October 5, 2998): 22.

Handy, Jim. *The Cache Memory Book.* Academic Press, 1998.

Halfhill, Tom R. "Today the Web, Tomorrow the World." [Java as a threat to Windows.] *Byte 22 (1): 68-80, 1997.*

Hickman, Angela and others. "A New Java OS is Born." *PCMagazine* 17 (12): 10, 1998.

Hilts, Paul. "Dazed and Confused." *Publishers Weekly* 245 (January 26, 1998), p. 32-33.

Hilts, Paul. "X Marks the Document." *Publishers Weekly* 245 (17) 25, 1998.

Hilts, Paul. "Publishers Back Microsoft Call for E-Book Standard." *Publishers Weekly* 245 (42): 10, 1998.

Hurwicz, Mike. "Cheaper Computing, Part 2: PCs Strike Back." *Byte* 22 (5): 81-88, 1997.

Lamparter, William C. "Digital Observations." *American Printer* 221 (1): 50-51, April, 1998.

Levy, Streven. "Code Warriors." *Newsweek* 133 (3): 60-62, 1999.

Lewis, Peter H. "Apple Shows Its Colors." *New York Times* (January 7, 1999): E1+.

Lewis, Peter H. "Many Updates Cause Profitable Confusion." *New York Times* (January 21, 1999): E1+.

Lewis, Peter H. "Whoosh! The Next Pentium." *New York Times* (January 14, 1999): E1+.

Lewis, Ted. "What to Do About Microsoft." *Computer* 31 (9):112, 1998.

Lidsky, David. "Home on the Web. [Search engines and Portals.]" *PC Magazine* 17 (15): 100-139, 1998.

Lohr, Steve. "Depth of Rift Over Software is Disclosed." *New York Times* (Monday, November 16, 1998) C1+.

Lohr, Steve. "Microsoft Presses Its View About Rivals 3-Way Deal." *New York Times* (January 7, 1999): C2.

Maler, Eve. *Developing SGML DTDs: From Text to Model to Markup.* Prentice Hall: 1996.

Markoff, John. "Oracle Data Base Takes Aim at Windows." *New York Times* (November 18, 1998): C5.

Miller, Micahel J. "Windows 98 Put to the Test." *PC Magazine* 17 (14): 100-135, 1998.

Mitchell, Russ. "Why AOL Really Clicks." *U.S. News and World Report* 125 (22): 52-53, December 7, 1998.

Potter, Ben. "Reed [Reed-Elsevier] Shares Leap on Gates Rumour." *The Daily Telegraph [London]* (December 17, 1998): 33.

Radosevich, Lynda, Marc Ferranti, and Rob Guth. "Windows Chips Away at Macintosh's Bastion." *InfoWorld* 20 (12): 32, March 23, 1998.

Rosenberg, Jim. "Prospect for *PostScript* RIPs." *Editor and Publisher* 131 (11): 32, March 14, 1998.

Ross, Chuck. "Gates Partners with Hachette." *Advertising Age* 69 (16): 52, April 20, 1998.

Sanders, James. "Linux, Open Source, and Software's Future." *IEEE Software* 15 (5): 88-91, 1998.

Schatz, Bruce, and others. "Federated Search of Scientific Literature. [SGML provides a robust basis for a multipublisher multidisciplinary electronic journal database with full article text.]" *Computer* 32 (2):51-59, 1999.

Schlieve, Paul L., and Michael P. Gilbert. *Developing Internet Information Services.* Wordware Publishing, 1997.

Schwartz, Candy. "Web Search Engines." *Journal of the American Society for Information Science* 49 (11): 973, 1998.

Schwartzwalder, Robert. "1997: A Quiet Year for Sci-Tech?" *Database* 20 (December, 1997): 59-61.

Schwarzwalder, Robert. "What Have We Learned From TULIP and Red Sage?" *Database* 21 (3): 63-64, June, 1998.

Seltzer, Larry. "Dynamic HTML." *PC Magazine* 16 (20): 108, November 18, 1997.

Sharples, Hadley. "Apple Computer Offers Web Consulting to Industry." *Graphic Arts Monthly* 70 (4): 98, April, 1998.

Southwick, Karen. "Found in the Crowd." *Inc.* 20 (13): 54-56, September 15, 1998.

Thrum, Scott. "Quark Tries to Catch a Fallen Hi-Tech Star. Once a Master of Fine Print, Adobe Slipped." *Wall Street Journal (Eastern Edition)* (August 27, 1998), p.B1+.

Travis, Brian E. *The SGML Implementation Guide.* Springer, 1996.

Tulloch, Mitch. *Administering IIS4 [Internet Information Server 4 Windows NT].* McGraw Hill, 1998.

Weibel, Bob. "Managing the Mix: Why Publishers are Blending Computer Platforms." *Publish* 13 (6): 50+, June, 1998.

Wilken, Earl. "Selling On-Demand Requires Solutions." *Graphic Arts Monthly* 70 (4): 86, April, 1998.

Wilken, Earl. "Solutions Debut at High-Tech Forum." *Graphic Arts Monthly* 70 (5): 94-95, May, 1998.

Wilken, Earl. "Xerox Zeroes In On Integrated Systems." *Graphic Arts Monthly* 70(4): 84, April, 1998.

Electronic Journal Concerns
and Strategies of Science Publishers

Tony Stankus

There are three main categories of science publishers: the college and university presses, the not-for-profit societies, and the for-profit publishers. To some degree they are competitors, but in many ways their concerns are more alike than critics within librarianship would like to admit. What follows is a survey of the distinctions between these categories, and how they are handling critical issues in publishing, both print and electronic, vis-à-vis the library community. This is followed by some key areas in which publishers of all these types are likely to be united.

THE UNIVERSITY PRESS AS SCIENCE JOURNAL PUBLISHERS: THE AMAZINGLY FEW, IF PROUD

It might strike intelligent people outside of academic libraries and publishing that one of two solutions to the complaints about the size, numbers, and costs of science journals would solve the problems. First, if successful science journal publishers that sell to university libraries as their primary market behave badly, why don't the universities simply become successful science publishers themselves, depriving the publishers of their primary market, and sell to their own captive audience of libraries? Second, alternatively, if it were true that at least the for-profit publishers were such stunningly successful profiteers, why wouldn't the universities with their hundreds of billions of dollars in collective endowments simply buy controlling interests in these publishers (for a few billion dollars) and pretty much run the publishing

[Haworth co-indexing entry note]: "Electronic Journal Concerns and Strategies of Science Publishers." Stankus, Tony. Co-published simultaneously in *Science & Technology Libraries* (The Haworth Press, Inc.) Vol. 18, No. 2/3, 1999, pp. 75-96; and: *Electronic Expectations: Science Journals on the Web* (Tony Stankus) The Haworth Press, Inc., 1999, pp. 75-96. Single or multiple copies of this article are available for a fee from The Haworth Document Delivery Service [1-800-342-9678, 9:00 a.m. - 5:00 p.m. (EST). E-mail address: getinfo@haworth pressinc.com].

75

house any way they chose, all the while raking in those run away profits for those endowments?

As the introductory paper suggests, there is little evidence that the librarians are particularly good at being science journal publishers, at least partly because collectively they don't particularly empathize with science or scientists, and partly because they themselves have no particularly great record as journal publishers, even if they are great lovers of books. Much the same can be said for university presses. Although there are dozens of distinguished university presses in the U.S. and abroad, there are perhaps only half a dozen that are distinguished publishers of significant numbers of science journals. Ironically, some of the same reasons for this lack of effort and interest in science apply to the rest of the remaining university presses as it does to university libraries. Their leaderships are far more likely to be drawn from humanities and the social sciences than from the sciences, and their hearts are with books. The little journals (in pagination and budgets, not necessary in importance to their intended audience) most university presses publish in the hundreds resemble in content the books they have published in the thousands over the last few decades: overwhelmingly focused on music and the arts, poetry and short fiction, literary and cultural criticism, archeology and history and world politics, social and political commentary, issues in education and various multicultural and feminist concerns. It might be argued that university based schools of business and law publish substantially larger journals that sometimes have substantial sales outside academia and which are closer in page counts and budgets to science journals than they are to many humanities-oriented titles. But this analogy excludes the fact that those professional schools are, in many respects, semi-autonomous institutions on campus whose accrediting bodies have virtually institutionalized requirements for such publications, and are often in possession and control of their own endowments.

THEIR HEARTS ARE IN THEIR BOOKS BUT THEIR BOOKS AREN'T ALLOWED TO BE PRINTED WITH RED INK ANYMORE

Because the People Who Write Their Budgets Are More Influential Than the People Who Write or Buy Their Books or Journals

Having said this, why aren't university presses happy and comfortable places in their chosen niches? This is because university presses are generally treated by the university's financial authorities at best as break-even adjuncts to the university's function, and at worst as enterprises that had better generate positive cash flow if they intend to stick around at all. University presses share most of the same pressures to reduce costs as do libraries, and have shared much of the same marginalization of influence as have some libraries in setting overall university priorities. Largely because external funds for libraries (the primary market for university press books) have not kept pace with other initiatives that generate income for universities, university financial officers no longer view building library collections as a kind of seed bed to grow even more external funds for the university. The percentage share of university revenues going to libraries has actually dropped, and it is already clear to the administrators who raise money and allocate expenditures, that they'll not gladly fund generously one enterprise (the university press) that sells primarily to another enterprise (the library) that they themselves have decided to downgrade in their list of spending priorities.

It wasn't always that way. Science and technology savvy universities (and their libraries), whose expansion in the World War II and the Cold War was often funded through direct grants from science foundations and the defense department or via indirect overhead revenues from STM research, initially embraced their STM faculty and their new publications. But the 1980s saw a strong backlash from those libraries when the financial officers at those very institutions that had profited from that external STM support began cutting back on the library spending. Monies that used to go to libraries now also went to a wide variety of other campus initiatives and departments, including wiring the entire campus for computing and funding the first generation of computers, a daunting challenge that had to be funded somehow (and which coincidentally, had become a sexier fundraising focus for parents, alumni, and corporate support campaigns). Faced with pressures to reduce costs, librarians saw the most expensive science journals as the likeliest cancellation targets to help them meet the expectations of their financial managers, although it is only fair to say that many humanities and social sciences books went unbought as well. The scientists, initially pleased and preoccupied by the advent of campus-wide computerization, seemed to be more irritated with the librarians who no longer supported their journal habit to the same degree as previously than aware of the fact that the accountants in Development were now in control of library budgets, at least in a negative sense. In any case, librarians began yelling at science publishers, while the scientists began yelling at the librarians–with no great effect in either case–because the ultimate truth was that neither the faculty nor the heads of university libraries or presses can yell at the top financial bosses on campus and keep their jobs.

FINDING TECHNOLOGY PARTNERS FOR UNIVERSITY SCIENCE JOURNAL PRESSES TO HANDLE THE ELECTRONIC PART OF THEIR JOURNALS

The Project Muse and Highwire Approaches

It is particularly ironic that the high end computerization needs of electronic science journal production, are likely to fall on deaf ears in university financial offices. Indeed, the one area where university scientists and their university press officers are now likely to be in synch is in disappointment. Both the scientists and the library presses have gotten the same response from the same financial administrators when they separately asked for yet another computer system upgrade to replace the ones they got in the 1980s through the mid-1990s: "Go get your own grant, and if you get it, we in administration will still take our usual administrative overhead cut." The sort of challenge led to Johns Hopkins University Press' Project Muse for electronic journals which, although not involving only science journals, is indeed a hugely successful grant-driven project. It was far more funded externally rather than internally, but it is interesting to note that it was the Milton S. Eisenhower Library which appeared to take the on-campus lead in organizing the project. Likewise it was the Stanford University Libraries and their Academic Information Resources Group that took the lead in setting up Highwire Press. Once again, it was initially partly grant-driven and involved publishing mostly electronic versions of existing print journals and has been hugely successful. What made it different was that from the start it focused on attracting journals from outside the Stanford research and publications community, mostly from STM societies rather than other university presses. (Rockefeller University Press is a notable exception.) Highwire will advise any not-for-profit publisher of good reputation on platforms, electronic manuscript mark-up and encoding standards and take care of their round-the-clock distribution network needs through hosting their electronic journals directly, or through providing a pointer server that links authorized subscribers to their respective publisher's host servers. The get-a-big-grant-path, while worthwhile initially, is now getting well-worn and losing novelty attraction to external agencies, much like what happened to the grant-driven electronic conversions of the library card catalog or the consortial union list of serials projects of the 1970s and 1980s.

SCIENTIFIC SOCIETIES, AMERICAN AND FOREIGN, AS PUBLISHERS

To some degree, American research libraries have it easier than many of their foreign counterparts for two reasons. First, nominally not-for-profit scientific societies publish most of the science journal articles written by Americans. American libraries do not have to pay import or for-profit prices to cover most of their own country's output. Second, most of these same journals are regarded as the world's best journals in given fields, a fact attested to in that they contain a high proportion of foreign papers. The problem, at least for librarians, is that not all American publish in domestic not-for-profit science society journals, and not all the necessary or best science emanates from America alone. What remains valued and needed seems irreducibly to account for about a third of the science journal subscriptions taken in American research libraries and over half the typical university budget for science serials.

One of the greatest frustrations of not-for-profit societies is that, despite this outstanding performance (American societies have less than 20% of the world's science PhDs and yet American societies publish such a disproportionate share of the science that just about everyone needs and uses worldwide) many libraries demonize their domestic not-for-profit publications as much as they do the foreign for-profits. Much of this has to do with the usual librarian's lack of understanding for the huge volume of science papers that many of the best journals of science typically feature. But an even greater source of resentment by librarians may be that subscriptions to society members cost only a fraction of what their libraries are charged. While the fairness of this issue can be debated endlessly, perhaps the greatest galling factor for librarians is that this practice suggests that most scientists are likely to identify more closely with the interests of their national society than the interests of their local research library or even their institution in general.

There are several reasons for this. In these recent years of widespread science journal cancellations, society members may well feel better served by their society than they are by the library. While it might be argued that libraries have more than one subject to serve, it is hard for scientists to argue with an organization that exists more or less solely to serve their subject needs alone, and in particular, tends not only not to question those needs, but lobbies nationally with governmental bodies, foundations, accrediting bodies, and even their university administrators on behalf of them. (Those university administrators cannot fire the society, and societies, through their accrediting power, have more power to defend their society members than the library has to defend the same scientists as one among many of their patrons). Moreover, in those cases when either the library or the administration find they cannot fund or tenure a scientist, the society is more likely to be a help to the disgruntled or dispossessed scientist in finding a new position.

Additionally, academic scientists are not the only members of many subject based scientific societies. Chemists in academia, for example, feel a kinship through their society with chemists in medicine, private industry, agriculture, governmental regulatory bodies, and the like. Academic chemists may well defer somewhat, depending on the issue involved, to these other colleagues for the good of chemistry. This is particularly true if they perceive that even though they are hired as teachers, the only measure of performance that, all things being equal, is largely in their own hands, is the new science they discover. The grades they give to students (who might sue them) or the endless administrative paperwork they fill out correctly for the bean counters (who are always threatening to cut their funding) are important, but may not be as satisfying or seemingly under their control. They are certainly more likely to receive actual awards, promotions to fellow-of-the-society, and the like, and to regard them as more honestly won, for their scientific achieve-ments as judged by their society colleagues than they are to receive positive enforcement from their students, deans or their librarians, in these conten-tious times. It has been clear for decades that scientists bring more money and fame to universities than do either most librarians or many university admin-istrators, but it is not clear that they have been thanked for it.

What scientists do know is that for virtually all of their professional lives, their professional society has kept up at least one journal with which they can identify, and from time to time, that society has added more pages or more journals as their fields have grown. With the advent of electronic versions of these journals, scientists are more likely to believe that both physically and metaphorically their society's journals will gladly be there for them, even if the libraries and librarians won't.

FINDING THEIR OWN COALITION PARTNERS:
OTHER ORGANIZATIONS LIKE THEMSELVES
AND LIBRARY ORGANIZATIONS THAT HAVE A CLUE

Some science societies, particularly those in the physical sciences and engineering, are big enough, rich enough, and technically versed to such a degree that they can take on their electronic publishing ventures with some confidence. But staying big, rich, and technically versed also means that they are confident enough to invite like-minded organizations to join them, and yet feel that they can retain control. These collaborations can proceed with their foreign counterparts within the same discipline, or with their domestic analogue societies in neighboring disciplines. Thus it is no sur-prise that the American Chemical Society's *ChemCenter* or the Royal Soci-ety of Chemistry's *chemsoc* electronic publishing ventures are collaborative and have partners and customers beyond their immediate discipline and their domestic colleagues, including some document delivery services and links to indexing-abstracting services. This is a natural progression from the earlier successes of these societies in setting up the internationally collaborative (and largely society-owned) STN search service which clearly dominates on-line and web-based searching in the sciences over commercial networks and some others initially pioneered or favored by library groups. The links of the new electronic centers with indexing-abstracting services are particularly important because the latter are the venues that lead searchers to their core products, the journals themselves (electronic and print) of the member societies. These society-driven efforts even sustain current visibility and viability by the seemingly counter-intuitive trend of attracting even some of their for-profit competitors into these electronic ventures because the societies have the controlling interest. These growing e-centers have the further potential of being one-stop sites likely to be visited by student scientists, ensuring their future visibility and viability. It is entirely possible that these sites will do more to shape young scientist loyalties and opinions of what constitutes a good or reasonable journal collection (print or electronic) than what their local university library has decided that it could afford or was worthwhile.

About the only prospect that libraries have had to form coalitions with physical science and engineering societies that are credible are when the libraries drive a much more discerning wedge between society publishers and for-profit publishers, without attacking or attempting to reform the publishing mores of the societies or the scientists in the bargain. The SPARC coalition, which basically puts library money into the coffers of a not-for-profit society that commands wide respect, in this case, the American Chemical Society, seems a first step to deal that has some prospects for success. The life sciences and medicine present a somewhat different picture, in that the link to indexing-abstracting services that matters the most is the National Libraries of Medicine web product, *PubMed*. Many not-for-profit societies, including HighWire members, are linking their journal article reference lists to *PubMed*. Unfortunately for librarians who are seeking any edge that will help them downsize for-profit publishers, the making of hot links to *PubMed* does not appear to be limited to the not-for-profit publishers as it is essentially in the public domain as a kind of federal government document.

THE FOR-PROFIT PRESS, BOTH DOMESTIC AND FOREIGN

Today's for-profit print publishers see themselves as the longest-standing organizers of efforts to initiate and sustain journals for the mutual benefit of scientists and themselves, and as the biggest risk-takers in the process, particularly in the early, characteristically money-losing early years of a journal. Many scientific fields that were without much clear market definition or solid publishing support but had some promise were staked ink, paper, postage and sympathy by entrepreneurial for-profit publishers. Specialties yearning to be recognized in the in the 1960s-1970s found considerably more support at Elsevier, Springer, Academic, Plenum and Wiley than they did at their parent professional organizations or their university presses. The STM for-profit firms, knowing that these new titles did not have the virtually automatic sales guaranteed via distribution through society membership, and seeing that their science journal emphasis did not fit into the overwhelming humanities and social science vein of the book-oriented university presses, realized that they were viable only through marketing and distribution to libraries. That strategy worked until well into the 1980s, when academic library budget shortfalls caused librarians to look for prospective cancellation targets and to demonize for-profit publishers in particular.

CONTINUING NICHE PUBLISHING, BUT LOOKING FOR NICHES THAT CORPORATE LIBRARIES ARE STILL WILLING TO PAY TO EXPLORE, AND TO TITLES THAT ARE GOING TO HAVE MULTIPLE READERS EVEN IN TIMES OF CORPORATE MERGERS

For-profit publishers have grown their empires at least as much on specialty niche publications as on competing head-to-head with the major not-for-profit societies in the major academic disciplines. Partly as a response to criticisms coming from American academic librarians, their rate of introducing new academic niche titles has slowed, particularly given the 5-7 year time span needed for new academic titles to become self-sustaining and profitable. Nonetheless new title introductions have not stopped entirely. Rather, for-profit libraries are being targeted, particularly in corporate biotech and hi-tech areas, which are continuing their rapid growth. With company expenditures so extravagant, a few thousand dollars here and there doesn't seem all that much given the greater financial risks of not keeping apace in competitive scientific information represents. Additionally, newsletters and certain titles more known for the high readability of the rather compact minireview articles they publish and for their deliberate focus on highly competitive research areas are positive growth areas. The paradigm here is Elsevier's *Trends* series, which is high cost per page, but is also in tremendous demand, and which was one of the first titles to go to an electronic version.

"THEY'LL ALWAYS HAVE PARIS". . .
AND "WHEN IN ROME DO AS THE ROMANS DO"
AND OTHER MOVIE LINES AND CLICHES
THAT SUGGEST THAT AMERICAN FOR-PROFIT COMPANIES
WILL INCREASE THEIR PRESENCE AND ASSUME A PARALLEL
"EUROIDENTITY" IN A GROWING EUROECONOMY

One of the few regions where the for-profit publishers hold most of the STM journal market is on the European Continent. This is not to say that European libraries are any happier than American libraries in paying for-profit prices. However, they may well have less of a choice in the matter because two segments of the American STM journal publishing market are substantially less independent and powerful on the Continent. There is no university press to speak of in STM journal publishing for most of Europe. England's Oxford University Press and Cambridge University Press are the biggest players in both print and electronic ventures, but to some degree the English are viewed as still reluctant partners in the accelerating Euro market. (The Scandinavian University Press is a rising player but still viewed as more narrowly Scandinavian than broadly European.) Additionally, a substantial portion of the Continental society sector is actually co-published by for-profits Springer, Kluwer and Elsevier in a manner that has actually increased their worldwide stature (and their American and Asian subscriptions) by a frank appeal to European unity (many of the individual national titles were consolidated and restyled with "*European Journal of* . . . titles") that pointedly included the encouragement to use American English as a neutral, international language. Many of these journals are now among the largest and most expensive STM journals in the world and, while criticized and threatened by massive cancellations in American libraries, there is virtually no chance of them being canceled at such a level in Europe because of their local co-sponsorship and because political and economic policies will strongly favor the maintenance of a "Europroduct line." (Consider ventures like the Airbus and various telecommunications companies that routinely run deficits, but are supported for reasons of "Europride.") Perhaps the key situation favoring a pan-European identity, as opposed to single-nation identity, has occurred in Germany. VCH was essentially the publishing arm of the strongest single-nation chemical society, the Deutsche Chemische Gesellschaft, in Europe. While it may have hoped for a substantial enhancement of its status through the reunification of the former East Germany with the West, the manuscripts, memberships, and subscriptions that resulted clearly disappointed expectations. This was at a time when VCH did not appear to have much in the way of an electronic publishing strategy, and felt it needed one if it was to remain competitive at all. This was in part because by the time that East Germans had decided to become West Germans, many West Germans had become Europeans or worse, Americans, in their publishing propensities. The solution to their mounting problems was extremely ironic, yet, upon reflection, sensible. The Germans sold their publishing arm with its several journals to Wiley, an American for-profit with a very strong presence in chemistry. Wiley is now in the process of Europeanizing the journals through signing on several other member societies to join with the Germans. In one stroke the Germans (and other Europeans) had gained additional American presence, while turning their decent old-line journals into world-class competitors with a growing electronic presence. Meanwhile, Wiley has qualified for the favorable legal and tax consequences granted to European firms (but not to wholly American firms or societies) in the consolidating Euromarket. Wiley also got some assurance that its approach to electronic journal publishing standards and practices would probably be defended by the European Internet community in chemistry, because Wiley's approach is, de facto, going to be Europe's approach.

FOR-PROFITS WILL CONTINUE TO COOPERATE WITH NOT-FOR PROFIT SOCIETIES, EVEN WHEN THE FOR-PROFIT PUBLISHER WILL REMAIN A JUNIOR PARTNER IN ANY JOINT DISCIPLINARY WEB SITE VENTURES

While it is clear that not-for-profit societies have begun to form some limited partnerships with libraries, it should be recognized that for-profit publishers have been quite willing to work with their seeming not-for-profit competitors for a lot longer. There are several reasons for this. First, the for-profit houses make fewer a priori demands, and walk into negotiations as opposed to riding in on a high horse. Second, most of the for-profit houses that matter in science publishing predominantly publish science, and talk the language of science already: they talk about the good of chemistry or geology or physics, not about saving the world via free access to scientific information. Third, for-profit houses can make necessary decisions and marshal cash more quickly, without having endless discussions and rounds of voting. Fourth, even though for-profit publishers compete with the not-for-profit societies, about a third of the scholarly output of a typical member of a not-for-profit American society is in for-profit journals. Those society members are not going to urge their not-for-profit society leadership to freeze out one-third of their manuscripts outlets and reading material. Fifth, in the tricky details of electronic publishing, such as special fonts, equational arrays, and technical illustrations, for-profit publishers and not-for-profit publishers are confronting issues on which they have a shared experience and a shared appreciation of getting it right.

IN RESPONSE TO UNCERTAINTY IN THE MARKET PLACE AND IN ELECTRONIC STANDARDS-SETTING, BUY YOUR COMPETITION AND STRENGTHEN YOUR BARGAINING HAND IN THE MARKETPLACE OR IN E-PUBLISHING TECHNOLOGY STANDARDS-SETTING

Several factors favor mergers and acquisitions in the for-profit sector. The Plenum case is indicative. First, smaller but reputable publishers like Plenum were looking for corporation-buying "white knights" that preserved their shareholders rights and equity without forcing the company to invest ever more heavily in e-journal launching and maintenance. Companies like Plenum had largely used OCLC as a technology partner, but sooner or later would probably have had to contribute financially more to journal aftercare than their 100 or so titles would have produced by way of offsetting revenue. Their takeover by Wolters-Kluwer, also initially an OCLC partner and sharing a similar electronic experience, seemed right on the money and the technology. Second, this is an optimum time for such transactions: investment banking interest rates and activity are highly favorable to mergers and acquisitions in the closing years of this decade. (Consider Chrysler and Daimler, a deal that dwarfs anything in publishing.) The middle men who broker these deals internationally are attuned to the needs and requirements of transatlantic deal-making as never before. Third, companies with experience in book selling, or electronic commerce, are looking for more journal content to vend or repackage as books. Owning a mixed book-journal product line guarantees German firms like Bertelesman (who recently bought the German family-owned, but internationally important, Springer Verlag) that they will have something to sell that they effectively own, keeping them from being boycotted by associations of rival publishers, sellers, or libraries on either side of the Atlantic. Fourth, economies of scale come into play with merged operations; perhaps sadly for publishing industry professionals, the cost of larger staffs can be reduced through layoffs. It is certainly clear that costs will come down for white-collar offices through reduced redundancy.

BACKGROUND ISSUE COMMON TO SCIENCE PUBLISHERS OF ALL TYPES: INCREASING NET REVENUE BY REDUCING REVENUE SHARING WITH MIDDLEMEN

One of the early hopes of today's for-profit print publishers was that in an electronic world they have another chance at effectively regaining the exclusive right or at least a greater financial benefit from distributing to fully paying subscribers the content of their journals with few or no intermediaries who would cut into their profits. In what for them would be an ideal electronic world, publishers would not lose so much financially to the aggregators: subscription services, document delivery companies, and indexing-abstracting services (which often demand free subscriptions). The publishers would basically mount the journals on their own servers without needing a subscription service to handle sales or revenue collection, and grant access only to authorized, paying subscribers (complete with an internal search engine that obviated external indexing-abstracting)–and only for as long as the libraries paid. This would represent a tremendous advantage to publishers, for although their legal rights to exclusive copyright and its resulting revenues would already appear to be strong in the current world of print journal statutory law, copyright enforcement had been rendered problematic by case law and a wide variety of practical barriers. In particular, almost all publishers have had to gear up for a new round of battles with universities over who gets copyright: the publisher or the author's sponsoring university.

BACKGROUND ISSUE:
REASSERTING COPYRIGHTS AND FIGHTING PIRACY
WITH AN ELECTRONIC ASSIST

The standard practice and legal necessity of most publishers, for-profit or otherwise, is that authors who wish to publish in one of their journals must sign over their copyrights for those articles to the publishers. This is a practice that particularly galls many academic insitutions and their libraries. In this way, no library, author, subscription service, indexing/abstracting agency, or subscriber gains the rights to resell or otherwise redistribute substantial portions of these articles–theoretically covering both print and electronic forms–without the express permission of the publisher/copyright owner. To some degree, an alert, legally well-staffed publisher can already legally block any other player (subscription service, indexer/abstracter, library) from getting into a regular pattern of print publication that includes material on which the publisher holds the copyright. However, legal initiatives by publishers against copyright violation or exploitation "beyond fair use," usually against academic institutions or libraries, or not-for-profit interlibrary loan networks, have to proceed with caution, and have had little success in securing additional income for publishers. Battles over copyright are one of the major venues where academic librarians hope to rein in for-profit presses, and they have tried, with mixed results at best, to keep academic authors from signing over rights to publishers of any type. Somewhat to the surprise of these academic librarians, not-for-profit society presses and for-profit publishers have teamed up against this proposition. Nonethless, the few prominent successes that publishers have had in cost recovery via lawsuits have involved for-profit photocopy businesses, and for-profit corporate networks.

Generally four things must be in place for the publisher to prevail in court in a meaningful way, that is, with results that defend their financial interests. First, the publisher must be able to clearly identify transgressors and detail specific transgressions. Second, the publisher must appear reasonable in having publicized an easily-interpreted and easily-complied-with rights and permissions policy, with a quick, convenient and workable mechanism for the alleged transgressor to have obtained permission in advance, or paid a reasonable after-use recompense, so as to have avoided becoming a transgressor. Third, the transgressor must have sufficient assets that can be traced and levied so as to make the financial recovery worth the effort. Fourth, the transgressor must not have so many sympathetic allies who are also subscribers that adverse third party cancellations or boycotts (for example, from other sympathetic libraries) do not cost the publisher more in collateral damage than he is likely to obtain as a matter of redress from this particular transgressor.

It is not clear that the political barriers to copyright prosecutions will fall appreciably, or that legal judgments gained from prosecutions will necessarily rise in an electronic world, but the costs of detection of unauthorized duplication on the web can be lowered through greater use of encryption, firewalls, network security firms, Publisher Item Identifiers and a theft detection variant of "cookie" technology.

Encryption is the deliberate encoding of text or other information so that only authorized servers might be able to read some of the content sent in by clients, and vice-versa. It is ironic that this is used at all in web publishing, because the historic technical problem challenging web publishing has long been the non-readability of transmitted content owing to interplatform incompatibility among the computers involved. Right now, most encryption strategies have focused on securing transfer of small-segment data, particularly blocking out access to confidential or financial information like passwords, and credit card or library account numbers.

Added to this modest encryption initiative are a number of automatic firewall technologies and the increased hiring of human-supervised network security firms. Firewalls are generally electronic gatekeepers mounted on the ports of publisher's servers that are designed to detect the electronic penetration of a proprietary server by an unauthorized client, or an authorized client with bad intentions. Firewalls are often purchased as packaged software. They generally run automated diagnostic checks, produce daily reports, and are intermittently upgraded to recognize new virus threats to the integrity of longer text files and any penetration to other files that operationally necessary for the publisher's business, but are of no business to subscribers.

Network security firms have human watchdogs working in tandem with the automated firewalls. Network security firms have historically served clusters of businesses on an ongoing retainer basis, and are now becoming yet another type of contractor with whom publishers will be dealing. These firms use all of the software technologies mentioned above, plus they develop and maintain more detailed profiles of patterns of expected usage of given files in expected time frames by given clients. In other words, they tend to have not only gatekeeper functions but a penchant to act as traffic monitor and security cop. Even authorized users who are in some way uncharacteristic in their time of initiation, extent of downloading or file transfer, or atypical subject-specific file usage are vulnerable to being detected, and possibly queried.

Thus far, publishing houses have had a joint emphasis on keeping their content unaltered by users–the hacker dilemma–and keeping non-paying users from getting at the content, even if no attempt to alter that content is made, but have yet to implement copyright infringement technology in the article-by-article case that has been seen in the unauthorized republishing of new collective works. But article-specific content may be on its way to its security assurance, with at least two possibilities. The first is based on what amounts to an electronically given tag to each article called a *Publisher Item Identifier*, or *PII*. The goal of this tag is similar to that of the copyright logo, although it adds features of indelibility, in the sense that it persists across all platforms and re-occurs every time an item is downloaded or printed as well. Right now, this initiative is primarily focused on simple identification, with the later possibility of its electronic presence later being used as evidence. It will keep pirates from claiming that they didn't know an item was copyrighted. It does not have a "pirate disarming device," but this might be possible if it was linked with "cookie technology."

"Cookies" are little electronic tags that identify the client computers accessing proprietary server sites on the web. Some servers tend to deposit a little reminder in your client computer's memory that a portion of their content was seen by you previously. This technology was developed by non-publishing retail and financial services firms doing business on the web for reasons of security, marketing analysis, and to alert benevolently your client computer when an update of a new software product or a new bit of information is being offered each time your client computer reconnects with their server. It is part of the general drive in the Internet business for "Push Technology," and it does make it easier to update server supplied software that is frequently changed. The cookies are designed to be inobtrusive but detectable. Indeed some web access companies will warn you if a file that came up in a search is cookie-tagged and allow you to reject opening that file it if you so choose. You can also search your own computer's hard drive for the cookies you have accumulated. But cookies are otherwise invisible to third parties (via encryption during transfer over the web) so that one client's use of cookie-tagged content is not revealed to another client who simultaneously or subsequently uses that cookie-tagged file. While ALA might suggest that this linkage of PIIs with cookies effectively violates the confidentiality of circulation records, publishers could very reasonably argue that this was more akin to maintaining lists of authorized subscribers to a journal, something that is clearly legal now. This combination would still not corrupt file content but could be attached to the content in such a way that it is difficult to remove or rebroadcast the content over the web. In an article-copyright protection mode, anyone running enough cookie-tagged content for any length of time will be running the cookies along with the contents. This could allow cookie-tagged articles to act as a homing device, much like transponders hidden in cars that are activated once a car owner reports a theft. It could then be possible for publisher-authorized server administrators to detect unauthorized use of their content over the web, by electronically searching the web for cookie signals. Pirates would probably have to construct rather expensive firewalls to protect themselves from detection, raising costs at their home base, and limiting their illegal reselling forays on the larger web.

BACKGROUND ISSUE:
MAKING CONSORTIA PAY CONSORTIAL FEES

The current mechanism for financial relief for publishers from losses caused by many unpursuable cases of individual losses by over-the-top ILL photocopying (the death by a thousand paper cuts)–the charging of all of the remaining individual library subscribers more for virtually all their remaining subscriptions (blood donations over a pint in volume)–is not be sustainable because the donors keep dying. Indeed, chronic financial anemia seems to be an academic epidemic whose first sign may be an institution's library dropping out of the competitive game of building expensive STM collections as an inducement to student enrollment and faculty recruiting. Indeed, the systematic bleeding caused by increasing STM journal prices has long overcome inter-school rivalry as a deterrent to joining in subscription-reducing library consortia. Schools that routinely fight over high school seniors with great SATs using generous financial aid packages, and bid for faculty with Nobel Prize-ability using endowed chairs, freely give each other library ammunition to fire back at one another. While publishers complain that this cooperation makes illegal ILLs among discreet consortial partners all too easy, librarians follow enough of the letter of the law, and keep up appearances, to avoid the rare prosecution, often using something like subsidized shuttle buses more as window-dressing than as the actual means by which the majority of photocopied articles are obtained. Historically, subsidized shuttle buses did offset a little of the annoyance factor to faculty and students, so that scholars from several institutions did commute to the sole remaining library that takes an expensive subscription. The consortia figured that it was cheaper to buy the buses, because it needed them for cross-enrollments, anyway, and the roads were already there.

Of course it can argued that other libraries in a consortium are offsetting the burden of one library taking expensive Journal A by taking other particularly expensive Journals B through Z, but this can be a difficult matter to manage and is rarely carefully balanced out. Formal written consortial agreements specifying individual responsibilities in great detail are quite rare and somewhat suspect legally under existing copyright and fair use law. Therefore most consortium library resource sharing plans are rather general and nonspecific and still depend on each institution have distinctly individual budgets for each library, arrived at internally on campus, with limited day-to-day invoice verification and plan adherence oversight allowed to other consortium members. There are even fewer consortiums which maintain veto powers over individual library downsizing and agreement enforcement rights. This is particularly the case with science journals, because most of the major core science titles are really required by just about every library in the consortium. Most schools in a consortium today are not really likely, for example, to lack a chemistry, physics, biology, or math department with expensive journal demands for each of these fields–that would be rather unusual, frankly–although some individual libraries might have genuinely different subspecializations, for example, lichenology or lunar geology. However, savings realized by having one library take these subspecialty titles are not likely to be actually large or real because the remaining consortial partners are not likely to have identically subspecialized faculty who would have asked that their own library subscribe to journals of lunar geology or lichenology in the first place. Most substantial savings from consortial arrangements today come from librarians at one or more institutions canceling something their resident science faculty really want and would use, but that no longer fits in their institution's library budget. While it is clear that librarians (most of whom are not scientists) can live with this, it is not clear that their faculty are really happy with it. Are the chemistry faculty at the one school that pays $20,000 for the *Journal Internationalis of Chemistry* "really" happy to do so because some partner in the consortium is taking the $500 *Bavarian Journal of Lunar Geology & Lichenology* or worse, some $50 humanities or social studies journal? Consortial arrangements such as this can hold together only as long as the librarians resent the high-priced publishers more that the faculty resent their librarians for not taking expensive needed journals. In other words, the faculty whose institutional librarians will not pay for a journal they need are actually making their scientists pay for it in the most expensive and resented unit of currency: time away from their labs, adding insult to injury.

The electronic world will allow publishers to crack, somewhat, these sometimes fragile gentlemen's agreements, underwritten by the shuttle bus, the fax machine, and the postal system, by taking advantage of the Internet just as nimbly as the libraries have used these other means of communication. This reassertion of the need for every partner within a consortium to treat all their scientists and their science publishers fairly could be done without requiring everyone in the consortium to be given a print copy (too expensive for the publisher, in the old regime) or forcing one library to bear the actual burden of paying for what everyone else in the consortium has to commute to. Publishers in an electronic mode could do two things that are hard to do in a print mode: offer what amounts to partial or subdivided prices for whole subscriptions for everyone in the consortium, and eliminate everyone's real commute for a virtual one. This would require an upgrade to an "A" or "B" class IP license, but ironically not require much by the way of electronic infrastructure improvement on the part of either the consortium or the publisher. Chances are, schools in a geographically based consortium, sharing the same highway network, area phone code, and postal distribution center today are also using the same "B" node on the Internet already, and the publisher has already a server hooked up to serve the one subscriber that he has under contract.

BACKGROUND ISSUE:
USING TECHNOLOGY DEFICITS AND DISCOUNTS
ON PACKAGE PLANS TO DETER DEFECTIONS
TO SELF-PUBLISHING MOVEMENTS

One of the more intriguing complications results when a publisher handles a journal for a not-for-profit professional society, a situation very common for associations having only a thousand members or fewer, and not having a large, paid headquarters administration. In these situations, subscriptions prices for libraries (the prime market for most scholarly journals) are generally quite a bit higher than for individual society members, and cannot be decreased to the point where the society's cut of revenue from the sale of its publication makes it unfeasible to continue the publisher-society contract. Dissatisfied or distressed societies rarely stop publishing a journal, they just move the journal to yet another publisher. These defections hurt the original for-profit publishers in lost start-up money.

Financial losses for the abandoned publisher are compounded because not only does that original publishing firm lose the account, but the competitor that subsequently wins the contract frequently gains in his or her pool of titles available to fund even more competitors to the original publisher's line. Indeed, in recent years, subscription services have taken to sorting out for libraries those publishers whose rates rise more significantly than average for the subject area or for the industry at large. . . . and this has the effect of making libraries even more angry at publishers who raised rates to keep their society partners happy. Moreover, some societies, goaded in part by librarians and the library press, where demonizations of for-profit publishers in particular have become commonplace, are now deciding to go it alone, without partnerships with any for-profit firms. This pleases library subscribers, at least for a short time, because the initial benefit is often some reduction in library subscription rates, funded by the society's not having to share revenue with the for-profit firm. But the learning curve for self-publishing is long and hard. Content may not be published as often or as quickly or as carefully. Libraries may pay less but may get even less than they pay for.

Electronic publishing may hold down the rate of defections to stand-alone status, because while defectors are conceivably likely to have enough computer power simultaneously to run print and maintain a single server for a single title, access to a multiple time-zone network of high-end servers is likely to be much more expensive. For-profit publishers may have to fear proposed alliances, however, between their former partners and major rival for-profit publishers, indexing-abstracting services or bibliographic utilities, because many of them already have such a network in place already.

Publishers can also offer package plan discounts that deter the rate of defection or self-publishing independence that is being encouraged by librarians. The publisher can effectively ask the library community that is encouraging society independence: Will there be enough of a savings through the single price reduction for this one journal for your library to offset the discount your library gets on all the remaining journals we publish electronically?

BACKGROUND ISSUE: REVITALIZING FACULTY DEMAND FOR NEW JOURNALS VIA MORE EFFECTIVE PROMOTIONS THAT BYPASS LIBRARIANS

New, less-page-and-postage intensive print journals have been one of the few ways that publishers had been able to recoup some losses from cancellations of their well established but voluminous and production-and-postage costly titles. But even the more affordable new print journals have been strongly resented by librarians for reasons of both direct costs of subscriptions and the hidden costs in library processing and housing. Librarians have become intensely sales-resistant and, if they can be made interested at all, often want what amounts to a free subscription for a prolonged time, and generally at a high expense that the publisher must bear alone without help from a subscription service, in order to even consider adding a new journal. Under the current print journal system, most publishers must wage an advertising campaign for their new titles. The publisher's principal tools are direct mail flyers, print advertisements in existing professional journals, booths at professional conferences, sponsoring of meetings for researchers in the subject area of the journal, free copy distribution for a limited time (sometimes via additional pages bound into, or a supplement within, a well-known print journal, at other times the mailing of an independent issue sent via the use of a mailing list), and in-person sales visits to professors by publisher. Virtually all of these costs require skilled marketing personnel, mail-list rental, travel, telecommunications, and consumable materials. Publishers are increasingly aware that some of this expensive access to the scientists can be limited by their librarians who are unsympathetic to new ventures. A lot of new journal advertisements get thrown out by librarians before they are ever seen by the faculty.

An electronic platform for a publisher's journals allows publisher-controlled promotion to new electronic journals by whomever is scanning their existing electronic journals. Many electronic publishers today allow the scanning of tables of contents (but not the full text) of their journals from their home page, or via links to electronic journals that are already licensed to a library system, as a subtle form of advertising. In an electronic world, the librarian could no longer intercept and discard the print junk mail ads, or excise the inserted pages of the new journal from the established journal prior to their being displayed or bound. The publisher need not make an in-person visit, or have to sponsor an in-person symposium: it can hot-link interested readers with a button to an ad, a running virtual symposium, or even allow for a time-limited personal subscription. Librarian-bypass for promotional purposes is a more readily accomplished surgery in an electronic world. The problem remains, however, that individual subscriptions are not a viable way to sustain a new journal. Viability comes only when the demand from faculty for the new journal causes enough pressure on the librarians that they have to place the order.

BIBLIOGRAPHY

Bibliography of Viewpoints from the Differing Segments of Publishing on

- *Electronic Publishing in General*
- *On Their Own Electronic Journals*

- *Copyright Ownership Debates*
- *Fighting Pirates and Hackers*
- *Privacy Issues*
- *Revenue Enhancement Through Advertising and CoBranding.*

Anonymous. "Journals Endorse "Electronic Linking Plan." *Science* 281: 747, 1998.

Anonymous. "Publishing Partners: The Press, the Library, and Academic Computing." *Library Journal* 123 (14): 143, September 1, 1998.

Baker, John F. "University Presses to the Rescue." *Publishers Weekly* 245 (22): 38-40, June 1, 1998.

Boyce, Peter B. "Electronic Publishing of Scientific Journals." *Physics Today* 49 (1): 42-47, 1996.

Case, Mary M. "University Presses: Balancing Academic and Market Values." *ARL Newsletter* 193. *http://www.arl.org/newsltr/193/up.html*

Case, Tony. "Waverly Latest in Spree of Medical Buyouts." *Folio: The Magazine for Magazine Management* 27 (5): 17, April 1, 1998.

Clausing, Jeri. "Intel Alters Plan Said to Undermine PC Users' Privacy." *New York Times* (January 26, 1999): A1 and C27.

Derricourt, Robin. *An Author's Guide to Scholarly Publishing.* Princeton, 1996.

DiMattia, Susan Smith, and Norman Oder. "OhioLINK Cuts $23 Million Deal With Elsevier for Journals." *Library Journal* 122: 12, June 15, 1997.

Dryden, Patrick. "Publisher Combats Network Gremlins." *Computerworld* 32: 25, August 10, 1998.

Eiblum, Paula, and Stephanie C. Ardito. "Royalty Fees, Part I: The Copyright Clearance Center and Publishers." *Online* 22 (March/April, 1998): 83-86.

Freeman, Lisa. "University Presses and Scholarly Communications: Dilemmas and Prospects in the New Age." *Library Acquisitions in the New Age." Library Acquisitions: Practice and Theory* 20: 329-339, 1996.

Friedman, Jessica R. "How to Protect Your Web Site's Name." *Folio: The Magazine for Magazine Management* (1998 Special Supplement): 236-237, 1998.

Gapper, John. "Latest Chapter in Reed's [Reed-Elsevier] History Does Not Make Happy Reading." *Financial Times [London]* (December 7, 1998), p. 26.

Garigliano, Jeff. "First Round in E-Rights Goes to Publishers." *Folio: The Magazine for Magazine Management* 26 (September, 1997): 12.

Gaudin, Sharon. "Hackers Disrupt N.Y. Times Site." *Computerworld* 32(38): 6, Sept. 21, 1998.

German, Greg. "To Catch a Hacker." *Library Hi Tech* 15 (1-2): 96-98, 1997.

Graham, Anne. "Peace Overtakes the Ad/Edit Conflict." *Folio: The Magazine for Magazine Management* 27 (9): 88-89, July, 1998.

Grant, Robert T. "Cooperation Between Libraries and University Presses." *In Renewing the ARL Agenda.* Association of Research Libraries, 1996.

Guernsey, Lisa and Vincent Kiernan. "Journals Differ on Whether to Publish Articles That Have Appeared on the Web." *Chronicle of Higher Education* 44 (45): A27-29, July 17, 1998.

Hunter, Karen. "Science Direct." *The Serials Librarian* 33(3-4): 287-97, 1998.

International Publisher's Copyright Council. "Libraries, Copyright and the Electronic Environment." *Http://www.ifla.org/documents/infopol.copyright/ipa/txt*

Joa, Harald. "Scandinavian University Press's Role as a Publisher in the Digital Future." *The Serials Librarian* 33 (1-2): 1998.

Kiernan, Vincent. "Publisher Loosens Rules on Sharing Electronic Journals." *Chronicle of Higher Education* 44 (43): A20, July 3, 1998.

Kiernan, Vincent. "Scholars Seek New Copyright Rule to Ease Dissemination of Research on the Web." *Chronicle of Higher Education* 45 (3): A32, September 11, 1998.

Kiernan, Vincent. "University Libraries Debate the Value of Package Deals on Electronic Journals." *Chronicle of Higher Education* 44 (3): A31-A33, September 12, 1997.

Kiernan, Vincent. "Use of "Cookies" in Research Sparks a Debate Over Privacy." *Chronicle of Higher Education* 45 (5): A31-A34, September 25, 1998.

LaVagnino, Merri Beth. "The ICAAP Project, Part One: A Continuum of Security Needs for the CIC Virtual Electronic Library." *Library Hi Tech* 15 (1-2): 72-76, 1997.

Lichtenberg, James. "Inching Towards E-Commerce." *Publishers Weekly* 244 (December 8, 1997): 35-37.

Liebly, Frank. "The Role of Content Management in a Digital Production Environment." *Direct Marketing* 60 (December, 1997): 30-33.

Long, John. "Faster Than a Fast Thing." *Against the Grain* 7 (November, 1995): 24.

Memon, Nasir and Ping Wah Wong. "Protecting Digital Media Content." *Communications of the ACM* 41 (7): 34-43, July, 1998.

Muir, Adrienne. "Publishers' Views of Electronic Short-Loan Collections and Copyright Clearance Issues." *Journal of Information Science* 24(4): 215-30, July/Aug. 1998.

Nauman, Mathew. "Institute of Physics Publishing." *Against the Grain* 10 (3): 56, 1998.

Peek, Robin P. "Privacy, Publishing, and Self Regulation." *Information Today* 15 (2): 38-39, 1998.

Perry, Phillip M. "Whose Rights: Old Contracts and New Media." *Folio: the Magazine for Magazine Management* 27 (13): 55+, September 15, 1998.

Phipps, Jennie L. "Ripping Off Writers or Justified New Profits?" *Editor and Publisher* 131 (22): 18+, May 30, 1998.

Potter, William Gray. "Scholarly Publishing, Copyright, and the Future of Resource Sharing." *Journal of Library Administration* 21 (1-2): 49-99, 1995.

Reid, Calvin. "WIPO: Publishers, Librarians Face-Off Over Copyright Bill." *Publishers Weekly* 245 (January 5, 1998): 11.

Richardson, Jean. "Taylor & Francis Plan Stock Market Flotation." *Publisher's Weekly* 2145 (16): 13, April 20, 1998.

Schwarzwalder, Robert. "The American Chemical Society." *Database* 21 (5): 64-66, 1998.

Schwarzwalder, Robert. "Electronic Publishing and the American Institute of Physics." *Database* 21(4): 79-81, 1998.

Sharp, Ellen Meyers. "Whose Copyrights?" *Editor and Publisher* 131 (February, 14, 1998): 14-15.

Shea, Christopher. "A Small, Respected University Press Fights Off a Push to Eliminate It." *Chronicle of Higher Education* 44 (32): A16-A17, April 17, 1998.

Shores, Clark. "Ownership of Faculty Works and University Copyright Policy." *ARL Newsletter* 189. *http://www.arl.org/newsltr/189/owner.html*

Singleton, Alan. "Journals and the Electronic Programme of the Institute of Physics." *The Serials Librarian* 30 (3-4): 149-161, 1997.

Spring, Jeffrey D. and Lorrin R. Garson. ""Electronic Publishing and the Journals of the American Chemical Society." *Journal of the National Institute of Standards and Technology* 101 (3): 357-360, 1996.

Stankus, Tony. "Ads Are Your Serials Budget Friends." *Technicalties* 16 (6): 10, 1996.

Stankus, Tony. "The Dearth of a Salesman: The Decline in Library Visits from Serials Marketers." *Technicalities* 17 (7): 11, 1997.

Stankus, Tony. " Journal Divorces." *Technicalities*. 18(1): 4-5, Jan. 1998.

Stankus, Tony, and Kevin Rosseel. "The Rise of Eurojournals: Their Success Can Be Ours." *Library Resources and Technical Services* 31 (3): 215-224, 1987.

Stone, Martha L. "Managing Your Cyber Liabilities." *Editor and Publisher* 131 (13): 18-19, March 28, 1998.

Stone, Martha L. "Protecting Against Web Image Theft." *Editor and Publisher* 131 (February 7, 1998): 39.

Taylor, Sally Adamson. "DOI: Digital Object Identifier or Disorganized Idea?" *Publishers Weekly* 244 (November 10, 1997): 13.

Tucker, Amy E. "Electronic Journals: Fulfilling a Mission at the Institute of Physics." *Serials Review* 23(3): 67-8, Fall 1997.

Weston, Beth, and Julia C. Blixrud. "Report of the SISAC General Meeting, Sunday, February 16, 1997: Digital Article Identifiers and Rights Management." *Serial Review* 23 (2): 89-91, 1997.

Yeung, Minerva, guest editor. "Digital Watermarking. [a series of related papers] *Communications of the ACM* 41(7): 31-77, 1999.

Electronic Journal Concerns and Strategies for Aggregators: Subscription Services, Indexing/Abstracting Services, and Electronic Bibliographic Utilities

Tony Stankus

Aggregators are those people and firms involved with serials that do not so much produce serials (like publishers) nor purchase and store them for use (like libraries) but deal with many publishers and many libraries along the way.

- They may bundle the orders from many libraries for the publications of many publishers.
- They may produce indexes and abstracts of articles from many publications for many library users.
- They may supply of many single documents from many publications for many users within libraries or otherwise.

The principal aggregators important for electronic journals today are subscription services (subscription agents), indexing/abstracting agencies and electronic bibliographic utilities. Some aggregating firms perform all of these services; others do only one or two.

THE SUBSCRIPTION SERVICE'S VIEWPOINT

Any move by publishers to sell web journals directly to institutions imperils subscription services. Subscription services view themselves as the indis-

[Haworth co-indexing entry note]: "Electronic Journal Concerns and Strategies for Aggregators: Subscription Services, Indexing/Abstracting Services, and Electronic Bibliographic Utilities." Stankus, Tony. Co-published simultaneously in *Science & Technology Libraries* (The Haworth Press, Inc.) Vol. 18, No. 2/3, 1999, pp. 97-110; and: *Electronic Expectations: Science Journals on the Web* (Tony Stankus) The Haworth Press, Inc., 1999, pp. 97-110. Single or multiple copies of this article are available for a fee from The Haworth Document Delivery Service [1-800-342-9678, 9:00 a.m. - 5:00 p.m. (EST). E-mail address: getinfo@haworthpressinc.com].

97

pensable middlemen between libraries and publishers. This job is very secure in the print world, but is going to require some inventiveness to retain that security in the web world. The most common strategy has been for subscription services, already among the most electronically adept in handling their business affairs, to expand their electronic staffs in areas of republishing, access services, and infrastructure consulting.

BACKGROUND ISSUE:
MAINTAINING THE SUBSCRIPTION SERVICE'S CORE ROLE
AS AN ESCROW AGENCY ARGUABLY FAVORABLE
TO BOTH PUBLISHERS AND LIBRARIES

Subscription services portray themselves as the professionals who are most capable of taking the eclectically and eccentrically bundled orders of thousands of libraries (orders that contain subscriptions involving hundreds of different publishers at each institution), untying those bundles, and uniformly rebundling them by publisher in a way that leads to a negotiated price from the publishers that is often lower than what the libraries, acting individually, and paying the publisher's list price, would be able to get for themselves. Publishers have been willing, or forced, depending on a variety of internal financial and human resource factors that would affect an individual publisher's attitude to this arrangement, to grant discounts to subscription services based on the increased volume of orders and lumps sum payments that subscription services provide along with these rebundled orders. In most cases, libraries also pay a single digit percentage surcharge of the total journal order to the subscription service (with the prices as published in the subscription service's catalog generally serving as a guide when compiling the total), in exchange for this money-and-time-saving representation of library interests.

Direct electronic promotion of electronic-only journals by publishers presents some threats to subscription services working only in the print world, but it has remained a diffused threat because librarians are habituated to ordering through subscription services. Only a little of the new orders and increased revenues resulting from publishers' ad campaigns to promote new print titles in the past ever reached publishers in the print-only world, without subscription services taking a cut, and this seems unlikely to change with electronic ads for new electronic journals placed within existing electronic journals. This galls some publishers for, in a sense, the subscription service gets to add to his volume of business through his commission on a new journal that the subscription service himself did not help promote. (Of course, the subscription service still has the argument that he has managed to secure the money up front from the libraries for the publisher.) It is already clear that most subscription services are willing and able to handle electronic journals so as to avoid loss of that revenue stream. They are banking, quite rightly, that the emphasis in libraries will be on the "journal" part of the phrase "electronic journals" and libraries will act accordingly in institutional buying strategies.

Even those subscription services who are not electronically adept still benefit in an increasingly electronic climate. Subscription services can vouch to publishers for the print subscriptions that are still often required by publishers for libraries to obtain access to electronic versions. Most subscription services, however, have long maintained such large server networks and such a large cadre of computing professionals to handle their existing computerized billing and subscription servicing, that they have a ready potential as a server warehouse utility for publishers whose own servers are underpowered. It is arguable that as small publishers go beyond the one or two titles that they can handle from their own server, they are going to need more capacity and especially more geo-dispersed capacity. Using subscription service servers as proxies or supplements for their own servers can diminish publisher server load and offset time-dependent traffic tie ups, as many subscription services are scattered over time zones, maintain dispersed regional offices, and have experienced computer mangers and troubleshooters.

BACKGROUND ISSUE:
WITH NEGOTIATION, FULFILLMENT AND BIBLIOGRAPHIC DETECTIVE WORK LESS OF A PROBLEM, WHAT OTHER SAVINGS IN TIME OR TROUBLE CAN SUBSCRIPTION SERVICES OFFER TO LIBRARIES?

Most subscription services have long presented themselves to libraries as advocates for the library in dealing with the publisher concerning journal issues that are late in delivery to the library, missing, or otherwise out of sequence during the subscription period. Traditionally, publishers also used subscription services to see to it that printed issues have actually reached intended, paying subscribers. Subscription services handled initial claims of non-delivery from libraries, and bundle demands for back-issues, enabling publishers to check on the reliability of their own production and shipping departments, or those of their contractors, and thereby resolve subscriber complaints. With web journals, lost, missing, or delayed issues are not likely to be much of a problem. This form of time savings historically attributed by libraries to subscription services, is likely to be diminished in an electronic world.

Subscription services have also cultivated a reputation for bibliographically identifying specific "trouble journals", particularly by being helpful in sorting out similarly named journals, journals that have undergone name changes, and dealing with journals from obscure places and publishers. This service will probably also see some devaluation, given that most web journals that are likely to matter are going to come from existing major print publishers, and that the hyperlinks from an old version to a newly named one are going to obviate some of the problems of discontinuity.

What remains as a special service opportunity is the one-stop electronic registration feature that subscription services could provide to libraries in their dealings with publishers. Filling out electronic registration forms on-line and continuously registering various configurations of computer servers and clients required under different publisher plans is getting to be as big a hassle for serials librarians as ordering from many different print publishers used to be.

This is particularly the case when libraries have difficulties with their own institution's internal information technology department. Subscription services historically have far congenial relations with librarians, whom the subscription services see as customers with cash. Campus computer center managers often see librarians as dinosaurs that compete with the computing center for institutional dollars while demanding special cabling, trouble-shooting, and newer or different equipment than what the computing center might wish to provide. To a substantial degree today's subscription services are more likely to have computer-capable staffers who can probe or map the library's portion of the campus intranet (with the library's permission). This can help the library greatly in site registration agreements with publishers, and can help the librarians in their arguments with computer center managers over bottlenecks and overloads that are not the result of the publishers or of the subscription services computer network, but of inadequacies or flaws in the campus allocation of internet access and resources given to the library.

Subscription services can also help libraries design their own electronic journal resources web-pages or front-ends on the campus computing network. This is becoming increasingly necessary as libraries add on dozens and dozens of different electronic journals or journal packages (often with a different internal search engine for each), and add listing after listing with links that hopefully match. Screen clutter is becoming a serious problem in the library portions of campus web pages. Given the often hostile relations that librarians have with their own computer departments, and the fact that many if not all of these journals are being ordered through the same subscription service, one finds the subscription service often motivated to help. Indeed, subscription services might make the most suitable of partners with librarians on setting up recommended standards for library serials web pages, a kind of super-MARC standard for electronic serials holdings and access.

THE SUBSCRIPTION SERVICE
AS ELECTRONIC JOURNAL CONTENT REPACKAGER
AND COLLECTION CUSTOMIZER

It is already becoming clear that subscription services are likely to have a better sense of the need for electronic journal format uniformity than do individual publishers or individual libraries. To some degree each publisher and each library has groped towards a web future that was uncertain both in terms of what web technology might bring, and what competing publishers and libraries were doing. Subscription services are uniquely positioned to know what each of these separate classes of participants in the game have been doing apart from one another, and what their internal competitors within a class have been up to. Right now, it may seem hard to get competing publishers to adopt one or more of their competitor's formats or protocols. It may seem too much like surrender. But, adopting the common format of a mutual party–namely the subscription service–may seem more palatable, particularly if the subscription service plans to crack open markets for journals that have been either resistant or difficult in recent years. Such is the case with lower "level-of-institution" or subject niche market libraries.

The toughest audience for science journals in recent years has been the junior college, small college and university branch market. While branch campuses of larger systems, and various community colleges and distance education sites have continued to open, sales for those branches or new sites have not increased correspondingly. While it was unthinkable in the past for colleges to open without a standard array of basic chemistry, biology, math and physics courses and library holdings to match, today's students are alleged to be so underprepared and the new schools so underfunded that these academically difficult and their traditionally expensive library needs have been getting short shrift. What is typically founded is a very limited print library, often one sharing space and funding with a video center or Internet classroom with traditional reading and quiet studying having no special status over viewing films and surfing the net as an educational activity. Nonetheless degrees or certificates for various biotech, hi-tech, and allied health sciences are being handed out routinely at these schools, and some ethical need and market clearly exists for modest holdings or specially tailored holdings of serious content. Librarians in these settings are taking only a few journals from a relatively few STM publishers for these programs, and it is likely that many other STM publishers would like to get a piece of even that diminished business, rather than have none of it at all. Subscription services have at least the possibility of designing multi-publisher electronic journal packages that either meet a small and affordable general journal package (an all-electronic collection that contains some science journals) or a tailored package (a small but focused collection stressing biotech, hi-tech, or allied health). By using various royalty schemes, more publishers could be induced by subscription services to sign up and get some revenue, where before there was none, unless one's titles were among the lucky few taken in print editions. In a sense, a subscription service is in a position to construct a kind of mutual fund in which these smaller libraries, who are otherwise unlikely to invest in individual journal stocks, can invest some sci-tech-med journal dollars. Part of the inducement for librarians is likely to be acceptance of a common format and common search engine for each package, with the most likely format and search engine not those of a single competitor, but something neutral that will be accepted by all publishers in the package. In a curious way, an all-electronic format would probably appeal to these students more so than traditional journals in a library.

PROSPECTS FOR SUBSCRIPTION SERVICE SUCCESS IN A WEB JOURNAL WORLD

Subscription services have had much better press than publishers in the librarian's professional literature. Moreover, while few publishers maintain a substantial in-person sales force any more, subscription services generally maintain quite a network of geographic account representatives who stoke the fires of a personal, working friendship with serials librarians. This had led librarians to believe, justly or otherwise, the literature that subscription services publish and/or distribute to libraries that claims that the now chronic increases in a library's serials costs are largely due to price rises initiated by the publisher, not due to the explicitly stated service charge of the subscription service, nor to any hidden percentage of the discount on subscription prices that the subscription service obtains from publishers, but does not pass on to the libraries. Nor, indeed, do most libraries ever hear about the cases where a subscription service holds on to the cumulated subscription money longer than it should, before passing it on to the publishers. Subscription services generally are allowed to hold on to that money for 90 days–or in some cases 180 days–and use that "float time" to make money in various short-term financial and currency markets, adding to subscription service revenues.

Publishers, despite their resentment at being demonized to some degree by the subscription services, still have the sense that subscription services are more likely to support the continued existence of publishers rather than their demise. While it is clear that subscription services will benefit from re-packaging some journal content electronically, few subscription services are likely to be able to become primary publishers of original content. While the largest subscription services are probably as wealthy as some of the larger publishers, subscription services lack the editorial and society recruitment skills that are necessary to sustain sci-tech-med journal publishing, and would find it hard to pay for developing this capacity in addition to the electronic upgrades that they are already having to bear. Moreover, such a boldy intrusive move would cause publishers to pull out of the primary revenue stream of most subscription services: making money on order bundling. Likewise, subscription services are aware that encouraging too much electronic independence away from print and away from commercial publishing (print or electronic) is likely to lead to subsequent abandonment by academia of not only publishers, but eventually of subscription services as well.

The strength of the subscription service's position is based on long-standing custom–90% of libraries take 90% of their scholarly journals through subscription services and have done so for over 25 years. Subscription services aid cash flow management on the part of both institutional subscribers– and although publishers are loathe to admit it–also on the part of the financial managers of journal publishers as well. The predictability of a publisher receiving one or two big checks a year, usually within 90 days of the start of the calendar year or fiscal year, confers a great deal of stability to financial planning and cost control. While libraries can complain with much justice about how hard it is to pay the inflated bills they see, they remain quite free to adjust their bills downward through cancellations in order to match available budget dollars. Likewise, publishers know pretty much well in advance what their revenues and costs are likely to be for 6 months to a year ahead. Publishers, in many cases, have a far better idea of how their business is going to be than the major makers of cars, appliances, or even computers, and can make adjustments to their operational costs much sooner than those other industries through downsizing or price adjustment (usually upwards). In a peculiar way, subscription services are like certified accountants for both publishers and subscribers. They take a piece of your money in return for handling a great deal of your money and providing you with strategic information. As long as the piece taken is not greater in value than the fuss avoided and information provided, these players are likely to have a good chance of surviving in the electronic journal world.

INDEXING SERVICES
AS ELECTRONIC JOURNAL DISTRIBUTORS

Virtually no publisher or subscription service directly controls or shapes the desire for scientists to see given papers. This is largely because scientists primarily seek to read papers of particular interest, rather than papers of particular publishers or particular subscription services. To the degree that a publisher packages journal content to match a specialty, and subscription services sell that journal, the publishers and the subscription services have some influence on reading and subscription strategy, but that influence is rarely exclusive or monopolistic for long. Prominent journals tend to be preferred as outlets for papers, and are browsed often, but there is a reasonable anxiety on the part of most scientists that a systematic search of the literature ought to be done just to make sure that nothing important that did not appear in a customarily browsed assortment of prominent journals was missed before a project is initiated or a manuscript is submitted.

This reassurance is overwhelmingly provided these days by electronic searches of indexing-abstracting sources. In the space of twenty-five years scientists have gone from a print-based searching method, to a dial-up modem-based on-line phase to the current state of web-based technology. With each step they have had access to increasing searching power and sophistication, and have been saving their research time, if not also the library's money. Part of this increase in confidence has to do with increasingly fast and memory-capacious electronics, but a good deal more has to do with the superior levels of insight that professional indexing and abstracting agencies have brought to understanding how scientists look at journals and papers. Some indexing and abstracting services have been looking at the ways scientists seek information for 75 years, and making notes of what those scientists find useful and, just as importantly, what annoys them or wastes their time. They have learned that scientists wish to reduce annoying false leads by creating hierarchies of relevance and weighting factors, and through greater vocabulary control. Essentially these services have learned that providing a thousand dubiously relevant citations to a search query–the bane of some general purpose search engines on the web–is no answer to the need to find a few dozen truly relevant ones. All that is needed for these indexing services to become dominant deliverers of information is the ability to provide the full text and figures from the journals themselves along with the abstract. Indexing and abstracting agencies have the power to become the de facto publishers of the ideal electronic journal: the one the scientist constructs for himself on the day of the search.

The problem with this dream is that the copyright to not only the full text and figures, but even in some cases to the abstract itself, is the property of the publishers, not the indexing-abstracting service. It is little appreciated that most indexing-abstracting services use the abstracts provided in the journal as the prime source for the abstracts it provides readers, and often incorporate author-supplied keywords as well. The role of the indexer-abstracter nowadays lies as much in editing out what is superfluous, adding what is missing, standardizing the format, language, and tagging of the search terms in the database, rather than in the original composition of abstracts for articles that have none. Indexers and abstracters are often called secondary publishers, but more accurately, they are really a kind of higher level editors and referees of key concepts. Indeed, many librarians will not subscribe to a journal unless it is covered by one or more prominent indexing-abstracting services. Partly for this reason, and partly because many indexing-abstracting services are not-for-profit, and do not themselves publish competitive primary journals, many publishers have essentially donated copies of their journals to these services, or sold them to indexing/abstracting firms at substantially lesser rates, so that they could be indexed and abstracted. Moreover, many journals abandoned detailed cumulative indexing of their journals precisely because both scientists and librarians looked for papers in the indexing-abstracting services much more so than in the now rare annual indexes of the publications themselves. This provided cost-savings for the publisher as well, in terms of reduced editorial staff.

The first chill in relations between publishers and indexing and abstracting services had to do with the rise of faxing document delivery services for scientists and their libraries in the 1980s. Indexing-abstracting services tended to form alliances with these new operations without too much regard for how this would play with the publishers themselves. Indexing-abstracting services needed to reinforce their historically good relations with libraries, because the costs of their own products to libraries had also been rising dramatically, to underwrite in most cases, the indexing-abstracting firm having to maintain simultaneous print, dial-up on-line and CD-ROM versions. The idea was that by providing libraries with a convenient way of obtaining photocopies or faxes to items featured in their database, the perceived value of the indexing-abstracting service would rise to the level of its necessarily high prices. Unfortunately, with relatively fixed dollars in library budgets, something had to give, and in most cases, it was subscriptions to the publisher's journals rather than subscriptions to the indexing-abstracting agencies.

Publishers, having lost most court fights with libraries and other not-for-profit agencies in the 1970s over photocopy-based interlibrary loan serving as a substitute for subscriptions, clearly sought to avoid further losses with the rise of the faxed-in document delivery industry. This new wave of document delivery agencies had a fair mixture of for-profit firms involved in selling photocopies, and these were clearly more vulnerable to legal challenges. Publishers hoped to gain some subscription-loss-offsetting secondary income through royalty payments from these new businesses, which were more or less forced to come to terms with the publishers. These new firms then had to offset increased costs from less favorable deals with the publishers. They could not raise their prices to libraries without suffering too great a drop off in business, so they sought greater internal efficiencies. Initially, some document delivery services accepted orders containing pretty much the same level of journal article identifying information that traditional interlibrary loan forms contained. Order clerks receiving these forms had to have a fairly high-level of bibliographic skills in order to retrieve the desired publication and fill the order accurately. Other document delivery companies attempted to construct their own table of contents, or other primitive search-engine-based electronic services, and offered lower rates to customers who used these services, because their orders would also contain physical file or electronic file location information that were tailored to the company in a way that made order fulfillment easier or cheaper for the company. But these identification and ordering features had neither the power, nor the ubiquity, nor the reputation of those of the established indexing-abstracting services. Deals were then made by the delivery companies with leading indexing abstracting services to incorporate, rather seamlessly, document ordering from the company as a simple extension of on-line searching with the index-ing-abstracting service. The combination of the fax-speed delivery of the document companies with the touch-of-a-keystroke, or click-of-the-mouse ordering of articles chosen through more precise searches from reputable indexing abstracting services seemed formidable. Only the budgetary uncertainty of per-item billing for the delivery, as opposed to the certainty of paying once for subscriptions to many journals or to the indexing-abstracting service, restrained this development among libraries.

Not surprisingly, publishers have initially responded to this step-up in document delivery activity by repeatedly raising the royalty rates paid by the document delivery companies, and in a few cases, some publishers have discontinued doing business with them. No serious publisher, however, has pulled their journals from coverage by a major indexing-abstracting service as a means of retaliation. These two players still need each other too much. The biggest test of the relationship between the publishers and indexing-abstracting services will come as more and more indexing-abstracting services seek to add full-text provision of articles to the web versions of their traditional databases. The question will become, once again, can the publisher offset further subscription erosion through secondary fee revenues from the indexing-abstracting services. Conversely, can enough libraries afford to pay indexing-abstracting services, who have already had to increase their prices once again to recover costs for developing web-based versions, to also offset what those services must pay publishers for the privilege of offering full text? To a substantial degree, publishers and indexing-abstracting services are motivated to make this deal to the exclusion of outside document delivery services, because it allows them both to cut out one partner. Library uncertainty over per-item billings can also be reduced by putting the sale of full-text back on a predictable annual subscription basis. The only way that indexing/abstracting services are going to stay in businesses as document deliverers or as partners with document delivery suppliers will be to make sure that their royalty payments are sufficiently generous to the copyright-holding primary publishers.

THE ELECTRONIC UTILITY AS ELECTRONIC SUBSCRIPTION AGENT AND INTERLIBRARY LOAN SERVICE: OCLC AND FIRSTSEARCH ELECTRONIC COLLECTIONS ONLINE

If there is anything as ubiquitous in science libraries as electronic index-ing-abstracting services, it's general purpose electronic bibliographic utilities. These were largely introduced into librarianship, including science librarianship, as a means of aiding the cataloging of books. If books were not a high priority item for most science libraries, OCLC's secondary function, the facilitation of interlibrary loan of not only books, but journal articles made it a necessity, at a time of generalized downsizing of book and journal literature.

OCLC is a late-comer to web publishing. But it brings two things that most web start-ups do not have: "brand recognition" with librarians who identify with its librarian-management roots (even though its current administration involves at least as many lawyers and MBAs as librarians), and a megaton of cash. Although nominally not-for-profit, OCLC has an operating budget, staff-ing, and infrastructure that would be the envy of all but the very largest publishers, largely because over 30,000 libraries have already budgeted thou-sands of library dollars for dozens of services for decades. OCLC also made a reputation by marketing a fair amount of discounted, already-loaded "turn-key" desktop hardware along with a strong dose of help-desk reassurance and workshop sponsorships to an often technologically-challenged traditionally print-skilled library audience. (It is interesting to note that much of OCLC-vended hardware is not, at the time of its sale, cutting-edge but safety-edge, a tradeoff many librarians seem to favor. OCLC does not frighten librarians although it does cost them more and more each year, largely because it is also the master tactician of the invasion of the subtly incremental budget snatchers.)

OCLC serves far more general librarians than science librarians, and serves far more institutions than those that support scientific research as a matter of course. Indeed, OCLC is wealthy enough to have failed in pre-In-ternet electronic journals and yet survived. OCLC has shown a willingness to abandon technological failures, even when hundreds of librarians held out hoping for ongoing persistence. No institution of any size has abandoned OCLC in reaction to its earlier electronic abortions, because even if parts of the product line failed, OCLC's ongoing presence in other necessary areas offset it. Moreover, OCLC could disappoint hundreds because tens of thou-sands remained reasonably happy. OCLC has been moving aggressively into electronic journal redistribution, and its *First Search Electronic Journals On-*

line is probably the paradigm for inclusion of just about all publishers and all aggregators and most libraries of any size. While there has been some informal grumbling about OCLC's choices of technology (they included *Catchword,* a less frequent choice among publishers as a formatting and display language), and about the rigidity of the terms of their agreements ("My way, or the highway," reported one source, albeit not for attribution), there seems to be an unstoppable cascade of parties signing on with OCLC of late. OCLC may well be the great leveler of inconsistencies in electronic journal publishing (it is a pioneer developer of ISO standards on electronic transfer of bibliographic information), but more details, apart from the many positive press releases, must be forthcoming in order to make a better assessment.

BIBLIOGRAPHY

Bibliography on Aggregators and Electronic Journals

Anonymous. "Academic Press to Make Journals Available to Electronic Collections Online." *OCLC Systems and Services* 14 (1): 9-19, 1998.

Anonymous. "EBSCO and OCLC Conclude FirstSearch Agreement." *OCLC Systems and Services* 13 (2): 40-42, 1997.

Anonymous. "EBSCO Publishing Expands EBSCOmed." *Information Today* 15 (7): 14, 1998.

Anonymous. "EBSCO Publishing Introduces EBSCOhost 3.0. Adds to Product Line." *Information Today* 15 (8): 59, 1998.

Anonymous. "First Group of Publishing Partners Announced for New OCLC FirstSearch Electronic Collections Online." *OCLC Systems and Services* 13 (2): 46-48, 1997.

Anonymous. "Johns Hopkins University Press to Join OCLC Electronic Collections Online." *OCLC Systems and Services* 14 (1): 5, 1998.

Anonymous. "OCLC Expands FirstSearch Subscription Options and Content." *Information Today* 15 (8) 56-57, 1998.

Anonymous. "OCLC to Integrate CatchWord Server into FirstSearch Electronic Collections Online." *OCLC Systems and Services* 13 (3): 81-82, 1997.

Anonymous. "Publishers Agree to Provide Full Text to EBSCO Online." *Information Today* 15 (8): 1, 1998.

Ardito, Stephanie C., and Paula Eiblum. "Royalty Fees: Copyright and Clearinghouses." *Online* 22 (4): 86-90, 1998.

Beddall, Jane, Sue Malin, and Kim Hallett. "Seamless and Integrated Access to the World of Electronic Journals." *The Serials Librarian* 33(3-4): 233-41, 1998.

Breeding, Marshall. "Telecommunications Options Connect OCLC and Libraries to the Future: The Co-Evolution of OCLC Connectivity Options and the Library Computing Environment." *Journal of Library Administration* 25 (2-3): 111-128, 1998.

Brunell, David Hays. "The Strategic Alliance Between OCLC and Networks: Partnerships That Work." *Journal of Library Administration* 25 (2-3): 19-29, 1998.

Cain, Randy, and Kirk Schwall. "Guiding Your Literature Searching." *CHEMTECH* 25 (8): 8-11, 1995.

Chepesiuk, Ronald. "Expanding Internationally–OCLC Gears Up." *American Libraries* 28 (10): 52-55, 1997.

Chepesiuk, Ronald. "The OCLC Connection." *American Libraries* 29 (7): 64-65, 1998.

Collins, Tim. "EBSCOs Plans for Handling Electronic Journals and Document Delivery." *Collection Management* 20 (3-4): 15-18, 1996.

Collins, Tim, and Beth Howell. "Journal Accessibility Factor: An Examination of Serials Value From the Standpoint of Access and Delivery." *Collection Management* 21 (1): 29-40, 1996.

Crump, Michele J. "Journal Costs in Academic Libraries Discussion Group, 'The Price We Pay: The Vendor's Influence'." *Serials Review* 22(4): 91-4, 1996.

Diedrichs, Carol Pitts. "An Interview with James T. Stephens and F. Dixon Brooke, Jr, EBSCO Industries." *Library Acquisitions: Practice and Theory* 22 (3): 311-327, 1998.

Douglas, Kimberly, and Dana Roth. "TOC/DOC: It Has Changed the Way I Do Science." *Science and Technology Libraries* 16 (3-4): 131-145, 1997.

Duranceau, Ellen Finnie. "Vendors and Librarians Speak out on Outsourcing, Cataloging, and Acquisitions." *Serials Librarian* 20(3): 69-83, 1994.

Guenette, David R. "Enterprising Information: The Retrieval/Data Storage/Network/Electronic Publishing Convergence." *EMedia Professional* 10 (November, 1997): 38-50+.

Kaiser, Jocelyn. "Journals Endorse Electronic Linking Plan." *Science* 281 (5378): 747, 1998.

Lenzini, Rebecca T., and Ward Shaw. "Facilitating Copyrights: The Role of the Middleman." *Current Legal Issues in Publishing* 1996.

Lenzini, Rebecca T. "Having our Cake and Eating it Too: Combining Aggregated and Distributed Resources." *Journal of Library Administration* 24(4): 39-48, 1997.

Lenzini, Rebecca. "New Partners for Collection Development." *Journal of Library Administration* 24 (1-2): 113-124, 1996.

Luther, Judy. "ATG Interview with Tim Colins, VP, Division General Manager, EBSCO Publishing." *Against the Grain* 9 (June, 1997): 36-37.

Martin, Murray S. "EBSCO Comes to Town." *The Bottom Line* 11 (1): 28-30, 1998.

McKay, Sharon Cline. "Partnering in a Changing Medium: The Challenge of Managing and Delivering E-Journals: The Subscription Agents' Point of View." *Library Acquisitions: Practice and Theory* 22(1): 23-7, Spring 1998.

Nilges, William. "Evolving an Integrated Electronic Journals Solution: OCLC FirstSearch Electronic Collections Online." *The Serials Librarian* 33(3-4): 299-318, 1998.

Peek, Robin P. "Will Abstracting-and-Indexing Services Become Passe." *Information Today* 15 (3): 46, March, 1998.

Prior, Albert. "Managing Electronic Serials: The Development of a Subscription Agent's Service." *The Serials Librarian.* 32(3-4): 57-65, 1997.

Prior, Albert. "Managing Electronic Serials: Development of a Subscription Agent's Service." *The Serials Librarian* 32 (3-4): 57-65, 1997.

Rogers, Michael. "Judge Rules Against UnCover in Copyright Suit." *Library Journal* 123 (19): 19, 1998.

Rogers, Michael. "Library Automation/Vendor Partnerships Continue in 1997." *Library Journal* 122(1): 27, Jan. 1997.

Rogers, Michael. "EBSCO Releases EBSCOHost Web 2.0 and Other Products." *Library Journal* 123 (6): 27, 1998.

Rogers, Michael. "OCLC Debuts Electronic Journal Licensing Program." *Library Journal.* 123(15): 27, Sept. 15, 1998.

Schwartz, Marla J. "Acquiring Electronic Journals: The Role of Vendors." *Library Acquisitions: Practice and Theory* 22 (3): 358-360, 1998.

Tenopir, Carol, and Jeff Barry. "EBSCO Publishing." *Library Journal* 123, 1997.

Waltner, Robb. "EBSCODOC Vs. CARL UnCover: A Comparison of Document Delivery Services at the University of Evansville." *Journal of Interlibrary Loan, Document Delivery, and Information Supply* 7 (3): 21-28, 1997.

The Best Original Scientific Research, Review, Methods and Symposia Journals with Their Current Web Addresses Ranked Within Their Primary Subject Category

Tony Stankus
Jeanne Marie Clavin
Richard Joslin

Methods: This list represents author Stankus' judgment of the most important titles in certain basic sciences and selected areas of medicine and engineering. There are certainly more titles than these 1,000+ titles available, but these represents much of the world's core literature, and should be considered for adoption first. Care was taken to ensure that only titles that are closely comparable to one another in scope and purpose were included. Within each category, journals that primarily feature research articles (full-length or "letters") or a mix of these and other features, are listed first. Journals that primarily feature reviews, symposia, or methods are then separately listed and judged. In areas where there were only a few competing titles, a ranking is sometimes omitted. In areas where subspecialized titles are important for the larger field whose listing precedes it, but which are not topically comparable among themselves, a listing without a ranking is provided. This list updates the relative rankings of journals in given fields originally analyzed in

---

Selection and ranking of titles by Tony Stankus.
Web address searching and reporting by Jeanne Marie Clavin and Richard Joslin.

[Haworth co-indexing entry note]: "The Best Original Scientific Research, Review, Methods and Symposia Journals with Their Current Web Addresses Ranked Within Their Primary Subject Category." Stankus, Tony, Jeanne Marie Clavin, and Richard Joslin. Co-published simultaneously in *Science & Technology Libraries* (The Haworth Press, Inc.) Vol. 18, No. 2/3, 1999, pp. 111-182; and: *Electronic Expectations: Science Journals on the Web* (Tony Stankus) The Haworth Press, Inc., 1999, pp. 111-182. Single or multiple copies of this article are available for a fee from The Haworth Document Delivery Service [1-800-342-9678, 9:00 a.m. - 5:00 p.m. (EST). E-mail address: getinfo@haworthpressinc.com].

111

the author Stankus' *Making Sense of Journals in the Physical Sciences and Making Sense of Journals in the Life Sciences,* and *Special Format Serials and Issues* including some new titles that have appeared since those works.

Web addresses are provided for the home page of each journal, when available, although some journals are also accessible via package plans with different URLs. Ideally, the address provided brought the reader directly to the journal itself. If this was not possible, it brought them to the publisher's home page. Occasionally, an academic or consortial site, that included an address for the journal was provided as a last resort. (This should not be taken, however, as an endorsement of any attempt to illegally access content by persons who do not fall within the license granted to these institutional or consortial site.) *Indeed, it should be noted that not all worthwhile journals have electronic journals or web sites yet.* When an address is missing here, a blank space is left for the reader to enter.

Many of the sites noted here contain internal links that provide readers with the opportunity to scan their recent tables of contents, editorial boards, frequency, subscription information, and in some cases, information for pro- spective authors. The reader should, however, be warned that although these addresses were checked at the time of their compiling, site shifting is not an uncommon occurrence among e-journal addresses and some publishers are better than others in ensuring continuity of home page address or in providing for transparent transfer to the new address.

Considerations for rankings, then and now, included heavy representation of authors from scientifically competitive countries, frequency of subscrip- tion within the collections of leading universities, clinics, and industrial re- search centers, and value for subscription price. Citation data over the years were consulted but were in no way the only means by which journals were chosen for inclusion, grouped by subject, or ranked. This list should not, be regarded as directly derivative, or as a substitute from the proprietary data published by the Institute for Scientific Information in their *Journal Citation Reports*™ series, although this author is happy to recommend their purchase and careful use by science librarians, and others in the publishing and library supply industry.

GENERAL CHEMISTRY– MIXED-FORMAT, PRIMARY RESEARCH AND LETTERS JOURNALS

1. *Journal of the American Chemical Society*
   http://pubs.acs.org/journals/jacsat/index.html
2. *Angewandte Chemie–International Edition in English*
   http://www.wiley-vch.de/vch/journals/2002.html

3. *Chemical Communications–A Journal of the Royal Society of Chemistry*
   http://www.rsc.org/is/journals/current/chemcomm/cccpub.htm
4. *Chemistry–A European Journal*
   http://www.wiley-vch.de/vch/journals/2111/index.html
5. *Canadian Journal of Chemistry*
   http://www.cisti.nrc.ca/cisti/journals/rjchem.html
6. *Helvetica Chimica Acta*
   http://www.wiley-vch.de/vhca/journals/2217.html
7. *New Journal of Chemistry*
   http://www.rsc.org/is/journals/current/newjchem/njc.htm
8. *Chemistry Letters*
   http://wwwsoc.nacsis.ac.jp/csj/journals/chem-lett/index-e.html
9. *Bulletin of the Chemical Society of Japan*
   http://wwwsoc.nacsis.ac.jp/csj/journals/bcsj/index-e.html
10. *Mendeleev Communications*
    http://www.rsc.org/is/journals/current/mendelev/mecpub.htm

GENERAL CHEMISTRY–
REVIEW, SYMPOSIA AND METHODS JOURNALS

1. *Accounts of Chemical Research*
   http://pubs.acs.org/journals/achre4/index.html
2. *Chemical Reviews*
   http://pubs.acs.org/journals/chreay/index.html
3. *Chemical Society Reviews*
   http://www.rsc.org/is/journals/current/chsocrev/csrpub.htm
4. *Topics in Current Chemistry*
   http://www.springer-ny.com/catalog/np/aug96np/DATA/3-540-
   61131-2.html
   Also some contents by gopher:
   gopher://trick.ntp.springer.de:70/11/chemistry/tcc/
5. *Pure & Applied Chemistry*
   http://www.blacksci.co.uk/products/journals/pac.htm

GENERAL ORGANIC CHEMISTRY–
MIXED-FORMAT, PRIMARY RESEARCH
AND LETTERS JOURNALS

1. *Journal of Organic Chemistry*
   http://pubs.acs.org/journals/joceah/index.html
2. *Tetrahedron Letters* (subscription required)
   http://oxford.elsevier.com/tis/

Some contents also available through ChemWeb (registration required)
http://chemweb.com/library
3. *Tetrahedron* (registration required)
http://oxford.elsevier.com/tis/
4. *Journal of the Chemical Society–Perkin Transactions I*
http://www.rsc.org/is/journals/current/perkin1/p1ppub.htm
5. *European Journal of Organic Chemistry*
http://www.wiley-vch.de/vch/journals/2046/index.html

GENERAL ORGANIC CHEMISTRY–
REVIEW, SYMPOSIA AND METHODS

1. *Organic Reactions*
http://catalog.wiley.com/
2. *Annual Reports on the Progress of Chemistry Section B–Organic Chemistry*
http://www.rsc.org/is/journals/current/anreport/arpcon.htm

SPECIALTIES WITHIN ORGANIC CHEMISTRY–
SYNTHETIC ORGANIC CHEMISTRY–
MIXED-FORMAT, PRIMARY RESEARCH
AND LETTERS JOURNALS

1. *Synlett*
http://www.thieme.com/chemistry/Chemfrm.htm
2. *Synthesis*
http://www.thieme.com/chemistry/Chemfrm.htm
3. *Synthetic Communications*
http://www.dekker.com/cgi-bin/webdbc/md/detail.
htx?d_cat_id=0039-7911
4. *Organic Preparations & Procedures International*
Published by Organic Preparations & Procedures, Inc., Newton
Highlands MA US
Information listed in Oxbridge Comm., Inc. MediaGuide-
http://www.oxbridge.com/spd/s0390037.cfm
5. *Journal of Synthetic Organic Chemistry of Japan*
http://wwwsoc.nacsis.ac.jp/ssocj/

SPECIALTIES WITHIN ORGANIC CHEMISTRY–
SYNTHETIC ORGANIC CHEMISTRY–
REVIEW, SYMPOSIA AND METHODS

1. *Organic Syntheses*
http://catalog.wiley.com/

2. *Contemporary Organic Synthesis*
   From 1998 on, COS will appear as a reviews section in the *Journal of the Chemical Society–Perkin Transactions 1*
   http://www.rsc.org/is/journals/current/perkin1/p1ppub.htm

SPECIALTIES WITHIN ORGANIC CHEMISTRY– PHYSICAL ORGANIC CHEMISTRY– MIXED-FORMAT, PRIMARY RESEARCH AND LETTERS JOURNALS

1. *Journal of the Chemical Society–Perkin Transactions 2*
   http://www.rsc.org/is/journals/current/perkin2/p2ppub.htm
2. *Journal of Physical Organic Chemistry*
   http://www.interscience.wiley.com/jpages/0894-3230/

SPECIALTIES WITHIN ORGANIC CHEMISTRY– PHYSICAL ORGANIC CHEMISTRY– REVIEW, SYMPOSIA AND METHODS

1. *Advances in Physical Organic Chemistry*
   http://www.apnet.com/
2. *Progress in Physical Organic Chemistry*
   http://catalog.wiley.com/
3. *Topics in Stereochemistry*
   http://catalog.wiley.com/

SPECIALTIES WITHIN ORGANIC CHEMISTRY– ORGANIC CHEMISTRY OF NATURAL PRODUCTS AND PHARMACOGNOSCY– MIXED-FORMAT, PRIMARY RESEARCH AND LETTERS JOURNALS

1. *Journal of Natural Products*
   http://pubs.acs.org/journals/jnprdf/index.html
2. *Phytochemistry*
   http://www.elsevier.nl/locate/phytochem
3. *Planta Medica*
   http://www.thieme.com/chemistry/aec.htm
4. *Journal of Ethnopharmacology*
   Lausanne Elsevier Sequoia
   http://www.elsevier.nl/

SPECIALTIES WITHIN ORGANIC CHEMISTRY– ORGANIC CHEMISTRY OF NATURAL PRODUCTS AND PHARMACOGNOSCY– REVIEW, SYMPOSIA AND METHODS

1. *Natural Product Reports*
   http://www.rsc.org/is/journals/current/npr/nprpub.htm
2. *Fortschritte der Chemie Organischer Naturstoffe (Progress in the Chemistry of Organic Natural Products)*
   http://www.springer-ny.com/catalog/np/jan96np/DATA/3-211-82695-5.html

SPECIALTIES WITHIN ORGANIC CHEMISTRY–MEDICINAL, PHARMACEUTICAL AND BIO-ORGANIC CHEMISTRY– MIXED-FORMAT, PRIMARY RESEARCH AND LETTERS JOURNALS

1. *Journal of Medicinal Chemistry*
   http://pubs.acs.org/journals/jmcmar/index.html
2. *Journal of Pharmaceutical Sciences*
   http://pubs.acs.org/journals/jpmsae/index.html
3. *Biorganic & Medicinal Chemistry Letters* (subscription required)
   http://oxford.elsevier.com/tis/

Some content available through ChemWeb (registration required):
   http://chemweb.com/library

4. *Bioorganic & Medicinal Chemistry* (subscription required)
   http://oxford.elsevier.com/tis/
   Some content available through ChemWeb (registration required)
   http://chemweb.com/library/
5. *European Journal of Medicinal Chemistry*
   http://www.elsevier.nl/locate/ejmedchem
6. *Chemical and Pharmaceutical Bulletin*
   published in Tokyo by the Pharmaceutical Society of Japan
   http://www.pharm.or.jp/

SPECIALTIES WITHIN ORGANIC CHEMISTRY– MEDICINAL, PHARMACEUTICAL, AND BIOORGANIC CHEMISTRY– REVIEW, SYMPOSIA AND METHODS

1. *Medicinal Research Reviews*
   http://www.interscience.wiley.com/jpages/0198-6325/

SPECIALTIES WITHIN ORGANIC CHEMISTRY– HETEROCYCLIC COMPOUNDS– MIXED-FORMAT, PRIMARY RESEARCH AND LETTERS JOURNALS

1. *Journal of Heterocyclic Chemistry*
   Published by HeteroCorporation, Provo, Utah US
2. *Heterocycles*
   http://www.elsevier.nl/locate/heterocycles

SPECIALTIES WITHIN ORGANIC CHEMISTRY– HETEROCYCLIC COMPOUNDS– REVIEW, SYMPOSIA AND METHODS

1. *Advances in Heterocyclic Chemistry*
   http://www.apnet.com/

GENERAL PHYSICAL CHEMISTRY AND CHEMICAL PHYSICS– MIXED-FORMAT, PRIMARY RESEARCH AND LETTERS JOURNALS

1. *Journal of Physical Chemistry A*
   http://pubs.acs.org/journals/jpcafh/index.html
2. *Journal of Chemical Physics*
   http://info.ripn.net:8080/infomag/journals/j006e/
3. *Chemical Physics Letters*
   http://www.elsevier.nl:80/inca/publications/store/5/0/5/7/0/7/
   Some contents available through ChemWeb (registration required):
   http://chemweb.com/library
4. *Journal of the Chemical Society–Faraday Transactions*
   http://www.rsc.org/is/journals/current/faraday/fappub.htm
5. *Berichte der Bunsen-Gesellschaft fuer Physikalische Chemie*
   http://www.wiley-vch.de/vch/journals/2018.html

GENERAL PHYSICAL CHEMISTRY AND CHEMICAL PHYSICS– REVIEW, SYMPOSIA AND METHODS JOURNALS

1. *Annual Review of Physical Chemistry*
   http://www.annualreviews.org/ari/pubs/pubs.htm
2. *International Reviews in Physical Chemistry*
   http://www.tandf.co.uk/jnls/rpc.htm

3. *Journal of the Chemical Society–Faraday Discussions*
http://www.rsc.org/is/journals/current/faraday/fadpub.htm

SPECIALTIES WITHIN PHYSICAL CHEMISTRY
AND CHEMICAL PHYSICS–
SURFACE SCIENCE–
MIXED-FORMAT, PRIMARY RESEARCH AND LETTERS JOURNALS

1. *Journal of Physical Chemistry B*
http://pubs.acs.org/journals/jpcbfk/index.html
2. *Langmuir*
http://pubs.acs.org/journals/langd5/index.html
3. *Journal of Colloid & Interface Science*
http://www.apnet.com/www/journal/cs.htm
4. *Surface Science*
http://www.elsevier.nl/locate/susc
5. *Thin Solid Films*
http://www.elsevier.nl/locate/tsf
6. *Journal of Vacuum Science & Technology A & B*
A–http://ojps.aip.org/jvsta/
B–http://ojps.aip.org/jvstb/

SPECIALTIES WITHIN PHYSICAL CHEMISTRY
AND CHEMICAL PHYSICS–
SURFACE SCIENCE-
REVIEW, SYMPOSIA AND METHODS JOURNALS

1. *Advances in Colloids & Interface Science*
http://www.elsevier.nl/locate/cis
2. *Progress in Surface Science*
http://www.elsevier.nl/cgi-bin/cas/tree/store/jpss/cas_free/browse/
browse.cgi
3. *Surface Science Reviews*
No web page available
4. *Surface Review & Letters* (World Publishing Co., Singapore)
http://www.wspc.com.sg/

SPECIALTIES WITHIN PHYSICAL CHEMISTRY
AND CHEMICAL PHYSICS–
COMPUTER MODELING, THEORETICAL
AND QUANTUM CHEMISTRY–
MIXED-FORMAT, PRIMARY RESEARCH AND LETTERS JOURNALS

1. *Journal of Computational Chemistry*
http://journals.wiley.com/0192-8651/

2. *Theoretica Chimica Acta*
   http://www.springer.de/
   Recent years on gopher:
   gopher://trick.ntp.springer.de/11/TOC/214/
3. *International Journal of Quantum Chemistry*
   http://www.interscience.wiley.com/jpages/0020-7608/
4. *Journal of Molecular Structure–THEOCHEM*
   http://www.elsevier.nl:80/inca/publications/store/5/0/0/8/5/1/

OTHER TOPICAL SPECIALTIES WITHIN PHYSICAL CHEMISTRY AND CHEMICAL PHYSICS

* *International Journal of Chemical Kinetics* (registration required)
  http://www2.interscience.wiley.com/
* *Journal of Solution Chemistry*
  http://www.plenum.com/title.cgi?2030
* *Journal of Chemical Thermodynamics*
  http://www.hbuk.co.uk/ap/journals/ct/
* *Biophysical Chemistry*
  http://www.elsevier.nl/locate/bpc
* *Photochemistry & Photobiology*
  http://www.kumc.edu/ASP/PAPHome/pap_home.html
* *Laser Chemistry*
  http://www.gbhap-us.com/journals/319/319-top.htm
* *Journal of Photochemistry*
  Lausanne Elsevier Sequoia
  http://www.elsevier.nl/

GENERAL ANALYTICAL CHEMISTRY– MIXED-FORMAT, PRIMARY RESEARCH AND LETTERS JOURNALS

1. *Analytical Chemistry*
   http://pubs.acs.org/journals/ancham/index.html
2. *Analytica Chimica Acta*
   http://www.elsevier.nl:80/inca/publications/store/5/0/2/6/8/1/
   Some contents available through ChemWeb (requires registration):
   http://chemweb.com/library
3. *The Analyst*
   http://www.rsc.org/is/journals/current/analyst/anlpub.htm
4. *Journal of the AOAC International*
   http://www.aoac.org/pubs/pubcatJN.htm

5. *Talanta*
   http://www.elsevier.nl:80/inca/publications/store/5/2/5/4/3/8/
6. *Fresenius' Journal of Analytical Chemistry*
   http://link.springer.de/link/service/00216/index.htm
7. *Analytical Letters*
   http://www.dekker.com/cgi-bin/webdbc/md/detail.
   htx?d_cat_id=0003-2719

GENERAL ANALYTICAL CHEMISTRY–
REVIEW, SYMPOSIA AND METHODS

1. *TrAC: Trends in Analytical Chemistry*
   http://www.elsevier.nl:80/homepage/saa/trac/
2. *CRC Critical Reviews in Analytical Chemistry*
   http://www.crcpress.com/jour/crac/crac.htm
3. *American Laboratory*
   http://www.iscpubs.com/pubs/al/a12.html

SPECIALTIES WITHIN ANALYTICAL CHEMISTRY–
CHROMATOGRAPHY AND SEPARATION SCIENCES–
MIXED-FORMAT, PRIMARY RESEARCH
AND LETTERS JOURNALS

1. *Journal of Chromatographic Science*
   http://www.j-chrom-sci.com/
2. *Journal of Chromatography A, with J of Chromatography B (Biomedical Sciences and Applications)*
   http://www.elsevier.nl:80/inca/publications/store/5/2/4/0/1/6/
3. *LC-GC: Magazine of Separation Science*
   http://www.lcgcmag.com/
4. *Separation & Purification Methods*
   http://www.dekker.com/
5. *Journal of Microcolumn Separations*
   http://www.interscience.wiley.com/jpages/1040-7685/
6. *JPC: Journal of Planar Chromatography*
   http://www.springer.de/chem/journals/journals.html
7. *Chromatographia*
   http://www.elsevier.nl:80/inca/publications/store/2/8/5/

SPECIALTIES WITHIN ANALYTICAL CHEMISTRY–
CHROMATOGRAPHY AND SEPARATION SCIENCES–
REVIEW, SYMPOSIA AND METHODS

1. *Advances in Chromatography*
   http://www.dekker.com/

SPECIALTIES WITHIN ANALYTICAL CHEMISTRY–
GENERAL SPECTROSCOPY–
MIXED-FORMAT, PRIMARY RESEARCH
AND LETTERS JOURNALS

1. *Applied Spectroscopy*
   http://www.s-a-s.org/journal.html
2. *Journal of Molecular Spectroscopy*
   http://www.apnet.com/www/journal/ms.htm
3. *Spectrochimica Acta A & B*
   Spectrochimica Acta Part A–Molecular and Biomolecular Spectroscopy
   http://www.elsevier.nl:80/inca/publications/store/5/2/5/4/3/6/
   Spectrochimica Acta Part B-Atomic Spectroscopy
   http://www.elsevier.nl:80/inca/publications/store/5/2/5/4/3/7/
4. *Journal of Analytical Atomic Spectroscopy*
   http://www.rsc.org/is/journals/current/jaas/jaaspub.htm
5. *Journal of Quantitative Spectroscopy & Radiative Transfer*
   http://www.elsevier.nl:80/inca/publications/store/2/7/2/

SPECIALTIES WITHIN ANALYTICAL CHEMISTRY–
MASS SPECTROMETRY–
MIXED-FORMAT, PRIMARY RESEARCH
AND LETTERS JOURNALS

1. *Journal of the American Society for Mass Spectrometry*
   http://www-east.elsevier.com/webjam/Menu.html
2. *Rapid Communications in Mass Spectrometry*
   http://www.interscience.wiley.com/jpages/0951-4198/
3. *Journal of Mass Spectrometry*
   http://www.interscience.wiley.com/jpages/1076-5174/
4. *International Journal of Mass Spectrometry* (formerly *International Journal of Mass Spectrometry and Ion Processes*)
   http://www.interscience.wiley.com/jpages/1076-5174/
5. *Organic Mass Spectrometry*
   Published by WileyUK-Heyden (London)
   http://www.wiley.co.uk/

6. *European Mass Spectrometry*
   http://www.impub.co.uk/ems.html

SPECIALTIES WITHIN ANALYTICAL CHEMISTRY–
MASS SPECTROMETRY–
REVIEW, SYMPOSIA AND METHODS

1. *Mass Spectrometry Reviews*
   http://journals.wiley.com/wilcat-bin/ops/
   ID0240942/0277-7037/prod

SPECIALTIES WITHIN ANALYTICAL CHEMISTRY–
NUCLEAR MAGNETIC RESONANCE IN CHEMISTRY–
MIXED-FORMAT, PRIMARY RESEARCH
AND LETTERS JOURNALS

1. *Journal of Magnetic Resonance*
   http://www.apnet.com/www/journal/mn.htm
2. *Magnetic Resonance in Chemistry*
   http://www2.interscience.wiley.com/zcgi/toc?ISSN=0749-1581

OTHER TOPICAL SPECIALTIES WITHIN ANALYTICAL
CHEMISTRY AND RELATED FIELDS–
MIXED-FORMAT, PRIMARY RESEARCH
AND LETTERS JOURNALS

- *Journal of Thermal Analysis and Calorimetry* (formerly *J. of Thermal Analysis)*
  http://www.wkap.nl/kapis/CGI-BIN/WORLD/journalhome.
  htm?1418-2874
- *Journal of Forensic Sciences*
  http://www.astm.org/forensic.htm
- *Clinical Chemistry*
  http://www.clinchem.org/
- *Analytical Biochemistry*
  http://www.apnet.com/www/journal/ab.htm
- *Microchemical Journal*
  http://www.apnet.com/www/journal/mj.htm
- *Journal of Electroanalytical Chemistry*
  http://www.elsevier.nl/inca/publications/store/5/0/4/0/8/7/

- *Electroanalysis*
  http://www.wiley-vch.de/vch/journals/2049/index.html
- *Journal of Food Science*
  http://www.ift.org/publ/publ_c00.html
- *Microscopy & Microanalysis*
  http://link.springer.de/link/service/journals/10005/index.htm

GENERAL INORGANIC AND ORGANOMETALLIC CHEMISTRY–
MIXED-FORMAT, PRIMARY RESEARCH,
AND LETTERS JOURNALS

1. *Inorganic Chemistry*
   http://pubs.acs.org/journals/inocaj/index.html
2. *Organometallics*
   http://pubs.acs.org/journals/orgnd7/index.html
3. *Journal of the Chemical Society, Dalton Transactions*
   http://www.rsc.org/is/journals/current/dalton/dappub.htm
4. *Journal of Organometallic Chemistry*
   http://www.elsevier.nl/inca/publications/store/5/0/4/0/9/0/
5. *Polyhedron*
   http://www.elsevier.nl:80/inca/publications/store/2/1/8/
6. *European Journal of Inorganic Chemistry*
   http://www.interscience.wiley.com/jpages/1434-1948/
7. *Inorganica Chimica Acta*
   http://www.elsevier.nl:80/inca/publications/store/5/0/4/0/8/6/
   Some contents available through ChemWeb (requires registration):
   http://chemweb.com/library
8. *Transition Metal Chemistry*
   http://www.wkap.nl/journalhome.htm/0340-4285

GENERAL INORGANIC AND ORGANOMETALLIC CHEMISTRY–
REVIEW, SYMPOSIA AND METHODS

1. *Inorganic Syntheses*
   http://catalog.wiley.com/
2. *Advances in Organometallic Chemistry*
   http://www.apnet.com/
3. *Structure & Bonding*
   http://www.springer.de
   available by gopher:
   gopher://trick.ntp.springer.de:70/11/chemistry/ struct_bonding

TOPICAL SPECIALTIES WITHIN INORGANIC AND ORGANOMETALLIC CHEMISTRY– MIXED-FORMAT, PRIMARY RESEARCH AND LETTERS JOURNALS

- *Journal of Solid State Chemistry*
  http://www.apnet.com/www/journal/sc.htm
- *Journal of Inorganic Biochemistry*
  http://www.elsevier.nl:80/inca/publications/store/5/0/5/7/7/2/
- *Metal Ions in Biological Systems*
  http://www.dekker.com/
- *Journal of Catalysis*
  http://www.apnet.com/www/journal/ca.htm
- Acta Crystallographica–
  Section A (Foundations of Crystallography)
  http://www.iucr.ac.uk/journals/acta/actaa.html
  Section B (Structural Science)
  http://www.iucr.ac.uk/journals/acta/actab.html
  Section C (Crystal Structure Communications)
  http://www.iucr.ac.uk/journals/acta/actac.html
  Section D (Biological Crystallography)
  http://www.iucr.ac.uk/journals/acta/actad.html
- *Journal of Coordination Chemistry*
  http://www.gbhap-us.com/journals/122/index.html
  table of contents, abstracts and some content available through ChemWeb (registration required):
  http://www.chemweb.com/library
- *Phosphorous, Sulfur and Silicon and the Related Elements*
  http://www.gbhap-us.com/journals/198/198-top.htm
- Available through ChemWeb (registration required):
  http://www.chemweb.com/library/
- *Journal of Fluorine Chemistry*
  http://www.elsevier.nl:80/inca/publications/store/5/0/4/0/8/8/

GENERAL POLYMER CHEMISTRY AND PHYSICS– MIXED-FORMAT, PRIMARY RESEARCH AND LETTERS JOURNALS

1. *Macromolecules*
   http://www.acsinfo.acs.org/journals/mamobx
2. *Macromolecular Rapid Communications*
   http://www.huethig.de/zeitschr/mrc/cc/19

3. *Polymer*
   http://www.elsevier.nl/inca/publications/store/3/0/index_05.html
4. *Journal of Polymer Science–Polymer Chemistry*
   http:// www.interscience.wiley.com/jpages/0887-624x/
5. *Journal of Polymer Science–Polymer Physics*
   http://www.interscience.wiley.com/jpages/0887-6266/
6. *Macromolecular Chemistry & Physics*
   http://www.huethig/de/zeitschr/mcp.html
7. *Journal of Macromolecular Science A–Pure & Applied Chemistry*
   http://www.dekker.com/e/p.pl/1060-1325
8. *Journal of Macromolecular Science B–Physics*

POLYMER CHEMISTRY AND PHYSICS–
REVIEW, SYMPOSIA AND METHODS

- *Advances in Polymer Science*
- *Progress in Polymer Science*
- *Journal of Macromolecular Science–Reviews in Macromolecular Chemistry and Physics*
   http://www.dekker.com/e/p.pl/0736-6574
- *Macromolecular Symposia*
   http://www.huethig.de/zeitschr/mms/mms.html

GENERAL MATERIALS SCIENCE (EXCEPTING POLYMERS)–
MIXED-FORMAT, PRIMARY RESEARCH
AND LETTERS JOURNALS

1. *Chemistry of Materials*
   http://pubs.acs.org/journals/cmatex/index.html
2. *Journal of Materials Chemistry*
   http://www.rsc.org/is/journals/current/jmc/mapcon.htm
3. *Advanced Materials*
   http://www.wiley-vch.de/vch/journals/2089.html
4. *Journal of Materials Research*
   http://www.mrs.org/publications/jmr/
5. *MRS Bulletin*
   http://www.mrs.org/publications/bulletin/
6. *Materials Research Bulletin*
   http://www.elsevier.nl/locate/matresbu
7. *Materials Letters*
   http://www.elsevier.nl/locate/matlet

8. *Journal of Materials Science*
   http://www.wkap.nl/journalhome.htm/0022-2461
9. *Materials Chemistry & Physics*
   http://www.elsevier.nl/locate/matchemphys
10. *Materials Science & Engineering: A*
    http://www.elsevier.nl/locate/msea
11. *JOM–Journal of Minerals, Metals & Materials Science*
    http://www.tms.org/pubs/journals/JOM/JOM.html

GENERAL MATERIALS SCIENCE
(EXCEPTING POLYMERS)–
REVIEW, SYMPOSIA AND METHODS

1. *Annual Review of Materials Science* http://www.annualreviews.org
2. *Progress in Materials Science*
   http://www.elsevier.nl/locate/pmatsci
3. *Materials Research Society Symposium Proceedings*
   http://dns.mrs.org/publications/books/index.html
4. *National SAMPE Technical Conference Series*
   SAMPE Publications homepage
   http://org.et.byu.edu/sampe/publicat.html or
5. SAMPE International Symposium and Exhibition Proceedings Compiled by Composite Materials Research Group University of Mississippi
   http://www.olemiss.edu/depts/compmatl/lit/sampe2.html
6. *Materials Characterization*
   http://www.elsevier.nl/locate/matchar

TOPICAL SPECIALTIES WITHIN MATERIALS SCIENCE
(EXCEPTING POLYMERS)–
MIXED-FORMAT, PRIMARY RESEARCH
AND LETTERS JOURNALS

- *Journal of Biomedical Materials Research*
  http://www.interscience.wiley.com/jpages/0021-9304/
- *Biomaterials*
- *Journal of the American Ceramic Society*
  http://www.acers.org/pubs/journal/journal.stm
- *Journal of Pulp & Paper Science*
  http://www.open.doors.cppa.ca/english/cppa/technic/public.htm
- *Journal of Wood Chemistry & Technology*
  http://www.dekker.com/cgi-bin/webdbc/md/detail.
  htx?d_cat_id=0277-3813

- *Cement & Concrete Research*
  http://www.elsevier.nl/locate/cemconres
- *Journal of Crystal Growth*
  http://www.elsevier.nl/locate/jcrysgro
- *Acta Metallurgica & Materialia*
  http://www.elsevier.nl/locate/actamat
- *Intermetallics*
  http://www.elsevier.nl/locate/intermet
- *Chemistry & Physics of Carbon*
  http://www.dekker.com/cgi-bin/webdbc/md/detail.
  htx?d_cat_id=1953-0
- *Chemical Vapor Deposition*
  http://www.wiley-vch.de/vch/journals/2112.html
- *Semiconductor Science & Technology*
  http://www.iop.org/Journals/ss
- *Journal of Electronic Materials*
  http://www.tms.org/pubs/Journals/JEM/jem.html
- *Surface & Coatings Technology*
  http://www.elsevier.nl/locate/surfcoat
- *International Journal of Fatigue*
  http://www.elsevier.nl/locate/ijfatigue
- *Journal of Engineering Materials–Transactions of the American Society of Mechanical Engineering*
  http://asme.org/pubs/journals/mattech/mattech.html

SOLID EARTH SCIENCES AND RELATED GEOPHYSICS– MIXED-FORMAT, PRIMARY RESEARCH AND LETTERS JOURNALS

1. *American Journal of Science*
   http://love.geology.yale.edu/~rye/ajs.html
2. *Geology*
   http://www.geosociety.org/pubs/geology.htm
3. *Geological Society of America Bulletin*
   http://www.geosociety.org/pubs/bulletin.htm
4. *Journal of Geology*
   http://www.journals.uchicago.edu/JG/home.html
5. *Earth & Planetary Science Letters*
   http://www.elsevier.nl/locate/epslet
6. *Journal of Geophysical Research*
   http://www.ess.ucla.edu/jgr/

7. *Geophysical Research Letters*
   http://www.agu.org/GRL/
8. *Geological Magazine*
   http://www.cup.cam.ac.uk/scripts/webjrn1.asp?issn=00167568
9. *Canadian Journal of Earth Sciences*
   http://www.cisti.nrc.ca/cisti/journals/earthep.html
10. *Geological Journal*
    http://journals.wiley.com/wilcat-bin/ops/ID0702104/0072-1050/prod

SOLID EARTH SCIENCES AND RELATED GEOPHYSICS– REVIEW, SYMPOSIA AND METHODS JOURNALS

1. *Annular Review of Earth & Planetary Sciences*
   http://www.ari.org
2. *Earth Science Reviews*
   http://www.elsevier.nl/locate/earscirev
3. *Surveys in Geophysics*
   http://kapis.www.wkap.nl/kapis/CGI-BIN/WORLD/journalhome.
   htm?0169-3298
4. *Revue Geophysique*
   http://earth.agu.org/kosmos/homepage.html

SOLID EARTH SCIENCES AND RELATED GEOPHYSICS– PETROLOGY, MINERALOGY AND GEOCHEMISTRY– MIXED-FORMAT, PRIMARY RESEARCH AND LETTERS JOURNALS

1. *Journal of Petrology*
   http://www.oup.co.uk/petroj/
2. *American Mineralogist*
   http://www.minsocam.org/AmMin/ammin.html
3. *Contributions to Mineralogy & Petrology*
   http://link.springer.de/link/service/journals/00410/index.htm
4. *Geochimica et Cosmochimica Acta*
   http://www.elsevier.nl/locate/gca
5. *Chemical Geology*
   http://www.elsevier.nl/locate/chemgeo

SOLID EARTH SCIENCES AND RELATED GEOPHYSICS– TOPICAL SPECIALTIES IN ECONOMIC GEOLOGY– MIXED-FORMAT, PRIMARY RESEARCH AND LETTERS JOURNALS

- *AAPG Bulletin*
  http://www.aapg.org/dataserv.html
- *Journal of Sedimentary Petrology*
- *Journal of Petroleum Geology*
- *International Journal of Coal Geology*
  http://www.elsevier.nl/locate/ijcoalgeo
- *Exploratory Mineralogy & Geology*
- *Rock Mechanics & Rock Engineering*
  http://link.springer.de/link/service/journals/00603/index.htm
- *Journal of Applied Geophysics*
  http://www.elsevier.nl/locate/jappgeo
- *Journal of Geochemical Exploration*
  http://www.elsevier.nl/locate/jgeoexp
- *Mineralium Deposita*
  http://link.springer.de/link/service/journals/00126/index.htm
- *Marine & Petroleum Geology*
  http://www.elsevier.nl/locate/marpetgeo
- *Ore Geology Review*
  http://www.elsevier.nl/locate/oregeorev

SOLID EARTH SCIENCES AND RELATED GEOPHYSICS– SOIL SCIENCE– MIXED-FORMAT, ORIGINAL RESEARCH AND LETTERS JOURNALS

1. *Soil Science Society of America Journal*
   http://link.springer-ny.com/link/service/journals/10089/index.htm
2. *Soil Science*
   http://www.hintze-online.com/sos/
3. *European Journal of Soil Science*
   http://www.blacksci.co.uk/~cgilib/jnlpage.
   bin?Journal=EJSS&File= EJSS&Page=aims
4. *Geoderma*
   http://www.elsevier.nl/locate/geoderma
5. *Canadian Journal of Soil Science*
   http://www.nrc.ca/aic-journals/cjss.html

SOLID EARTH SCIENCES–
SOIL SCIENCE–
AGRONOMY–
MIXED-FORMAT,
PRIMARY RESEARCH AND LETTERS

1. *Plant & Soil*
   http://www.wkap.nl/journalhome.htm/0032-079X
2. *Soil Biology & Biochemistry*
   http://www.elsevier.co.jp/locate/soilbio
3. *Biology & Fertility of Soils*
   http://link.springer.de/link/service/journals/00374/index.htm
4. *Soil & Tillage Research*
   http://www.elsevier.nl/locate/still
5. *Soil Use & Management*
   http://www.cabi.org/catalog/journals/primjour/sum/sum.htm
6. *Soil Science & Plant Nutrition*
   http://wwwsoc.nacsis.ac.jp/jssspn/SSPN.html
7. *Journal of Soil & Water Conservation*
   http://www.swcs.org/JSWCwelcom.htm
8. *Transactions of the American Society of Agronomy Engineers*
   Home page of organization not of periodical
   http://asae.org/
9. *Communications in Soil Science & Plant Analysis*
   http://www.dekker.com/cgi-bin/webdbc/md/detail.
   htx?d_ cat_id=0010-3624
10. *Land Degradation & Development*
   http://www.wiley.com/journals/ldr/

SOLID EARTH SCIENCES AND RELATED GEOPHYSICS–
TECTONICS, SEISMOLOGY, STRUCTURAL
GEOLOGY, VOLCANOLOGY–
MIXED-FORMAT, PRIMARY RESEARCH
AND LETTERS JOURNALS

1. *Tectonics*
   http://www.agu.org/pubs/agu_jourtect.html
2. *Journal of Structural Geology*
   http://www.elsevier.nl/locate/jstrugeo
3. *Tectonophysics*
   http://www.elsevier.nl/locate/tecto
4. *Bulletin of the Seismological Society of America*
   http://www.seismosoc.org/htdocs/publications.html#BSSA

5. *Journal of Geodynamics*
   http://www.elsevier.nl/locate/jgeodyn
6. *Physics of the Earth and Planetary Interiors*
   http://www.elsevier.nl/locate/pepi
7. *Bulletin of Volcanology*
   http://link.springer.de/link/service/journals/00445/index
8. *Journal of Volcanology & Geothermal Research*
   http://www.elsevier.nl/locate/jvolgeores

SOLID EARTH SCIENCES AND RELATED GEOPHYSICS– PALEONTOLOGY– MIXED-FORMAT, ORIGINAL RESEARCH AND LETTERS JOURNALS

1. *Paleobiology*
   http://www.uic.edu/orgs/paleo/paleobio.htm
2. *Palaeontology*
   http://www.ucmp.berkeley.edu/Paleonet/PalAss/index.html
3. *Journal of Palenotology*
   http://www.uic.edu/orgs/paleo/JP.html
4. *Lethaia*
   http://www.scup.no/journals/en/j-109.html
5. *Palaios*
   http://www.ngdc.noaa.gov/mgg/sepm/palaios/
6. *Journal of Vertebrate Paleontology*
   http://eteweb.lscf.ucsb.edu/svp/jvp/

TOPICAL SPECIALTIES TRANSITIONAL FROM SOLID EARTH SCIENCES AND RELATED GEOPHYSICS TO OCEANIC AND ATMOSPHERIC SCIENCES– REMOTE SENSING AND MEASUREMENT SCIENCES

- *Remote Sensing of the Environment*
  http://www.elsevier.nl/locate/rse
- *IEEE Tranactions on Geoscience & Remote Sensing* (Table of contents page)
  http://www.ieee.org/pub_preview/grs_toc.html
- *Photogrammetric Engineering & Remote Sensing*
  http://www.asprs.org/asprs/publications/journal/pers.html
- *Journal of Geodesy*
  http://link.springer.de/link/service/journals/00190/index.htm

TOPICAL SPECIALTIES TRANSITIONAL FROM SOLID EARTH SCIENCES AND RELATED GEOPHYSICS TO OCEANIC AND ATMOSPHERIC SCIENCES– BASIC HYDROLOGY AND APPLIED WATER RESOURCES TECHNOLOGY– MIXED-FORMAT, ORIGINAL RESEARCH AND LETTERS

- *Water Resources Research*
  http://www.agu.org/pubs/agu_jourwrr.html
- *Water Research*
  http://www.elsevier.nl/locate/watres
- *Journal of Hydrology*
  http://www.elsevier.nl/locate/jhydrol
- *Hydrological Processes*
  http://journals.wiley.com/wilcat-bin/ops/
  ID0702104/0885-6087/prod
- *Journal of the American Water Works Association*
  http://www.awwa.org/journal/jfeature.htm
- *Journal of Contaminant Hydrology*
  http://www.elsevier.nl/locate/jconhyd
- *Ground Water Monitoring & Remediation*
  http://www.h2o-ngwa.org/publication/gwmrinfo.html

TOPICAL SPECIALTIES TRANSITIONAL FROM SOLID EARTH SCIENCES AND RELATED GEOPHYSICS TO OCEANIC AND ATMOSPHERIC SCIENCES– QUATERNARY SCIENCE, PHYSICAL GEOGRAPHY AND CLIMATOLOGY– MIXED-FORMAT, ORIGINAL RESEARCH AND LETTERS JOURNALS

- *Quaternary Research*
  http://www.apnet.com/www/journal/qr.htm
- *Geomorphology*
  http://www.elsevier.nl/locate/geomorph
- *Journal of Quaternary Science*
  http://www.interscience.wiley.com/jpages/0267-8179/
- *Terra Nova*
  http://www.gly.bris.ac.uk/WWW/TerraNova/terranova.html
- *Geographie Physique et Quaternaire*
  http://ftp.lemig.umontreal.ca/gpq/rgpq.htm
- *Journal of Climate*
  http://ams.allenpress.com/cgi-bin/omisapi.dll/
  ams?request=frames&link= all-jour

- *Physical Geography*
- *Journal of Glaciology and Geocryology*
  http://www.geodata.soton.ac.uk/ipa/ipa_publications.html
- *Global Biogeochemical Cycles*
  http://www.agu.org/pubs/agu_jourgbc.html
- *Arctic & Alpine Research*
  http://www.colorado.edu/INSTAAR/arctical pine/
- *Paleogeography, Paleoecology, Paleoclimatology*
  http://www.elsevier.nl/locate/palaeo
- *Polar Research*
- *Earth Surface Processes & Landforms*
  http://www.wiley.com/journals/esp/

TOPICAL SPECIALTIES TRANSITIONAL FROM SOLID EARTH SCIENCES TO OCEANIC AND ATMOSPHERIC SCIENCES– REVIEW, METHODS AND SYMPOSIA

- *Progress in Physical Geography*
  http://www.arnoldpublishers.co.uk/Journals/Journpages/
  03091333.htm

GENERAL OCEANIC AND ATMOSPHERIC SCIENCES– MIXED-FORMAT, ORIGINAL RESEARCH AND LETTERS JOURNALS

1. *Journal of Geophysical Research*
   http://www.agu.org/pubs/agu_jourjgro.html
2. *Geophysical Research Letters*
   http://www.agu.org/GRL/
3. *Tellus A–Dynamic Meteorology & Oceanology*
   http://www.munksgaard.dk/tellusa/
4. *Dynamics of Atmospheres & Oceans*
   http://www.elsevier.nl/locate/dynatmoce
5. *Atmosphere–Ocean*
   http://www.meds.dfo.ca/cmos/aotitabs.html

OCEANIC AND ATMOSPHERIC SCIENCES– PHYSICAL OCEANOGRAPHY– MIXED-FORMAT, ORIGINAL RESEARCH AND LETTERS JOURNALS

1. *Journal of Physical Oceanography* (AMS page to journals)
   http://ams.allenpress.com/cgi-bin/omisapi.dll/
   ams?request= frames&link=all-jour

2. *Journal of Marine Research*
   http://stormy.geology.yale.edu/kgl/Dept_Information/Journals/
   jmr.html
3. *Limnology & Oceanography*
   http://www.aslo.org/lo/
4. *Marine Geophysical Researches*
   http://www.wkap.nl/journalhome.htm/0025-3235

OCEANIC AND ATMOSPHERIC SCIENCES–
ATMOSPHERIC SCIENCES

1. *Journal of Atmospheric Sciences AMS page*
   http://ams.allenpress.com/cgi-bin/omisapi.dll/
   ams?request=frames&link=all-jour
2. *Atmospheric Environment*
   http://www.elsevier.nl/locate/atmosenv
3. *Journal of Atmospheric Chemistry*
   http://kapis.www.wkap.nl/kapis/CGI-BIN/WORLD/journal home.
   htm?0167-7764
4. *Meteorology and Atmospheric Physics*
   http://link.springer.de/link/service/journals/00703/index.htm
5. *Journal of Atmospheric & Terrestrial Physics*
   http://scienceserver.orionsci.com/elsevier/00219169/

OCEANIC AND ATMOSPHERIC SCIENCES–
METEOROLOGY

1. *Bulletin of the American Meteorological Society* (AMS page)
   http://ams.allenpress.com/cgi-bin/
   omisapi.dll/ams?request=frames&link=all-jour
2. *Monthly Weather Review* (AMS page)
   http://ams.allenpress.com/cgi-bin/
   omisapi.dll/ams?request=frames&link=all-jour
3. *Boundary-Layer Meteorology*
   http://kapis.www.wkap.nl/kapis/CGI-BIN/
   WORLD/journalhome.htm?0006-8314
4. *Weather & Forecasting* (AMS page)
   http://ams.allenpress.com/cgi-bin/
   omisapi.dll/ams?request=frames&link=all-jour
5. *Journal of Applied Meteorology* (AMS page)
   http://ams.allenpress.com/cgi-bin/
   omisapi.dll/ams?request=frames&link=all-jour

MODERN GENERAL PHYSICS–
ORIGINAL RESEARCH–
MIXED-FORMAT AND LETTERS JOURNALS

1. *Physical Review Letters*
   http://publish.aps.org/PRL/
2. *Europhysics Letters*
   http://www.iop.org/Journals/el
3. *Physics Letters A*
   http://www.elsevier.nl/locate/physleta
4. *Annals of Physics NY*
   http://www.apnet.com/www/journal/ph.htm
5. *Journal of Physics A–Mathematical & General*
   http://www.iop.org/Journals/ja
6. *Journal of the Physical Society of Japan*
   http://nabext.riken.go.jp/jps/jps/jposj/
7. *Physica A*
   http://www.elsevier.nl/locate/physa
8. *Canadian Journal of Physics*
   http://www.cisti.nrc.ca/cisti/journals/rjphys.html
9. *International Journal Modern Physics A*
   http://www.wspc.com.sg/journals/ijmpa/ijmpa.html
10. *Journal of Experimental & Theroretical Physics*
    http://ojps.aip.org/jetp/

MODERN GENERAL PHYSICS–
REVIEW, SYMPOSIA AND METHODS

1. *Reviews of Modern Physics*
   http://rmp.aps.org/
2. *Reports on Progress in Physics*
   http://www.iop.org/Journals/rp
3. *Physics Reports*
   http://www.elsevier.nl/locate/physrep

HIGH ENERGY NUCLEAR PHYSICS, PARTICLES AND FIELDS–
ORIGINAL RESEARCH–
MIXED-FORMAT AND LETTERS JOURNALS

1. *Physics Letter B* (need password)
   http://scienceserver.orionsci.com/elsevier/03702693/

2. *Nuclear Physics B*
   http://www.elsevier.nl/locate/npb
3. *Physical Review D–Particles and Fields*
   http://publish.aps.org/PRDO/prdohome.html
4. *European Physical Journal C*
   http://link.springer.de/link/service/journals/10052/index.htm
5. *International Journal of Modern Physics A*
   http://www.wspc.com.sg/journals/ijmpa/ijmpa.html

NUCLEAR STRUCTURE AND HEAVY ION PHYSICS– ORIGINAL RESEARCH– MIXED-FORMAT AND LETTERS JOURNALS

1. *Physical Review C*
   http://publish.aps.org/PRC/
2. *European Physical Journal A*
   http://link.springer.de/link/service/
   journals/10050/bibs/8001001/80010007.htm
3. *Journal of Physics G: Nuclear and Particle Physics*
   http://www.iop.org/Journals/jg

NUCLEAR AND PARTICLE PHYSICS AT ALL ENERGY LEVELS– REVIEW, SYMPOSIA AND METHODS

1. *Annual Review of Nuclear & Particle Science* (AR Link Homepage)
   http://www.annualreviews.org/ibbin/
   ibGate.exe?LOADPAGE=%2fARI%2fpubs%2falpha.htm
   (Journal homepage: 7 pages long)
2. *Progress in Particle and Nuclear Physics*
   http://www.elsevier.nl/locate/ppartnuclphys
3. *Nuclear Instruments & Methods in Physics Research A*
   http://www.elsevier.nl/locate/nima
4. *Particle Accelerators*

ATOMIC AND MOLECULAR PHYSICS– ORIGINAL RESEARCH– MIXED-FORMAT AND LETTERS JOURNALS (SEE ALSO GENERAL PHYSICAL CHEMISTRY AND CHEMICAL PHYSICS)

1. *Physical Review A (Atomic, Molecular, and Optical Physics)*
   http://ojps.aip.org/prao/

2. *Journal of Physics B: Atomic, Molecular and Optical Physics*
   http://www.iop.org/Journals/jb
3. *European Physics Journal D*
   http://link.springer.de/link/service/journals/10053/index.htm
4. *Journal of Optical Society of America B*
   http://www.osa.org/pub_svc/journals/josab/default1.htm
5. *Molecular Physics*
   http://www.tandf.co.uk/JNLS/mph.htm

ATOMIC AND MOLECULAR PHYSICS–
REVIEW, SYMPOSIA AND METHODS (SEE ALSO GENERAL
PHYSICAL CHEMISTRY AND CHEMICAL PHYSICS)

1. *Advances in Atomic, Molecular & Optical Physics*

PLASMA PHYSICS–
ORIGINAL RESEARCH–
MIXED-FORMAT AND LETTERS

2. *Physical Review E*
   http://preo.aps.org/
3. *Physics of Plasmas*
   http://www.aip.org/journals/php/php.html
4. *Plasma Physics and Controlled Fusion*
   http://www.ioppublishing.com/Journals/Catalogue/PP
5. *IEEE Transactions on Plasma Science*
   http://www.ieee.org/pub_preview/ps_toc.html
6. *Journal of Plasma Physics*
   http://www.cup.org/journals/jnlscat/pla/pla.html

PLASMA PHYSICS–REVIEWS, SYMPOSIA AND METHODS

1. *Annual Review of Fluid Mechanics* (ARI Link Homepage)
   http://www.annualreviews.org/ibbin/ibGate.
   exe?LOADPAGE=%2fARI%2fpubs%2falpha.htm
   The journal homepage URL is 4 lines long.

ASTRONOMY AND ASTROPHYSICS–
ORIGINAL RESEARCH–
MIXED-FORMAT AND LETTERS

1. *Astrophysical Journal* (include Letters and Supplements)
   http://www.journals.uchicago.edu/ApJ/

Monthly Notice of the Royal Astronomical Society
http://www.blacksci.co.uk/~cgilib/jnlpage.
bin?-Journal=MNRAS&File=MNRAS&Page=aims
2. *Astronomy & Astrophysics* (includes Supplements)
http://www.edpsciences.com/docinfos/AAS/OnlineAAS.html
3. *Astronomical Journal*
http://www.journals.uchicago.edu/AJ/journal/index.html
4. *Acta Astronomica*
http://www.astrouw.edu.pl/~udalski/acta.html
5. *Publications of the Astronomical Society of the Pacific*
http://www.journals.uchicago.edu/PASP/journal/index.html
6. *Astrophysical Letters & Communications*
http://www.gbhap-us.com/journals/105/105-top.htm

TOPICAL SPECIALTIES IN ASTRONOMY AND ASTROPHYSICS– SOLAR AND PLANETARY SCIENCES– ORIGINAL RESEARCH– MIXED-FORMAT AND LETTERS

- *Solar Physics*
  http://www.wkap.nl/journalhome.htm/0038-0938
- *Icarus*
  http://astrosun.tn.cornell.edu/Icarus/Icarus.html
- *Planetary & Space Sciences*
  http://www.elsevier.nl/locate/planspasci
- *Earth, Moon & Planets*
  http://www.wkap.nl/journalhome.htm/0167-9295
- *Journal of Geophysical Research–Planets*
  http://www.agu.org/pubs/agu_jourjgrp.html

ASTRONOMY AND ASTROPHYSICS– REVIEW, SYMPOSIA AND METHODS

1. *Annual Review of Astronomy & Astrophysics*
http://www.annualreviews.org/
ibbin/ibGate.exe?LOADPAGE=%2fARI%2fpubs%2falpha.htm
2. *Astronomy & Astrophysics Review*
http://link.springer.de/link/service/journals/00159/index.htm
3. *Space Science Reviews*
http://www.wkap.nl/journalhome.htm/0038-6308

4. *IAU Symposia*
   http://www.intastun.org/pastsympub.html
5. *Annual Review of Earth & Planetary Sciences*
   http://www.annualreviews.org/ibbin/
   ibGate.exe?LOADPAGE=%2fARI%2fpubs%2falpha.htm

MODERN GENERAL PHYSICS
MATHEMATICAL METHODS AND MODELING–
ORIGINAL RESEARCH–
MIXED-FORMAT AND LETTERS

1. *Communications on Mathematical Physics*
   http://link.springer.de/link/service/journals/00220/index.htm
2. *Journal of Computational Physics*
   http://www.apnet.com/www/journal/cp.htm
3. *Journal of Mathematical Physics*
   http://www.aip.org/journals/jmp/jmp.html
4. *Letters in Mathematical Physics*
   http://www.wkap.nl/journalhome.htm/0377-9017
5. *Journal of Geometry & Physics*
   http://www.jgp.unifi.it/
   and
   http://www.elsevier.nl/locate/jgeomphy

TOPICAL SPECIALTIES
IN MATHEMATICS PHYSICS AND MODELING

- *Chaos, Solitons & Fractals*
  http://www.ieee.org/pub_preview/mi_toc.html
- *Nonlinearity*
  http://www.iop.org/Journals/no
- *Archives of Rational Mechanics & Analysis Inverse Problems*
  http://www.iop.org/Journals/ip
- *Journal of Nonlinear Science*
  http://link.springer.de/link/service/journals/00332/index.htm
- *Ergodic Theory & Dynamical Systems*
  http://www.cup.cam.ac.uk/scripts/webjrn1.asp?mnemonic=ets
- *Waves in Random Media*
  http://www.iop.org/Journals/wr
- *Classical & Quantum Gravity*
  http://www.iop.org/Journals/cq

- *GRG Journal*
  http://www.plenum.com/title.cgi?2061
- *Journal of Fluid Mechanics*
  http://www.cup.org/journals/jnlscat/flm/flm.html
- *International Journal of Numerical Methods in Fluids for heat and fluid flow??*
  http://www.mcb.co.uk/hff.htm

CONDENSED MATTER/SOLID STATE PHYSICS– ORIGINAL RESEARCH– MIXED-FORMAT AND LETTERS JOURNALS

1. *Physical Review B*
   http://publish.aps.org/PRB/prbinfo.html
2. *European Physics Journal B*
   http://link.springer.de/link/service/journals/10051/index.htm
3. *Journal of the Mechanics & Physics of Solids*
   http://www.elsevier.nl/locate/jmps
4. *Philosophical Magazine Letters*
   http://www.tandf.co.uk/JNLS/phl.htm
5. *Journal of Physics* (Condensed Matter)
   http://www.ioppublishing.com/Journals/Catalogue/JD/
6. *Solid State Communications*
   http://www.elsevier.nl/locate/ssconline
7. *Philosophical Magazine A*
   http://www.tandf.co.uk/JNLS/PHMa.HTM
8. *Physica B*
   http://www.elsevier.nl/locate/physb

CONDENSED MATTER/SOLID STATE PHYSICS– REVIEW, SYMPOSIA AND METHODS

1. *Solid State Physics*
2. *Advances in Physics*
   http://www.tandf.co.uk/JNLS/adp.htm
3. *Critical Reviews in Solid State & Materials Science*
   http://www.crcpress.com/www/index.htm

GENERAL APPLIED PHYSICS– ORIGINAL RESEARCH– MIXED-FORMAT AND LETTERS JOURNALS

1. *Applied Physics Letters*
   http://ojps.aip.org/aplo/

2. *Journal of Applied Physics*
   http://www.aip.org/journals/jap/jap.html
3. *Journal of Physics D–Applied*
   http://www.ioppublishing.com/Journals/Catalogue/JD/
4. *International Journal of Modern Physics B*
   http://www.wspc.co.uk/wspc/Journals/ijmpb/ijmpb.html

GENERAL APPLIED PHYSICS–
REVIEW, SYMPOSIA AND METHODS

• *Topics in Applied Physics*
   http://www.springer.de/cgi-bin/search_book.pl?link=/link/service/
   svcat/deutsch2/series/560.html

APPLIED PHYSICS–
SOLID STATE ELECTRONICS AND ELECTRONIC MATERIALS
SCIENCE ORIGINAL RESEARCH–
MIXED-FORMAT AND LETTERS JOURNALS

1. *Solid State Ionics*
   http://www.elsevier.nl/locate/inca/521129
2. *Philosophical Magazine B*
   http://www.tandf.co.uk/JNLS/PHMb.HTM
3. *Semiconductor Science & Technology*
   http://www.iop.org/Journals/ss
4. *Journal of Magnetism & Magnetic Materials*
   http://www.elsevier.nl/locate/inca/521182
5. *Solid State Electronics*
   http://www.elsevier.nl/locate/sse
6. *Solid State Technology*
   http://www.solid-state.com/
7. *Journal of Materials Science–Materials in Electronics*
   http://www.wkap.nl/journalhome.htm/0957-4522

APPLIED PHYSICS–
SOLID STATE ELECTRONICS
AND ELECTRONIC MATERIALS SCIENCE–
SUPERCONDUCTIVITY–
ORIGINAL RESEARCH–
MIXED-FORMAT AND LETTERS JOURNALS

1. *Superconductor Science & Technology*
   http://www.iop.org/Journals/su

2. *Journal of Superconductivity (Solid State Electronics)*
   http://www.elsevier.nl/locate/sse (see above section)
3. *Superlattices & Microstructures*
   http://www.hbuk.co.uk/ap/journals/sm.htm
4. *Applied Superconductivity*
   http://www.elsevier.nl/locate/inca/30993
   http://www.elsevier.nl/locate/sse (see above section)
5. *Physica D*
   http://www.elsevier.nl/locate/physd

APPLIED PHYSICS–
OPTICS–
ORIGINAL RESEARCH–
MIXED-FORMAT AND LETTERS JOURNALS

1. *Optics Letters*
   http://w3.osa.org/pub_svc/journals/ol/default5.htm
2. *Journal of The Optical Society of America A–Optics & Image Science*
   http://www.osa.org/pub_svc/journals/josaa/default1.htm
3. *Journal of Modern Optics*
   http://www.tandf.co.uk/JNLS/mop.htm
4. *Optics Communications*
   http://www.lfw.com/www/lfw/publist.htm
5. *Applied Optics*
   http://www.osa.org/pub_svc/journals/ao/default1.htm
6. *Journal of Optics*
   http://www.ioppublishing.com/Journals/jo
7. *Optics & Spectroscopy*
   http://www.osa.org/pub_svc/journals/other/default4.htm

APPLIED PHYSICS–
OPTICS–
REVIEW, METHODS, AND SYMPOSIA

1. *Progress in Optics*
   http://www.elsevier.nl/locate/isbn/0444867368
2. *SPIE Proceedings–Society of Photo-Optical Instrumentation Engineers Proceedings*
   http://www.spie.org/web/abstracts/abstracts_home.html

APPLIED PHYSICS–
OPTICS–
LASERS–
ORIGINAL RESEARCH–
MIXED-FORMAT AND LETTERS JOURNAL

1. *Journal of Lightwave Technology*
   http://www.ieee.org/pubs/transjour/j_lt/
2. *Quantum and Semiclassical Optics: Journal of the European Optical Society Part B*
   http://www.iop.org/journals/qs
3. *IEEE Photonics Technology Letters*
   http://www.ieee.org/pub_preview/ptl_toc.html
4. *Journal of Nonlinear Optical Physics & Materials*
5. *Laser Physics*
6. *Optics & Lasers in Engineering*
   http://www.lfw.com/www/lfw/publist.htm
7. *Optics & Laser Technology*
   http://www.elsevier.nl/locate/optlastec
8. *Journal of Laser Applications*

APPLIED PHYSICS–
OPTICS–
LASERS–
REVIEW, SYMPOSIA AND METHODS

- *Laser Focus World*
  http://www.lfw.com/

APPLIED PHYSICS–
GENERAL MEDICAL PHYSICS AND GENERAL IMAGING–
ORIGINAL RESEARCH–
MIXED-FORMAT AND LETTERS

- *Medical Physics*
  http://www.aip.org/journals_program/html/medphys.html
- *IEEE Transactions on Medical Imaging*
  http://www.ieee.org/pub_preview/mi_toc.html
- *Physics in Medicine & Biology*
  http://www.iop.org/Journals/pb

APPLIED PHYSICS–
TOPICS IN MEDICAL PHYSICS–
SPECIFIC IMAGING METHODS, NUCLEAR METHODS
AND RADIATION HAZARDS–
ORIGINAL RESEARCH–
MIXED-FORMAT AND LETTERS JOURNALS

- *Health Physics: The Radiation Protection Journal*
  http://lww.com/store/products?0017-9078
- *Magnetic Resonance in Medicine*
  http://www.wwilkins.com/MAG/
- *JMRI–Journal of Magnetic Resonance Imaging*
  http://www.wwilkins.com/MRI/
- *Ultrasound in Medicine & Biology*
- *Journal of Computer Assisted Tomography*
  http://lww.com/store/products?0363-8715
- *Ultrasonic Imaging*
  http://www.idealibrary.com/cgi-bin/fai.idealibrary.
  com_8100/fetch/0103015e040401010f0500030d5303530
  f000001565b50030b0c5452095b54500557095401025d0004055c0508
  5704 0b0802045a0003/130:1114:1028/48
- *NMR Biomedicine Nuc. Mag. Resonance*
- *Journal of Nuclear Medicine*
  http://www.snm.org/jnm.html
- *American Journal of Roentgenology*
  http://www.arrs.org/ajr/
- *Radiology*
  http://www.rsna.org/REG/publications/rad/rad.html
- *Radiation and Environmental Biophysics*
- *Radiation Protection Dosimetry*

APPLIED PHYSICS–
MEDICAL PHYSICS–
REVIEW, SYMPOSIUM AND METHODS

- *Seminars in Nuclear Medicine*
- *Radiological Clinics of North America*
- *Seminars in Ultrasound & Clinical Tomography*
- *Critical Reviews in Diagnostic Imaging*

GENERAL LIFE SCIENCES AND GENERAL SCIENCE JOURNALS WITH A PREPONDERANCE OF BIOLOGY– ORIGINAL RESEARCH– MIXED-FORMAT AND LETTERS JOURNALS

- *Nature*
  http://second.nature.com/
- *Science*
  http://science-mag.aaas.org/
- *FASEB Journal*
  http://www.fasebj.org/
- *Proceedings of the National Academy of Science*
  http://www.pnas.org/
- *Proceedings of the Royal Society of London B-Biological Sciences*
  http://www.pubs.royalsoc.ac.uk/publish/pro_bs/index.htm
- *Experientia*

GENERAL LIFE SCIENCES–REVIEW, SYMPOSIA AND METHODS

- *Current Biology*
  http://biomednet.com/gateways/cub
- *Bioessays*
  http://www.bioessays.demon.co.uk/
- *Biological Reviews*
  http://www.cup.cam.ac.uk/scripts/webjrn1.asp?mnemonic=bre
- *Quarterly Review of Biology*
  http://www.journals.uchicago.edu/QRB/home.html
- *Bioscience*
  http://www.aibs.org/latitude/latpublications.html

GENERAL BIOCHEMISTRY AND MOLECULAR BIOLOGY– ORIGINAL RESEARCH– MIXED-FORMAT AND LETTERS JOURNALS

1. *Journal of Biological Chemistry*
   http://www.jbc.org/
2. *EMBO Journal*
   http://www.emboj.org/
3. *Nature Structural Biology*
   http://structbio.nature.com/
4. *Journal of Molecular Biology*
   http://www.jbc.org/

5. *Biochemistry*
   http://pubs.acs.org/journals/bichaw/index.html
6. *Biochemical Journal*
   http://bj.portlandpress.co.uk/
7. *European Journal of Biochemistry*
   http://link.springer.de/link/service/journals/00225/index.htm
8. *FEBS Letters*
   http://www.elsevier.com/inca/publications/store/5/0/6/0/8/5/index. htm
9. *Biochemical & Biophysical Research Communications*
   http://www.apnet.com/www/journal/rc.htm
10. *Archives of Biochemistry & Biophysics*
    http://www.apnet.com/www/journal/bb.htm

GENERAL BIOCHEMISTRY AND MOLECULAR BIOLOGY– REVIEW, SYMPOSIA AND METHODS

1. *Annual Review of Biochemistry*
   http://biomedical.annualreviews.org/current/1.shtml/
2. *Trends in Biochemical Sciences*
   http://www.oup.co.uk/proeng/
3. *Annual Review of Biophysics and Biomolecular Structure*
   http://biomedical.annualreviews.org/current/2.shtml/
4. *Current Opinion in Structural Biology*
   http://biomednet.com/gateways/stb
5. *Analytical Biochemistry*
   http://www.apnet.com/www/journal/ab.htm
6. *Clinical Chemistry*
   http://www.bio.net/bioarchives/BIO-JOURNALS/CLIN_CHEM/

SUBSTANCE SPECIALTIES IN BIOCHEMISTRY AND MOLECULAR BIOLOGY– PROTEINS AND PRECURSORS– ALL FORMATS

- *Protein Profile*
- *Protein Science*
  http://www.prosci.uci.edu/
- *Proteins*
  http://www.interscience.wiley.com/jpages/0887-3585/
- *Protein Engineering*
  http://www.oup.co.uk/proeng/

- *Peptide Research*
- *Amino Acids*
  http://link.springer.de/link/service/journals/00726/index.htm
- *Advances in Enzymology and Related Areas of Molecular Biology Interscience*
- *Advances in Protein Research*
- *Methods: A Companion to Methods in Enzymology*
  http://www.apnet.com/www/journal/me.htm

SUBSTANCE SPECIALTIES IN BIOCHEMISTRY AND MOLECULAR BIOLOGY– NUCLEIC ACIDS– ALL FORMATS

- *Nucleic Acids Research*
  http://www.oup.co.uk/nar/
- *RNA*
  http://www.cup.cam.ac.uk/journals/rna/rna.html
- *Progress in Nucleic Acids Research & Molecular Biology*
- *PCR Methods & Applications*
  http://www.genome.org

SUBSTANCE SPECIALTIES IN BIOCHEMISTRY AND MOLECULAR BIOLOGY– LIPIDS– ALL FORMATS

- *Lipids*
  http://www.aocs.org/lipids1.htm
- *Journal of Lipid Research*
  http://www.jlr.org/
- *Chemistry & Physics of Lipids*
  http://www.elsevier.nl/inca/publications/
  store/5/0/6/0/3/6/?menu=cont.astc0009308+4
- *Advances in Lipid Research*
- *Progress in Lipid Research*
  http://www.elsevier.nl/locate/plipres

SUBSTANCE SPECIALTIES IN BIOCHEMISTRY AND MOLECULAR BIOLOGY– CARBOHYDRATES– ALL FORMATS

- *Journal of Carbohydrate Chemistry*
  http://www.dekker.com/cgi-bin/webdbc/md/detail.
  htx?d_cat_id=0732-8303
- *Starch–Starke*
  http://www.wiley-vch.de/vch/journals/2041.html
- *Advances in Carbohydrate Chemistry and Biochemistry*
  http://chem-www.mps.ohio-state.edu/~lowary/advances.html
- *Glycobiology*
  http://www.oup.co.uk/glycob/contents/
- *Glycoconjugate Journal*
  http://www.wkap.nl/journalhome.htm/0282-0080

GENERAL CELL BIOLOGY– ORIGINAL RESEARCH– MIXED-FORMAT AND LETTERS JOURNALS

1. *Cell*
   http://www.cell.com/
2. *Journal of Cell Biology*
   http://www.jcb.org/
3. *Molecular & Cell Biology*
   http://mcb.asm.org/
4. *Molecular Biology of the Cell*
   http://www.ascb.org/ascb/mbc/mbcf.html
5. *Journal of Cell Science*
   http://www.biologists.com/JCS/
6. *Experimental Cell Research*
   http://www.apnet.com/www/journal/ex.htm
7. *European Journal of Cell Biology*
8. *DNA: A Journal of Cell Biology*
   http://www.liebertpub.com/new/pubs/10445498.htm

GENERAL CELL BIOLOGY–REVIEW, SYMPOSIA AND METHODS

- *Annual Review of Cell & Developmental Biology*
  http://biomedical.annualreviews.org/current/3.shtml/

- *Current Opinion in Cell Biology*
  http://biomednet.com/library/cel
- *Trends in Cell Biology*
  http://www.elsevier.com/inca/publications/store/4/2/2/5/5/2/
  index.htm
- *International Review of Cytology*
- *Methods in Cell Biology*

CELL BIOLOGY– CELLULAR PHYSIOLOGY AND CULTURE– ORIGINAL RESEARCH– MIXED-FORMAT AND LETTERS JOURNALS

1. *Journal of Cellular Physiology*
   http://www2.interscience.wiley.com/issn/0021-9541/
2. *American Journal of Physiology: Cell Physiology*
   http://ajpcell.physiology.org/
3. *Journal of Cellular Biochemistry*
   http://www.interscience.wiley.com/jpages/0730-2312/
4. *In Vitro: Cell & Developmental Biology* (animal)
   http://www.sivb.org/pubs/publicat.htm
5. *In Vitro: Cell & Developmental Biology* (plant)
   http://www.sivb.org/pubs/publicat.htm
6. *Cell Physiology and Biochemistry*
   http://www.karger.ch/journals/cpb/cpbdes.htm

TOPICAL SPECIALTIES IN CELL BIOLOGY– CYTOLOGY, HISTOLOGY AND STAIN TECHNOLOGY

1. *Journal of Histochemistry & Cytochemistry*
   http://www.jhc.org/
2. *Cell & Tissue Research*
   http://www.bio.net/bioarchives/BIO
3. *Histochemistry & Cell Biology*
   http://www.bio.net/bioarchives/BIO
4. *Histochemical Journal*
   http://www.wkap.nl/journalhome.htm/0018-2214

DEVELOPMENTAL BIOLOGY–
ORIGINAL RESEARCH–
MIXED-FORMAT AND LETTERS JOURNALS

1. *Genes and Development*
   http://www.genesdev.org/
2. *Developmental Biology*
   http://www.academicpress.com/db
3. *Development*
   http://www.biologists.com/Development/
4. *Genes, Development and Evolution*
   http://gort.ucsd.edu/newjour/http://link.springer.de/link/service/
   journals/00 427/index.htm
5. *Developmental Dynamics*
   http://www.interscience.wiley.com/jpages/1058-8388/

TOPICAL SPECIALTIES IN DEVELOPMENTAL BIOLOGY–
DEVELOPMENTAL PATHOLOGIES AND TUMOR BIOLOGY

* *Teratology*
  http://www2.interscience.wiley.com/issn/0040-3709/
* *Cell Growth & Differentiation*
  http://www.aacr.org/cllgrwt.htm
* *Tumor Biology*
  http://www.karger.ch/journals/tbi/tbides.htm
* *Teratogenesis, Carcinogenesis, Mutagenesis*
  http://www.interscience.wiley.com/jpages/0270-3211/
* *Oncogene*
  http://www.stockton-press.co.uk/onc/http://www.stockton-
  press.co.uk/onc/
* *Journal of Craniofacial Genetics & Developmental Biology*
* *Clinical Dysmorphology*
  http://hermes.chaphall.co.uk/cd.html

DEVELOPMENTAL BIOLOGY–
REVIEW, SYMPOSIA AND METHODS

* *Current Topics in Developmental Biology*

GENERAL GENETICS–
ORIGINAL RESEARCH–
MIXED-FORMAT AND LETTERS JOURNALS

1. *Nature Genetics*
   http://genetics.nature.com/

2. *Genetics*
   http://www.genetics.org/
3. *Molecular & General Genetics*
   http://link.springer.de/link/service/journals/00438/index.htm
4. *Somatic Cell & Molecular Genetics*
   http://www.plenum.com/title.cgi?2012
5. *Chromosoma*
   http://www.springer-ny.com/lifesci/journals/chromosoma.html
6. *Gene*
   http://www.elsevier.nl/locate/gene

GENERAL GENETICS–REVIEW, SYMPOSIA AND METHODS

- *Annual Review of Genetics*
  http://www.annualreviews.org/ibbin/ibGate.
  exe?LOADPAGE=%2fARI%2fpub s%2falpha.htm
- *Trends in Genetics*
  http://www.elsevier.nl/locate/tig

GENERAL GENETICS–SEQUENCING STUDIES

- *Genomics*
  http://www.apnet.com/www/journal/ge.htm
- *Mammalian Genome*
  http://www.springer-ny.com/lifesci/journals/mammalian_
  genome.html
- *DNA Sequence*
- *Genetic Analysis–Biomolecular Engineering*
  http://www.elsevier.nl/locate/geneanabioeng

GENETICS–
GENERAL MUTATION RESEARCH–
MIXED-FORMAT AND LETTERS

1. *Environmental & Molecular Mutagenesis*
   http://www2.interscience.wiley.com/issn/0893-6692/
2. *Mutagenesis*
   http://www.oup.co.uk/mutage/
3. *Mutation Research*
   http://www1.elsevier.nl/journals/mutres/menu.htm
4. *Molecular Carcinogenesis*
   http://www.interscience.wiley.com/jpages/0899-1987/

GENETICS–
GENERAL CLINICAL GENETICS–
ORIGINAL RESEARCH–
MIXED-FORMAT AND LETTERS

1. *American Journal of Human Genetics*
   http://www.journals.uchicago.edu/AJHG/journal/
2. *American Journal of Medical Genetics*
   http://www2.interscience.wiley.com/issn/0148-7299/
3. *Annals of Human Genetics*
   http://www.cup.org/journals/jnlscat/hge/hge.html
4. *European Journal of Human Genetics*
   http://www.karger.ch/journals/ehg/ehgdes.htm
5. *Human Genetics*
   http://link.springer.de/link/service/journals/00439/index.htm

GENETICS–
HUMAN MUTATION RESEARCH AND GENE THERAPY

1. *Human Gene Therapy*
   http://www.liebertpub.com/new/pubs/10430342.htm
2. *Gene Therapy*
   http://www.stockton-press.co.uk/gt/index.html
3. *Human Molecular Genetics*
   http://www.oup.co.uk/hmg/
4. *Human Mutation*
   http://journals.wiley.com/wilcat-bin/ops/
   ID0159376/1059-7794/prod
5. *Journal of Molecular Medicine*
   http://link.springer.de/link/service/journals/00109/index.htm
6. *Disease Markers*
   http://www.iospress.nl/html/node415.html

GENETICS IN AGRICULTURE–
ORIGINAL RESEARCH–
MIXED-FORMAT AND LETTERS

1. *Journal of Heredity*
   http://www.oup.co.uk/jnls/list/jhered/contents/
2. *Theoretical & Applied Genetics*
   http://link.springer.de/link/service/journals/00122/index.htm
3. *Animal Genetics*
   http://www.blacksci.co.uk/products/journals/agen.htm

GENETICS IN EVOLUTION–
ORIGINAL RESEARCH, MIXED-FORMAT AND LETTERS

1. *Molecular & Phylogenetic Evolution*
   http://www.apnet.com/www/journal/fy.htm
2. *Journal of Molecular Evolution*
   http://link.springer.de/link/service/journals/00239/index.htm
3. *Biochemical Genetics*
   http://www.plenum.com/title.cgi?2067
4. *Molecular Biology and Evolution*
   http://apt.allenpress.com/cgi-bin/omisapi.dll/
   apt?request=get-journal&journal=mbev

GENERAL MICROBIOLOGY AND BACTERIOLOGY–
ORIGINAL RESEARCH–
MIXED-FORMAT AND LETTERS

1. *Journal of Bacteriology*
   http://jb.asm.org/
2. *Molecular Microbiology*
   http://www.blackwell-science.com/products/journals/mole.htm
3. *Microbiology*
   http://www.socgenmicrobiol.org.uk/mic_main.htm
4. *Archives of Microbiology*
   http://link.springer.de/link/service/journals/00203/index.htm
5. *FEMS Microbiology Letters*
   http://www.elsevier.nl/inca/publications/store/5/0/6/0/5/8/
6. *Antonie Von Leewenhoek J. Microbiology*
   http://www.wkap.nl/journalhome.htm/0003-6072
7. *Canadian Journal of Microbiology*
   http://www.cisti.nrc.ca/cisti/journals/tocmicr.html

GENERAL MICROBIOLOGY AND BACTERIOLOGY–
REVIEW, SYMPOSIA AND METHODS

1. *MMBR (Microbiology & Molecular Biology Reviews, American Society of Microbiology)*
   http://mmbr.asm.org/
2. *Annual Review of Microbiology*
   http://www.annualreviews.org/ibbin/ibGate.
   exe?LOADPAGE=%2fARI%2f pubs%2falpha.htm
3. *Critical Reviews of Microbiology*
   http://www.crcpress.com/cgi-bin/SoftCart.exe/jour/catalog/
   micrb.htm?E+storecrc

4. *Journal of Microbiological Methods*
   http://www.elsevier.nl/inca/publications/store/5/0/6/0/3/4/

APPLIED, ENVIRONMENTAL AND FOOD MICROBIOLOGY–MIXED-FORMAT AND LETTERS JOURNALS

1. *Applied & Environmental Microbiology*
   http://aem.asm.org/
2. *Microbial Ecology*
   http://link.springer.de/link/service/journals/00248/index.htm
3. *Journal of Applied Bacteriology*
   http://marlin.utmb.edu/~jwhill/
4. *International Journal of Food Microbiology*
   http://www.elsevier.nl/inca/publications/store/5/0/5/5/1/4/
5. *Food Microbiology*
   http://www.academicpress.com/foodmicro

APPLIED, ENVIRONMENTAL AND FOOD MICROBIOLOGY–REVIEW, SYMPOSIA AND METHODS

- *Advances in Applied Microbiology*
- *Advances in Microbial Physiology*
- *Advances in Microbial Ecology*
  http://www.plenum.com/title.cgi?0306455595

MICROBIOLOGY IN MEDICINE–ORIGINAL RESEARCH–MIXED-FORMAT AND LETTERS

1. *Journal of Infectious Disease*
   http://www.journals.uchicago.edu/JID/home.html
2. *Infection & Immunity*
   http://iai.asm.org/
3. *Journal of Clinical Microbiology*
   http://jcm.asm.org/
4. *Clinical Infectious Disease*
   http://www.journals.uchicago.edu/CID/home.html
5. *Journal of Medical Microbiology*
6. *Medical Microbiology & Immunity*
   http://link.springer.de/link/service/journals/00430/index.htm
7. *Diagnostic Microbiology & Infectious Disease*
   http://www.elsevier.nl/inca/publications/store/5/0/5/7/5/9/

8. *FEMS Immunology & Medical Microbiology*
    http://www.elsevier.nl/inca/publications/store/5/0/6/0/1/9/
9. *European Journal of Clinical Microbiology*
    http://link.springer.de/link/service/journals/10096/index.htm
10. *Journal of Infection*
    http://www.hbuk.co.uk/wbs/jin/

MICROBIOLOGY IN MEDICINE– REVIEW, SYMPOSIA AND METHODS

*   *Infectious Agents & Disease–Reviews, Issues and Commentary*
*   *Infectious Disease Clinics of North America*
    http://167.208.232.26/catalog/wbs-prod.pl?0891-5520
*   *Current Opinion in Infectious Diseases*
    http://www.biomednet.com/library/rapid/display.exe?jcode=jinf

MICROBIOLOGY IN MEDICINE– ANTIBIOTICS– ORIGINAL RESEARCH– MIXED-FORMAT AND LETTERS

*   *Antimicrobial Agents & Chemotherapy*
    http://aac.asm.org/
*   *Journal of Antimicrobial Chemotherapy*
    http://www.oup.co.uk/janmic/
*   *Journal of Antibiotics*
*   *Agents and Actions*

MICROBIOLOGY IN MEDICINE– MICROBIAL EPIDEMIOLOGY AND INFECTION CONTROL

1. *American Journal of Public Health*
    http://www.apha.org/news/publications/Journal/AJPH2.html
2. *American Journal of Tropical Medicine & Hygiene*
    http://www.astmh.org/journal.html
3. *Journal of Clinical Epidemiology*
    http://www.elsevier.nl/inca/publications/store/5/2/5/4/7/2/
4. *Epidemiology & Infection*
    http://www.cup.cam.ac.uk/journals/jnlscat/hyg/hyg.html
5. *Infection Control & Hospital Epidemiology*
    http://www.slackinc.com/general/iche/ichehome.htm

6. *American Journal of Infection Control*
   http://www1.mosby.com/mosbyscripts/mosby.
   dll?action=searchDB&search DBfor=home&ID=ic
7. *Journal of Hospital Infection*
   http://www.hbuk.co.uk/wbs/jhi/
8. *Bulletin of the World Health Organization*
   http://www.who.int/pub/
9. *Public Health Reports*

MICROBIOLOGY–
GENERAL VIROLOGY–
ORIGINAL RESEARCH–
MIXED-FORMAT AND LETTERS JOURNALS

1. *Journal of Virology*
   http://jvi.asm.org/
2. *Virology*
   http://www.apnet.com/www/journal/vy.htm
3. *Journal of General Virology*
   http://www.socgenmicrobiol.org.uk/vir_main.htm
4. *Archives of Virology*
   http://link.springer.de/link/service/journals/00705/index.htm
5. *Virus Research*
   http://www.elsevier.nl/inca/publications/store/5/0/6/0/5/4/

MICROBIOLOGY–
GENERAL VIROLOGY–
REVIEW, SYMPOSIA AND METHODS

* *Advances in Virus Research*
* *Seminars in Virology*
   http://www.hbuk.co.uk/ap/journals/vi/
* *Journal of Virologica Methods*
   http://www.elsevier.nl/inca/publications/store/5/0/6/0/8/0/

VIROLOGY–
VIRUSES IN MEDICINE–
ORIGINAL RESEARCH–
MIXED-FORMAT AND LETTERS JOURNALS

* *AIDS*
   http://www.aidsonline.com/

- *Journal of Acquired Immunodeficiency Syndrome*
  http://www.ccspublishing.com/j_aids.htm
- *AIDS Research & Human Retroviruses*
- *Journal of Medical Virology*
  http://www.interscience.wiley.com/jpages/0146-6615/
- *Antivirus Research*
  http://www.elsevier.nl/inca/publications/store/5/2/1/8/5/2/

VIROLOGY–
VIRUSES IN MEDICINE–
REVIEW, SYMPOSIA AND METHODS

- *Review of Medical Virology*
  http://www.interscience.wiley.com/jpages/1052-9276/

GENERAL IMMUNOLOGY–
ORIGINAL RESEARCH–
MIXED-FORMAT AND LETTERS JOURNALS

1. *Immunity*
   http://www.immunity.com/
2. *Journal of Immunology*
   http://www.jimmunol.org/
3. *European Journal of Immunology*
   http://www2.interscience.wiley.com/issn/0014-2980/
4. *Immunology*
   http://www.blackwell-science.com/products/journals/imm.htm
5. *International Immunology*
   http://www.oup.co.uk/intimm/

GENERAL IMMUNOLOGY–REVIEW, SYMPOSIA AND METHODS

1. *Immunology Today*
   http://www.elsevier.nl/inca/publications/store/4/0/5/9/1/4/
2. *Current Opinion in Immunology*
   http://www.biomednet.com/gateways/imm
3. *Advances in Immunology*
4. *Immunological Reviews*
   http://www.munksgaard-service.dk/munksgaard/tidsskrifter.nsf/
   bc60b2fb96a45473412565b60031388f/58d69c9af42b5b90412566
   4b0048523c?OpenDocument

5. *Critical Reviews in Immunology*
   http://www.begellhouse.com/crim/crim.html
6. *Springer Seminars in Immunology*
   http://link.springer.de/link/service/journals/00281/index.htm
7. *Journal of Immunological Methods*
   http://www.elsevier.nl/inca/publications/store/5/0/6/0/2/2/

IMMUNOLOGY–
GENERAL CLINICAL IMMUNOLOGY–
ORIGINAL RESEARCH–
MIXED-FORMAT AND LETTERS JOURNALS

1. *Journal of Experimential Medicine*
   http://www.jem.org/
2. *Clinical & Experimental Immunology*
   http://www.blackwell-science.com/products/journals/cei.htm
3. *Clinical Immunology & Immunopathology*
   http://www.apnet.com/www/journal/ii.htm
4. *Human Immunology*
   http://www.elsevier.nl/inca/publications/store/5/0/5/7/6/3/
5. *Journal of Clinical Immunology*
   http://www.plenum.com/title.cgi?2046

CLINICAL IMMUNOLOGY–
OTHER TOPICAL SPECIALTIES
IN CLINICAL IMMUNOLOGY–
MIXED-FORMAT AND LETTERS JOURNALS

- *Immunogenetics*
  http://link.springer.de/link/service/journals/00251/index.htm
- *Tissue Antigens*
  http://www.munksgaard-service.dk/munksgaard/tidsskrifter.nsf/
  bc60b2fb96a45473412565b60031388f/c9c410391799d28d4125665d0
  03d2d29?OpenDocument
- *Transplantation*
  http://www.wwilkins.com/TP/
- *Bone Marrow Transplantation*
  http://www.stockton-press.co.uk/bmt/index.html
- *Vaccine*
  http://www.elsevier.com/inca/publications/store/3/0/5/2/1/
- *Journal of Inflammation*
  http://www.interscience.wiley.com/jpages/1078-7852/

- *Journal of Autoimmunity*
  http://www.apnet.com/www/journal-uk/au.htm
- *Lupus*
  http://www.stockton-press.co.uk/lup/

CLINICAL IMMUNOLOGY–
ALLERGY–
ORIGINAL RESEARCH–
MIXED-FORMAT AND LETTERS JOURNALS

1. *Journal of Allergy & Clinical Immunology*
   http://www1.mosby.com/mosbyscripts/mosby.
   dll?action=searchDB&searchDBfor=home&id=ai
2. *Clinical & Experimental Allergy*
   http://www.blacksci.co.uk/~cgilib/jnlpage.
   bin?Journal=cea&File=cea&Page=aims
3. *Allergy*
   http://www.munksgaard-service.dk/munksgaard/tidsskrifter.nsf/
   bc60b2fb96a45473412565b60031388f/d59ed45029b3829d412566
   60003ee4a8?OpenDocument

GENERAL PHYSIOLOGY–
ORIGINAL RESEARCH–
MIXED-FORMAT–
LETTERS JOURNALS

1. *Journal of General Physiology*
   http://www.jgp.org/
2. *American Journal of Physiology*
   http://ajpcon.physiology.org/
3. *Journal of Physiology*
   http://physiology.cup.cam.ac.uk/JPhysiol/
4. *Pflugers Archiv–European Journal of Physiology*
   http://link.springer.de/link/service/journals/00424/index.htm
5. *Canadian Journal of Physiology and Pharmacology*
   http://link.springer.de/link/service/journals/00424/index.htm
6. *Journal de Physiologie (Paris)*
   http://www.elsevier.com/locate/jphysparis

GENERAL PHYSIOLOGY–
REVIEW, SYMPOSIA AND METHODS JOURNALS

1. *Physiological Reviews*
   http://physrev.physiology.org/

2. *Annual Review of Physiology*
   http://biomedical.annualreviews.org/
3. *Review of Physiology, Biochemistry & Pharmacology*

GENERAL AND CLINICAL ORGAN SYSTEM PHYSIOLOGY– HEART AND CIRCULATORY– ORIGINAL RESEARCH– MIXED-FORMAT AND LETTERS JOURNALS

1. *Journal of the American College of Cardiology*
   http://www.elsevier.nl/locate/issn/07351097
2. *Cardiovascular Research*
   http://www.elsevier.nl/locate/cardiores
3. *Journal of Molecular & Cellular Cardiology*
   http://www.apnet.com/www/journal-uk/mc.htm
4. *American Journal of Cardiology*
   http://www.elsevier.com/locate/amjcard
5. *Heart (formerly the British Heart Journal)*
   http://www.bmjpg.com/data/hea.htm
6. *American Journal of Physiology–Heart & Circulatory*
   http://ajpheart.physiology.org/

GENERAL AND CLINICAL ORGAN SYSTEM PHYSIOLOGY– RESPIRATORY, EXERCISE AND OCCUPATIONAL

1. *American Journal of Respiratory & Critical Care Medicine*
   http://www.thoracic.org/ajrccm.html
   or http://ajrcmb.atsjournals.org/
2. *American Journal of Respiratory Cell & Molecular Biology*
   http://ajrcmb.atsjournals.org/
3. *European Respiratory Journal*
   http://www.munksgaard-service.dk/munksgaard/tidsskrifter.nsf/
4. *Thorax*
   http://www.bmjpg.com/data/tho.htm
5. *Chest*
   http://journals.chestnet.org/chest
   (Allen Pr.)
   http://www.allenpress.com/catalogue/index/chest/index.html
6. *Experimental Lung Research*
   http://www.tandf.co.uk/JNLS/elr.htm
7. *Respiration Physiology*
   http://www.elsevier.nl/locate/resphysiol

GENERAL AND CLINICAL ORGAN SYSTEM PHYSIOLOGY–
DIGESTIVE SYSTEM–
ORIGINAL RESEARCH–
MIXED-FORMAT AND LETTERS JOURNALS

1. *Gastroenterology*
   http://www.elsevier.nl/locate/gastroenterology
2. *Gut*
   http://www.gutjnl.com/
3. *American Journal of Gastroenterology*
   http://www.elsevier.com/locate/amjgastro
4. *Digestive Diseases & Sciences*
   http://www.digestive-diseases.com/
5. *American Journal of Physiology–Gastrointestinal & Liver*
   http://ajpgi.physiology.org/

TOPICAL SPECIALTIES IN DIGESTIVE SYSTEM PHYSIOLOGY

- *Hepatology*
  (Hepatology web site)
  http://www.hepatology.org/
  (WB Saunders)
  http://www.wbsaunders.com/catalog/wbs-prod. pl?0270-9139
- *Journal of Hepatology*
  http://www.munksgaard-service.dk/munksgaard/tidsskrifter.nsf/
- *Diseases of the Colon & Rectum*
  http://www.wwilkins.com/DCR/
- *Gastrointestinal Endoscopy*
  http://www1.mosby.com/periodicals/temp-med.html

GENERAL AND CLINICAL ORGAN SYSTEM PHYSIOLOGY–
RENAL AND ELECTROLYTE–
ORIGINAL RESEARCH–
MIXED-FORMAT AND LETTERS JOURNALS

1. *Journal of the American Society of Nephrology*
   http://www.wwilkins.com/JASN/
2. *Kidney International*
   http://www.blacksci.co.uk/products/journals/XKI.HTM
3. *American Journal of Kidney Diseases*
   http://www.ajkdjournal.org/

4. *Journal of Urology*
   http://www.wwilkins.com/urology/
5. *American Journal of Physiology–Renal & Electrolyte Physiology*
   http://ajprenal.physiology.org/
6. *Nephron*
   http://www.karger.ch/journals/nef/nefdes.htm
7. *Experimental Nephrology*
   http://www.karger.ch/journals/exn/exndes.htm

GENERAL AND CLINICAL ORGAN SYSTEM PHYSIOLOGY– REPRODUCTIVE– ORIGINAL RESEARCH– MIXED-FORMAT AND LETTERS JOURNALS

1. *Biology of Reproduction*
   http://www.biolreprod.org/
2. *Human Reproduction*
   http://www.oup.co.uk/humrep/
3. *Journal of Reproduction & Fertility*
   http://www.journals-of-reproduction.org.uk/
4. *Fertility & Sterility*
   http://www.asrm.org/profession/fertility/fspage.html
5. *American Journal of Obstetrics & Gynecology*
   http://www1.mosby.com/periodicals/temp-med.html
6. *Obstetrics & Gynecology*
   http://www.elsevier.nl/locate/issn/00297844

GENERAL AND CLINICAL ORGAN SYSTEM PHYSIOLOGY– ENDOCRINOLOGY– ORIGINAL RESEARCH– MIXED-FORMAT AND LETTERS JOURNALS

1. *Endocrinology* (E)
   http://endo.edoc.com/end/
2. *Journal of Clinical Endocrinology & Metabolism*
   http://endo.edoc.com/jcem/
3. *Molecular Endocrinology*
   http://endo.edoc.com/mend/
4. *Journal of Endocrinology*
   http://www.endocrinology.org/sfe/journals.htm#joe
5. *General & Comparative Endocrinology*
   http://www.apnet.com/www/journal/gc.htm

ENDOCRINOLOGY–
REVIEW, SYMPOSIA AND METHODS JOURNALS

1. *Endocrine Reviews*
   http://endo.edoc.com/edr/
2. *Trends in Endocrinology & Metabolism*
   http://www.elsevier.nl/locate/tem
3. *Recent Progress in Hormone Research*
   http://www.apcatalog.com/

GENERAL NEUROSCIENCE–ORIGINAL RESEARCH

1. *Journal of Neuroscience*
   http://www.allenpress.com/catalogue/index/j_of_neurosci/
   index.html
2. *Neuroscience*
   http://www.elsevier.nl/locate/neuroscience
3. *Journal of Neurobiology*
   http://www.interscience.wiley.com/jpages/0022-3034/
4. *EJN: The European Journal of Neuroscience*
   http://www.blacksci.co.uk/products/journals/EJN.HTM
5. *Journal of Neurophysiology*
   http://jn.physiology.org/
6. *Experimental Brain Research*
   http://link.springer.de/link/service/journals/00221/index.htm
7. *Brain Research Bulletin*
   http://www.elsevier.nl/locate/brainresbull
8. *Neuroscience Letters*
   http://www.elsevier.nl/locate/neulet
9. *Journal of Comparative Neurology*
   http://www.interscience.wiley.com/jpages/0021-9967/
10. *Experimental Neurology*
    http://www.apnet.com/www/journal/en.htm

GENERAL NEUROSCIENCE–
REVIEW, SYMPOSIA AND METHODS JOURNALS

1. *Annual Review of Neuroscience*
   http://biomedical.annualreviews.org/
2. *Trends in Neurosciences*
   http://www.elsevier.nl/locate/tins

3. *Behavioral & Brain Sciences*
   http://www.princeton.edu/~harnad/bbs.html
4. *Brain Research Reviews*
   http://www.elsevier.nl/locate/bri
5. *Neuroscience & Biobehavioral Reviews*
   http://www.elsevier.nl/locate/neubiorev
6. *Progress in Neurobiology*
   http://www.elsevier.nl/locate/pneurobio
7. *Current Opinion in Neurobiology*
   http://current-biology.com/journals.htm
8. *Critical Reviews in Neurobiology*
   http://www.begellhouse.com/crn/crn.html
9. *Current Opinion in Neurology*
   http://www.ramex.com/rs/rs-neuro.html
10. *Journal of Neuroscience Methods*
    http://www.elsevier.nl/locate/jneumeth

NEUROSCIENCE– GENERAL PSYCHOBIOLOGY– ORIGINAL RESEARCH– MIXED-FORMAT AND LETTERS JOURNALS

1. *Behavioral Neuroscience*
   http://www.apa.org/journals/bne.html
2. *Physiology & Behavior*
   http://www.elsevier.nl/locate/physbeh
3. *Psychobiology*
   http://www.sig.net/~psysoc/pbi.htm
4. *Behavioural Brain Research*
   http://www.elsevier.nl/locate/bbr
5. *Neuropsychobiology*
   http://www.karger.ch/journals/nps/npsdes.htm

NEUROCIENCE–PSYCHOBIOLOGY–NEUROENDOCRINOLOGY

1. *Journal of Neuroendocrinology*
   http://www.blacksci.co.uk/products/journals/jneur.htm
2. *Hormones & Behavior*
   http://www.apnet.com/www/journal/hb.htm
3. *Neuroendocrinology*
   http://www.karger.ch/journals/nen/nendes.htm

4. *Psychoneuroendocrinology*
   http://www.elsevier.nl/locate/psyneuen
5. *Neuroendocrinology Letters*

REVIEWS, SYMPOSIA AND METHODS IN NEUROENDOCRINOLOGY

1. *Frontiers in Neuroendocrinology*
   http://www.apnet.com/www/journal/fn.htm

NEUROSCIENCE– DRUGS, BRAIN AND BEHAVIOR– ORIGINAL RESEARCH– MIXED-FORMAT AND LETTERS JOURNALS

1. *Journal of Clinical Psychopharmacology*
   http://www.wwilkins.com/JCP/
2. *Psychopharmacology*
   http://link.springer.de/link/service/journals/00213/index.htm
3. *Neuropharmacology*
   http://www.elsevier.nl/locate/neuropharm
4. *Pharmacology, Biochemistry & Behavior*
   http://www.elsevier.nl/locate/pharmbiochembeh
5. *Behavioral Pharmacology*
   http://lww.com/store/products?0955-8810
6. *Progress in Neuro-Psychopharmacology & Biological Psychiatry*
   http://www.elsevier.nl/locate/pnpbp
7. *European Neuropsychopharmacology*
   http://www.elsevier.nl/locate/euroneuro

NEUROSCIENCE– COGNITIVE NEUROPSYCHOLOGY– ORIGINAL RESEARCH– MIXED-FORMAT AND LETTERS JOURNALS

1. *Journal of Cognitive Neuroscience*
   http://mitpress.mit.edu/journal-home.tcl?issn=0898929X
2. *Cognitive Brain Research*
   http://www.elsevier.nl/locate/cogbri
3. *Neuropsychology*
   http://www.apa.org/journals/neujnlde.html

4. *Journal of Neuropsychiatry & Clinical Neurosciences*
   http://www.appi.org/jnptoc.html
5. *Brain & Cognition*
   http://www.apnet.com/www/journal/br.htm

NEUROSCIENCE–
MOLECULAR AND CELLULAR APPROACHES–
ORIGINAL RESEARCH–
MIXED-FORMAT AND LETTERS JOURNALS

1. *Neuron*
   http://www.neuron.org/
2. *Journal of Neurochemistry*
   http://www.jneurochem.com/
3. *MCN: Molecular & Cellular Neuroscience*
   http://www.apnet.com/www/journal/cn.htm
4. *Molecular Neurobiology*
   http://www.humanapress.com/journals/
5. *Cellular & Molecular Neurobiology*
   http://www.plenum.com/title.cgi?2064

NEUROSCIENCE–CLINICAL NEUROLOGY

1. *Annals of Neurology*
   http://lww.com/store/products?0364-5134
2. *Journal of Neuropathology & Experimental Neurology*
   http://www.allenpress.com/catalogue/index/j_of_neuropath/
   index.html
3. *Neurology*
   http://www.aan.com/journal_f.html
4. *Archives of Neurology*
   http://www.ama-assn.org/public/journals/neur/neurhome.htm
5. *Brain: A Journal of Neurology*
   http://www.oup.co.uk/brainj/

TOPICAL SPECIALTIES IN CLINICAL NEUROLOGY

1. *Schizophrenia Bulletin*
   http://www.medscape.com/govmt/NIMH/SchizophreniaBulletin/
   public/about.SB.html

2. *Pain*
   Http://www.elsevier.nl/locate/painonline
3. *Stroke*
   http://stroke.ahajournals.org/
4. *Dementia & Geriatric Cognitive Disorders*
   http://www.karger.ch/journals/dem/demdes.htm
5. *Epilepsia*
   http://www.epilepsia.com/
6. *Movement Disorders*
   http://www.mssm.edu/neurology/movejrnl/movejrnl.html
7. *Sleep*
   http://www.journalsleep.org/
8. *Headache*
   http://www.allenpress.com/catalogue/index/headache/index.html
9. *American Journal of Neuroradiology*
   http://www.asnr.org/ajnr/
10. *Developmental Medicine & Child Neurology*
    http://www.cup.org/journals/jnlscat/dmc/dmc.html
11. *Neuromuscular Disorders*
    http://www.elsevier.nl/locate/nmd
12. *Neuroepidemiology*
    http://www.karger.ch/journals/ned/neddes.htm
13. *Spine*
    http://journals.lrpub.com/spine/

GENERAL AND ANIMAL ECOLOGY–
ORIGINAL RESEARCH–
MIXED-FORMAT AND LETTERS JOURNALS

1. *American Naturalist*
   http://www.journals.uchicago.edu/AN/home.html
2. *Ecology*
   http://www.allenpress.com/catalogue/index/ecology/index.html
3. *Ecological Monographs*
   http://www.allenpress.com/catalogue/index/ecol_mono/index.html
4. *Journal of Animal Ecology*
   http://www.blacksci.co.uk/products/journals/JANIM.HTM
5. *Oecologia*
   http://link.springer.de/link/service/journals/00442/index.htm
6. *Oikos*
   http://www.munksgaard-service.dk/munksgaard/tidsskrifter.nsf/

7. American Midland Naturalist
   http://www.allenpress.com/catalogue/index/am_midland_nat/index.html
8. *Canadian Field-Naturalist*
   http://www.achilles.net/ofnc/cfn.htm
9. *Great Basin Naturalist*
   http://lib.byu.edu/~nms/

ECOLOGY–
PLANT ECOLOGY AND BIOGEOGRAPHY–
ORIGINAL RESEARCH–
MIXED-FORMAT AND LETTERS JOURNALS

1. *Journal of Ecology*
   http://www.blacksci.co.uk/products/journals/JECOL.HTM
2. *Journal of Vegetation Science*
   http://www2.passagen.se/opulus.com/jvspage/jvshome.htm
3. *Ecography*
   http://www.munksgaard-service.dk/munksgaard/tidsskrifter.nsf/
4. *Journal of Biogeography*
   http://www.blacksci.co.uk/products/journals/JBIOG.HTM
5. *Plant Ecology* (formerly *Vegetatio*)
   http://www.wkap.nl/journalhome.htm/1385-0237

ECOLOGY–
BIOLOGICAL CONSERVATION AND WILDLIFE MANAGEMENT

1. *Ecological Applications*
   http://esa.sdsc.edu/public.htm#PubsA.html
2. *Conservation Biology*
   http://www.blacksci.co.uk/products/journals/XCONB.HTM
3. *Journal of Wildlife Management*
   http://www.allenpress.com/catalogue/index/wildlife_soc/index.html
4. Wildlife Monographs (supplements to *J. of Wildlife Management*)
   http://www.wildlife.org/monograph_list.html
5. *Journal of Applied Ecology*
   http://www.blacksci.co.uk/products/journals/JAPPL.HTM
6. *Biological Conservation*
   http://www.elsevier.com/locate/biocon
7. *Biodiversity and Conservation*
   http://www.wkap.nl/journalhome.htm/1385-0237
8. *Animal Conservation*
   http://www.cup.cam.ac.uk/scripts/webjrn1.asp?mnemonic=ani

BIOLOGICAL CONSERVATION AND WILDLIFE MANAGEMENT–REGIONAL OR ECOLOGICAL NICHE SPECIALTIES

1. *Polar Biology*
   http://link.springer.de/link/service/journals/00300/index.htm
2. *Biotropica*
   http://atb.botany.ufl.edu/index.html
3. *Wetlands*
   http://www.allenpress.com/catalogue/index/wetlands/index.html
4. *Journal of Tropical Ecology*
   http://www.cup.cam.ac.uk/journals/tro/
5. *Journal of Range Management*
   http://uvalde.tamu.edu/jrm/jrmhome.htm
6. *Journal of Arid Environments*
   http://www.apnet.com/www/journal-uk/ae.htm
7. *African Journal of Ecology*
   http://www.blacksci.co.uk/products/journals/AFJE.HTM
8. *Amazoniana*
   http://www.mpil-ploen.mpg.de/mpiltj.htm

AQUATIC BIOLOGY AND ECOLOGY–PREDOMINANTLY SALTWATER JOURNALS

1. *Limnology & Oceanography*
   http://aslo.org/lo/
2. *Marine Biology*
   http://link.springer.de/link/service/journals/00227/index.htm
3. *Marine Ecology–Progress Series*
   http://www.int-res.com/journals/meps/
4. *Journal of Experimental Marine Biology & Ecology*
   http://www.elsevier.nl/locate/jembe
5. *Biological Bulletin*
   http://www.mbl.edu/html/BB/
6. *Journal of the Marine Biological Association of the United Kingdom*
   http://www1.npm.ac.uk/mba/journal.htm

AQUATIC BIOLOGY AND ECOLOGY–FISHERIES, PREDOMINANTLY COMMERCIAL AND SALTWATER JOURNALS

1. *Canadian Journal of Fisheries & Aquatic Science*
   http://www.nrc.ca/cisti/journals/cjfas.html

2. *Fishery Bulletin–NOAA*
   http://spo.nwr.noaa.gov/
3. *Transactions of the American Fisheries Society*
   http://www.allenpress.com/catalogue/index/afs1/index.html
4. *ICES–Journal of Marine Science*
   http://www.apnet.com/www/journal-uk/jm.htm
5. *Fisheries Research*
   http://www.elsevier.nl/locate/fishres
6. *Fisheries Science*
   (Pub.) Japanese Society for Fisheries Science, Tokyo
7. *Fisheries* (F)
   http://www.fisheries.org/publications/journals/index.html#fisheries
   (Allen Pr.)
   http://www.allenpress.com/catalogue/index/afs1/index.html

AQUATIC BIOLOGY AND ECOLOGY–
PREDOMINANTLY FRESHWATER JOURNALS

1. *Limnology & Oceanography*
   http://aslo.org/lo/
2. *Freshwater Biology*
   http://www.blacksci.co.uk/products/journals/FWB.HTM
3. *Journal of the North American Benthological Society*
   JNABS: http://www.benthos.org/jnabs/index.asp Allen Pr.:
   http://www.allenpress.com/catalogue/index/j_of_n_am_benth_soc/
   index.html
4. *Hydrobiologia*
   http://www.wkap.nl/journalhome.htm/0018-8158
5. *Journal of Freshwater Ecology*
   Pub. Oikos Pub., La Crosse WI (oikosjourn@aol.com)

GENERAL PLANT SCIENCES–
GENERAL PLANT PHYSIOLOGY–
ORIGINAL RESEARCH–
MIXED-FORMAT AND LETTERS JOURNALS

1. *Plant Physiology* (PP)
   http://www.plantphysiol.org/
   (Allen Pr.)
   http://www.allenpress.com/catalogue/index/plant_physiology/
   index.html

2. *The Plant Journal*
   http://www.blacksci.co.uk/products/journals/TPJ.HTM
3. *Planta*
   http://link.springer.de/link/service/journals/00425/index.htm
4. *American Journal of Botany*
   AJB home http://www.botany.org/bsa/ajb/index.html
   (Allen Pr.)
   http://www.allenpress.com/catalogue/index/am_j_of_botany/index.
   html
5. *Journal of Experimental Botany*
   http://www.oup.co.uk/exbotj/
6. *New Phytologist*
   http://www.cup.cam.ac.uk/journals/anp/
7. *International Journal of Plant Sciences*
   http://www.journals.uchicago.edu/IJPS/home.html
8. *Botanical Journal of the Linnean Society of London*
   http://www.apnet.com/www/journal-uk/bt.htm
9. *Annals of Botany*
   http://www.apnet.com/www/journal-uk/bo.htm
10. *Canadian Journal of Botany*
    http://www.cisti.nrc.ca/cisti/journals/cat.html#Journals

GENERAL PLANT SCIENCES–
MOLECULAR AND CELLULAR PLANT PHYSIOLOGY–
ORIGINAL RESEARCH–
MIXED-FORMAT AND LETTERS JOURNALS

1. *The Plant Cell*
   http://www.allenpress.com/catalogue/index/plant_cell/index.html
2. *In Vitro Cellular & Developmental Biology–Plant*
   http://www.allenpress.com/catalogue/index/in_vitro/index.html
3. *Plant Molecular Biology*
   http://www.wkap.nl/journalhome.htm/0167-4412
4. *Plant, Cell & Environment*
   http://www.blacksci.co.uk/products/journals/PCE.HTM
5. *Plant & Cell Physiology*
   http://www.nacos.com/jspp/jspp04.html
6. *Plant Cell Tissue & Organ Culture*
   http://www.wkap.nl/journalhome.htm/0167-6857
7. *Plant Cell Reports*
   http://link.springer.de/link/service/journals/00299/index.htm

GENERAL PLANT SCIENCES–
MOLECULAR AND CELLULAR PLANT PHYSIOLOGY–
REVIEW, SYMPOSIA AND METHODS JOURNALS

- *Annual Review of Plant Physiology & Plant Molecular Biology*
  http://biomedical.annualreviews.org/
- *Critical Reviews in Plant Sciences*
  http://www.crcpress.com/catalog/07352689.htm
- *The Botanical Review*
  http://www.allenpress.com/catalogue/index/botanical_review/
  index.html

PLANT SCIENCES–
TREES AND FORESTRY–
ORIGINAL RESEARCH–
MIXED-FORMAT AND LETTERS JOURNALS

1. *Tree Physiology*
   http://HeronPublishing.com/tphome.html
2. *Trees (Structure & Function)*
   http://link.springer.de/link/service/journals/00468/index.htm
3. *Canadian Journal of Forest Research*
   http://www.cisti.nrc.ca/cisti/journals/cat.html#Journals
4. *Forest Ecology & Management*
   http://www.elsevier.nl/locate/foreco
5. *Forest Science* (FS)
   http://www.safnet.org/pubs/forscience/index.html
   (Allen Pr.)
   http://www.allenpress.com/catalogue/index/for_sci/index.html
6. *Forestry*
   http://www.oup.co.uk/foresj/
7. *Journal of Forestry*
   http://www.safnet.org/pubs/jof/index.html
8. *Scandinavian Journal of Forest Research*
   http://www.scup.no/journals/en/j-417.html

PLANT SCIENCES–HORTICULTURE

1. *Journal of the American Society for Horticular Science*
   http://www.ashs.org/serialpubs/journal/journal.html
2. *Journal of Horticulture & Practical Gardening*
   (Journal not found on web)

3. *HortScience*
   http://www.ashs.org/serialpubs/hortscience/hortscience.html

PLANT SCIENCES–PLANT PATHOLOGY

1. *Phytopathology* (PP)
   http://www.scisoc.org/journals/phyto/
   (Allen Pr.)
   http://www.allenpress.com/catalogue/index/phytopath/index.html
2. *Physiological & Molecular Plant Pathology*
   http://www.apnet.com/www/journal-uk/pp.htm
3. *Molecular Plant Pathology*
   http://194.247.68.33/mppol/
4. *European Journal of Plant Pathology*
   http://www.wkap.nl/journalhome.htm/0929-1873
5. *Plant Pathology*
   http://www.blacksci.co.uk/products/journals/PPATH.HTM
6. *Plant Disease* (PD)
   http://www.scisoc.org/journals/pd
   (Allen Pr.)
   http://www.allenpress.com/catalogue/index/plant_disease/index.html

PLANT SCIENCES–
PLANT PATHOLOGY–
REVIEW, SYMPOSIA AND METHODS JOURNALS

* *Annual Review of Plant Physiology & Plant Molecular Biology*
  http://biomedical.annualreviews.org/

GENERAL ZOOLOGY–
ORIGINAL RESEARCH–
MIXED-FORMAT AND LETTERS JOURNALS

* *Integrative Biology*
  http://www.interscience.wiley.com/jpages/1093-4391/
* *Zoological Journal of the Linnean Society of London*
  http://www.apnet.com/www/journal-uk/zj.htm
* *Canadian Journal of Zoology*
  http://www.cisti.nrc.ca/cisti/journals/cat.html#Journals

- *Journal of Zoology*
  http://www.cup.cam.ac.uk/journals/zoo/
- *Zoologica Scripta*
  http://www.blacksci.co.uk/products/journals/ZSC.HTM

GENERAL ZOOLOGY–
REVIEW, SYMPOSIA AND METHODS JOURNALS

- *American Zoologist*
  http://www.allenpress.com/catalogue/index/am_zoologist/
  index.html

ZOOLOGY–
COMPARATIVE PHYSIOLOGY–
ORIGINAL RESEARCH–
MIXED-FORMAT AND LETTERS JOURNALS

1. *Journal of Experimental Biology*
   http://www.biologists.com/JEB/
2. *Experimental Biology Online*
   http://link.springer.de/link/service/journals/00898/index.htm
3. *Physiological Zoology*
   http://www.journals.uchicago.edu/PZ/home.html
4. *Journal of Comparative Physiology A: Sensory, Neural & Behavioral Physiology*
   http://link.springer.de/link/service/journals/00359/index.htm
5. *Journal of Comparative Physiology B: Biochemical, Systemic & Environmental Physiology*
   http://link.springer.de/link/service/journals/00360/index.htm
6. *Journal of Experimental Zoology*
   http://www.interscience.wiley.com/jpages/0022-104X/
7. *Comparative Biochemistry & Physiology Part A: Molecular & Integrative Physiology*
   http://www.elsevier.nl/locate/cbpa
8. *Comparative Biochemistry & Physiology Part B: Biochemistry & Molecular Biology*
   http://www.elsevier.nl/locate/cbpc
9. *Comparative Biochemistry & Physiology Part C: Pharmacology, Toxicology & Endocrinology*
   http://www.elsevier.nl/locate/cbpc

ZOOLOGY–
COMPARATIVE ANATOMY–
ORIGINAL RESEARCH–
MIXED-FORMAT AND LETTERS JOURNALS

1. *Journal of Morphology*
   http://www.interscience.wiley.com/jpages/0362-2525/
2. *Zoomorphology*
   http://link.springer.de/link/service/journals/00435/index.htm
3. *Journal of Anatomy*
   http://www.cup.cam.ac.uk/journals/ana/
4. *European Journal of Morphology*
   http://www.swets.nl/sps/journals/ejm.html
5. *Annals of Anatomy* (formerly *Anatomischer Anzeiger*)
   http://www.gfischer.de/docs/journals/anatomy.htm

ZOOLOGY–
COMPARATIVE PSYCHOLOGY AND ETHOLOGY–
ORIGINAL RESEARCH–
MIXED-FORMAT AND LETTERS JOURNALS

1. *Behavioral Ecology & Sociobiology*
   http://link.springer.de/link/service/journals/00265/index.htm
2. *Animal Behaviour*
   http://www.apnet.com/www/journal-uk/ar.htm
3. *Journal of Comparative Psychology*
   http://www.apa.org/journals/com.html
4. *Behaviour*
   http://www.brill.nl/catalogue/productinfo.asp?product=8582
5. *Ethology & Sociobiology*
   http://www.elsevier.nl/locate/inca/522397
6. *Ethology* (formerly *Zeitschrift fur Tierpsychologie*)
   http://www.blacksci.co.uk/products/journals/XETH.HTM
7. *Ethology, Ecology, Evolution*
   http://www.unifi.it/unifi/dbag/eee/
8. *Journal of Ethology*
   http://meme.biology.tohoku.ac.jp/JE/JE_J.html
   http://ethol.zool.kyoto-u.ac.jp/JE.html

ZOOLOGY–MAMMALS

1. *Journal of Mammalogy*
   http://www.allenpress.com/catalogue/index/j_of_mammalogy/
   index.html

2. *Mammal Review*
   http://www.blacksci.co.uk/products/journals/MAM.HTM
3. *Mammalia*
   http://www.mnhn.fr/mnhn/meo/mammal_e.htm
4. *Marine Mammal Science* (MMS)
   http://pegasus.cc.ucf.edu/~smm/mms.htm
   (Allen Pr.)
   http://www.allenpress.com/catalogue/index/marine_mammal_sci/
   index.html

ZOOLOGY–BIRDS

1. *Auk*
   http://www.allenpress.com/catalogue/index/auk/index.html
2. *Condor*
   http://www.nmnh.si.edu/BIRDNET/COS/authors.html
3. *Wilson Bulletin* (WB)
   http://www.ummz.lsa.umich.edu/birds/bulletin.html
   (Allen Pr.)
   http://www.allenpress.com/catalogue/index/wilson_bull/
   index.html
4. *Journal of Avian Biology*
   http://www.munksgaard-service.dk/munksgaard/tidsskrifter.nsf/
5. *Ibis*
   http://www.allenpress.com/catalogue/index/ibis/index.html
6. *Journal of Field Ornithology*
   http://www.allenpress.com/catalogue/index/j_of_field_ornith/
   index.html
7. *Journal fur Ornithologie*
   http://www.blackwell.de/jo.htm
8. *Ardea*
   http://www.nioz.nl/en/deps/mee/ardea/homepage.htm
9. *The Emu*
   http://avoca.vicnet.net.au/~birdsaus/emu/emu.html
10. *Ostrich*
    http://www.birdlife.org.za/whatweoffer.htm

ZOOLOGY–HERPETOLOGY

1. *Copeia*
   http://www.utexas.edu/depts/asih/pubs/copeiapr.html
   http://www.allenpress.com/catalogue/index/copeia/index.html

2. *Herpetologica*
   http://fishead.by.ua.edu/HL/Titles.html
3. *Journal of Herpetology*
   http://falcon.cc.ukans.edu/~gpisani/publink.html
4. *Herpetological Journal*
   http://www.herplit.com/contents/HerpJ.html
5. *Herpetological Review*
   http://falcon.cc.ukans.edu/~gpisani/publink.html

ZOOLOGY–
FISHES
(SEE ALSO AQUATIC BIOLOGY AND ECOLOGY–
FISHERIES)

1. *Copeia*
   http://www.allenpress.com/catalogue/index/copeia/index.html
2. *Environmental Biology of Fishes*
   http://www.wkap.nl/journalhome.htm/0378-1909
3. *Journal of Fish Biology*
   http://www.apnet.com/www/journal-uk/jb.htm
4. *Japanese Journal of Ichthyology*
   http://wwwsoc.nacsis.ac.jp/isj/index-e.html

ZOOLOGY–
ASSORTED INVERTEBRATES
(EXCEPT INSECTS AND ARACHNIDS)

- *Invertebrate Biology*
  http://www.allenpress.com/catalogue/index/invert_bio/index.html
- *Journal of Nematology* (JN)
  http://129.93.226.138/nematode/son/jon.htm
  http://www.allenpress.com/catalogue/index/j_of_nematology/index.html
- *Nematologica: International Journal of Nematological Research*
  http://www.brill.nl/catalogue/productinfo.asp?product=7392
- *Journal of Helminthology*
  http://www.cabi.org/catalog/journals/primjour/joh/joh.htm
- *Journal of Crustacean Biology*
  http://www.lam.mus.ca.us/~tcs/jcb.html
- *Crustaceana*
  http://www.brill.nl/catalogue/productinfo.asp?product=7188

- *The Veliger*
  http://www.ucmp.berkeley.edu/mologis/Veliger.html
- *Malacologia*
  http://www.ucmp.berkeley.edu/mologis/Malcogia.html
- *American Malacological Bulletin*
  http://www.ucmp.berkeley.edu/mologis/AMUBull.html
- *Nautilus*
  http://www.allenpress.com/catalogue/index/nautilus/index.html
- *Journal of Eukaryotic Microbiology*
  http://www.allenpress.com/catalogue/index/j_of_euk_micro/
  index.html
- *Journal of Conchology*
  Conchological Society Of Great Britain and Ireland

ZOOLOGY–
INSECTS AND RELATED ARTHROPODS–
GENERAL AND APPLIED MIXED-FORMAT JOURNALS

1. *Annals of the Entomological Society of America*
   http://www.entsoc.org/annals.htm
2. *Entomologia Experimentalis et Applicata*
   http://www.wkap.nl/journalhome.htm/0013-8703
3. *Journal of Economic Entomology*
   http://www.entsoc.org/jee.htm
4. *Bulletin of Entomological Research*
   http://www.cabi.org/catalog/journals/primjour/ber/ber.htm
5. *Environmental Entomology*
   http://www.entsoc.org/ee.htm
6. *European Journal of Entomology*
   http://www.entu.cas.cz/eje/
7. *Journal of Medical Entomology*
   http://www.entsoc.org/jme.htm
8. *Journal of Applied Entomology*
   http://www.blacksci.co.uk/products/journals/XJAE.HTM
9. *Canadian Entomologist* (CE)
   http://www.biology.ualberta.ca/esc.hp/canent.htm
   (Allen Pr.)
   http://www.allenpress.com/catalogue/index/can_ent/
   index.html
10. *The Entomologist*
    (Pub. London–also known as *Newman's Entomologist*)

ZOOLOGY–
INSECTS AND RELATED ARTHROPODS–
MOLECULAR, CELLULAR AND PHYSIOLOGICAL STUDIES

1. *Insect Biochemistry & Molecular Biology*
   http://www.elsevier.nl/locate/ibmb
2. *Journal of Insect Physiology*
   http://www.elsevier.nl/locate/jinsphys
3. *Physiological Entomology*
   http://www.blacksci.co.uk/products/journals/PENT.HTM
4. *Archives of Insect Biochemistry & Physiology*
   http://www.interscience.wiley.com/jpages/0739-4462/
5. *Pesticide Biochemistry & Physiology*
   http://www.apnet.com/www/journal/pb.htm

ZOOLOGY–
INSECTS AND RELATED ARTHROPODS–
REVIEW, SYMPOSIA AND METHODS JOURNALS

- *Annual Review of Entomology*
  http://biomedical.annualreviews.org/
- *Advances in Insect Physiology*
  http://www.apcatalog.com/

ZOOLOGY–
INSECTS AND RELATED ARTHROPODS–
BEHAVIORAL ECOLOGY

1. *Ecological Entomology*
   http://www.blacksci.co.uk/products/journals/EENT.HTM
2. *Sociobiology*
   (Irregular; Calif. State Univ. at Chico, Dept. of Biological Sciences)
   http://www.csuchico.edu/biol/
3. *Journal of Insect Behavior*
   http://www.plenum.com/title.cgi?2042
4. *Insectes Sociaux*
   http://www.birkhauser.ch/journals/4000/4000_tit.htm

EVOLUTION–
ORIGINAL RESEARCH–
MIXED-FORMAT AND LETTERS JOURNALS
(SEE ALSO GENETICS)

1. *Evolution–International Journal of Organic Evolution*
   http://www.allenpress.com/catalogue/index/evolution/index.html

2. *American Naturalist*
   http://www.journals.uchicago.edu/AN/home.html
3. *Biological Journal of the Linnean Society*
   http://www.apnet.com/www/journal-uk/bj.htm
4. *Journal of Evolutionary Biology*
   http://www.birkhauser.ch/journals/3600/3600_tit.htm
5. *Evolutionary Ecology*
   http://www.wkap.nl/journalhome.htm/0269-7653

EVOLUTION– SYSTEMATICS– ORIGINAL RESEARCH– MIXED-FORMAT AND LETTERS JOURNALS

- *Systematic Biology*
  http://www.tandf.co.uk/JNLS/SYB.htm
- *Taxon*
  http://bgbm3.bgbm.fu-berlin.de/IAPT/taxon/
- *Journal of Zoological Systematics & Evolutionary Research (Zeitschrift fur Zoologische Systematik und Evolutionsforschung)*
  http://www.blackwell-science.com/products/journals/jnltitle.htm
- *Systematic Botany*
  http://www.allenpress.com/catalogue/index/systematic_botany/index.html
- *Systematic Entomology*
  http://www.blacksci.co.uk/products/journals/SENT.HTM
- *Systematic Parasitology*
  http://www.wkap.nl/journalhome.htm/0165-5752

PLANT SCIENCES– MOLECULAR AND CELLULAR PLANT PHYSIOLOGY– REVIEW, SYMPOSIA AND METHODS JOURNALS

- *Annual Review of Plant Physiology & Plant Molecular Biology*
  http://biomedical.annualreviews.org/
- *Critical Reviews in Plant Sciences*
  http://www.crcpress.com/catalog/07352689.htm
- *The Botanical Review*
  http://www.allenpress.com/catalogue/index/botanical_review/index.html

PLANT SCIENCES–
TREES AND FORESTRY–
ORIGINAL RESEARCH–
MIXED-FORMAT AND LETTERS JOURNALS

1. *Tree Physiology*
   http://HeronPublishing.com/tphome.html
2. *Trees (Structure & Function)*
   http://link.springer.de/link/service/journals/00468/index.htm
3. *Canadian Journal of Forest Research*
   http://www.cisti.nrc.ca/cisti/journals/cat.html#Journals
4. *Forest Ecology & Management*
   http://www.elsevier.nl/locate/foreco
5. *Forest Science* (FS)
   http://www.safnet.org/pubs/forscience/index.html
   (Allen Pr.)
   http://www.allenpress.com/catalogue/index/for_sci/index.html
6. *Forestry*
   http://www.oup.co.uk/foresj/
7. *Journal of Forestry*
8. *Scandinavian Journal of Forest Research*

PLANT SCIENCES–HORTICULTURE

1. *Journal of the American Society for Horticular Science*
2. *Journal of Horticulture & Practical Gardening*
3. *HortScience*

PLANT SCIENCES–PLANT PATHOLOGY

1. *Phytopathology* (PP)
   http://www.scisoc.org/journals/phyto/
   (Allen Pr.)
   http://www.allenpress.com/catalogue/index/phytopath/
   index.html
2. *Physiological & Molecular Plant Pathology*
   http://www.apnet.com/www/journal-uk/pp.htm
3. *Molecular Plant Pathology*
   http://194.247.68.33/mppol/
4. *European Journal of Plant Pathology*
   http://www.wkap.nl/journalhome.htm/0929-1873

5. *Plant Pathology*
   http://www.blacksci.co.uk/products/journals/PPATH.HTM
6. *Plant Disease* (PD)
   http://www.scisoc.org/journals/pd
   (Allen Pr.)
   http://www.allenpress.com/catalogue/index/plant_
   disease/index.html

REFERENCES

Stankus, Tony. *Making Sense of Journals in the Life Sciences.* Binghamton: The Haworth Press, Inc. 1992.

Stankus, Tony. *Making Sense of Journals in the Physical Sciences.* Binghamton: The Haworth Press, Inc. 1992.

Stankus, Tony. Special Format Serials and Issues: Annual Review of. . ., Advances in. . ., Symposia on. . ., Methods in . . . Haworth Press, 1995.

Index

[Index compiled by Kathleen J. Patterson]